浙江省"十一五"重点教材建设项目

# 第二语言习得导论
## （英文版）

Second Language Acquisition: An Introductory Course

沈昌洪　刘喜文　季忠民　编

图书在版编目(CIP)数据

第二语言习得导论/沈昌洪,刘喜文,季忠民编. —北京:北京大学出版社,2010.6
(21世纪英语专业系列教材)
ISBN 978-7-301-17135-6

Ⅰ.第… Ⅱ.①沈…②刘…③季… Ⅲ.第二语言—高等学校—教材 Ⅳ.H003

中国版本图书馆CIP数据核字(2010)第072727号

书　　　名:第二语言习得导论
著作责任者:沈昌洪　刘喜文　季忠民 编
责 任 编 辑:叶　丹
标 准 书 号:ISBN 978-7-301-17135-6/H·2486
出 版 发 行:北京大学出版社
地　　　址:北京市海淀区成府路205号　100871
电 子 邮 箱:zbing@pup.pku.edu.cn
电　　　话:邮购部 62752015　发行部 62750672　编辑部 62754382
　　　　　　出版部 62754962
印　刷　者:北京虎彩文化传播有限公司
经　销　者:新华书店
　　　　　　650毫米×980毫米　16开本　15.5印张　246千字
　　　　　　2010年6月第1版　2022年1月第4次印刷
定　　　价:56.00元

未经许可,不得以任何方式复制或抄袭本书之部分或全部内容。
版权所有,侵权必究　举报电话:010- 62752024
　　　　　　电子邮箱:fd@pup.pku.edu.cn

## 《21世纪英语专业系列教材》编写委员会

(以姓氏笔画排序)

王守仁　王克非　申　丹
刘意青　李　力　胡壮麟
桂诗春　梅德明　程朝翔

# 总 序

  北京大学出版社自 2005 年以来已出版《语言与应用语言学知识系列读本》多种,为了配合第十一个五年计划,现又策划陆续出版《21世纪英语专业系列教材》。这个重大举措势必受到英语专业广大教师和学生的欢迎。

  作为英语教师,最让人揪心的莫过于听人说英语不是一个专业,只是一个工具。说这些话的领导和教师的用心是好的,为英语专业的毕业生将来找工作着想,因此要为英语专业的学生多多开设诸如新闻、法律、国际商务、经济、旅游等其他专业的课程。但事与愿违,英语专业的教师们很快发现,学生投入英语学习的时间少了,掌握英语专业课程知识甚微,即使对四个技能的掌握也并不比大学英语学生高明多少,而那个所谓的第二专业在有关专家的眼中只是学到些皮毛而已。

  英语专业的路在何方?有没有其他路可走?这是需要我们英语专业教师思索的问题。中央领导关于创新是一个民族的灵魂和要培养创新人才等的指示精神,让我们在层层迷雾中找到了航向。显然,培养学生具有自主学习能力和能进行创造性思维是我们更为重要的战略目标,使英语专业的人才更能适应 21 世纪的需要,迎接 21 世纪的挑战。

  如今,北京大学出版社外语部的领导和编辑同志们,也从教材出版的视角探索英语专业的教材问题,从而为贯彻英语专业教学大纲做些有益的工作,为教师们开设大纲中所规定的必修、选修课程提供各种教材。《21 世纪英语专业系列教材》是普通高等教育"十一五"国家级规划教材和国家"十一五"重点出版规划项目《面向新世纪的立体化网络化英语学科建设丛书》的重要组成部分。这套系列教材要体现新世纪英语教学的自主化、协作化、模块化和超文本化,结合外语教材的具体情况，既要解决语言、教学内容、教学方法和教育技术的时代化，也要坚持弘扬以爱国主义为核心的民族精神。因此，今天北京大学出版社在大力提倡专业英语教学改革的基础上，编辑出版各种英语专业技能、英语专业知识和相关专业知识课程的教材，以培养具有创新性思维的和具有实际工作能力的学生，充分体现了时代精神。

北京大学出版社的远见卓识，也反映了英语专业广大师生盼望已久的心愿。由北京大学等全国几十所院校具体组织力量，积极编写相关教材。这就是说，这套教材是由一些高等院校有水平有经验的第一线教师们制定编写大纲，反复讨论，特别是考虑到在不同层次、不同背景学校之间取得平衡，避免了先前的教材或偏难或偏易的弊病。与此同时，一批知名专家教授参与策划和教材审定工作，保证了教材质量。

当然，这套系列教材出版只是初步实现了出版社和编者们的预期目标。为了获得更大效果，希望使用本系列教材的教师和同学不吝指教，及时将意见反馈给我们，使教材更加完善。

航道已经开通，我们有决心乘风破浪，奋勇前进！

胡壮麟

北京大学蓝旗营

# Preface

This is a coursebook for Second Language Acquisition (SLA). As such, it deals with the process in which the second languages (L2) are learned. The general aim of this coursebook is to provide an up-to-date, introductory overview of the current trends of SLA studies.

SLA is a field of research with potential to make its own distinctive contribution to fundamental understandings, for instance, of the workings of the human mind or the nature of language. It also has the potential to inform the improvement of social practice in some other fields, most obviously in language learning and teaching. The coursebook presents the interest in SLA from both perspectives, and intends to make it intelligible to the widest possible audience.

The coursebook is designed to make the information available to students with a wide variety of linguistic and applied linguistic knowledge. The coursebook can be used by those with a background in language and/or linguistics and others with little or no background in the field. The book develops out of the belief that the complexities of the field can and should be brought to the attention of language teachers and adult language learners, both those who are intending to delve further into the field and those who are only curious about the pervasive phenomenon of learning a second language.

Thus, its intended audience is wide: undergraduates accomplishing their first degree in language or linguistics; graduate students embarking on courses in foreign language education or applied linguistics; and a broader audience of in-service teachers involving themselves in second-language education and research.

The coursebook takes a multidisciplinary approach in that what has been included and presented is the result of research emanating from well-established disciplines. The content is limited, for the most part, to a discussion of adult L2 learning.

The SLA research is old and new at the same time. It is old in the sense that scholars for centuries have been fascinated by the questions posed by the nature of foreign language learning and language teaching. It is new in the sense that the field, as it is now represented, only goes back about 40 years. In the earlier part of the modern phase, most scholarly articles emphasized language teaching and only had a secondary interest in language learning. In other words, the impetus for studying language learning was derived from pedagogical concerns.

Although the SLA research has been extremely active and productive in recent decades, it has not yet arrived at a unified or comprehensive view as to how L2s are learned. This coursebook therefore is organized as an introduction to a number of SLA theories, linguistically, psycholinguistically and socio-linguistically.

Indeed, the SLA research largely reflects the fact that strands of research already active 20 years ago have continued to flourish. The most obvious example is the ongoing linguistic research inspired by the Universal Grammar Theory of Noam Chomsky. However, while this vein of theorizing and empirical investigation remains active and productive, it has not succeeded in capturing the whole field, nor indeed has it attempted to do so. No single theoretical position has achieved dominance, and new theoretical orientations continue to appear. Whether or not this is a desirable state of affairs has been an issue of some controversy for SLA researchers.

On the whole, though language teachers and researchers accept fully the arguments for the need of cumulative programmes of research within the framework of a particular theory, they incline towards a pluralist view of SLA theorizing. In any case, it is obvious that students entering the field today need a broad introduction to a range of theoretical positions, with the tools to evaluate their goals, strengths and limitations, and this is what this introductory book aims to offer.

For nearly 40 years, the SLA research has developed into an independent and autonomous discipline, complete with its own research agenda. In addition, SLA researchers have witnessed an increase in the number of conferences (of both a general and a topical nature) dealing exclusively with SLA as well as special sessions on SLA as part of larger conferences. Furthermore, the field now has journals devoted exclusively to research in the field (*Studies in SLA; Language Learning; Second Language Research*) as well as others in which reports of second language studies comprise a major part (e. g. *Applied Linguistics; Applied Psycholinguistics*). Finally, there are now numerous edited volumes dealing with subareas of the field (e. g. Language Transfer; Language Input; Language Variation; Universal Grammar; Critical Period Hypothesis; Interaction; Interlanguage) and in recent years various books concerned with subareas of the field and with research methodology.

What is particularly noteworthy about the SLA research is its interdisciplinary characteristic. The research is concerned with the general question: *How are second languages learned?* Scholars approach this question from a wide range of backgrounds: sociology, psychology, education, and linguistics, to name a few. This has both positive and negative effects on the field.

On one hand, the advantage is that through the multiplicity of perspectives, people are able to see a richer picture of acquisition, a picture that appears to be more representative of the phenomenon of acquisition in that learning a second language undoubtedly involves factors relating to sociology, psychology, education, and linguistics. On the other hand, multiple perspectives on what purports to be a single discipline bring confusion, because it is frequently the case that scholars approaching SLA from different (often opposing and seemingly incompatible) frameworks are not able to talk to one another. This is so because each perspective brings with it its own way of approaching data and its own research methodology.

This coursebook attempts to bring together these disparate threads, to place them within a coherent framework, and importantly, to make the field accessible to large numbers of language researchers and second language learners.

Shen Changhong, Liu Xiwen, Ji Zhongmin<br>2010, 02

# Contents

**Chapter 1 Introduction: Key Concepts and Issues in SLA** …… (1)
  1.1 Language Acquisition and SLA ………………………… (1)
  1.2 Some Definitions of SLA ………………………………… (2)
  1.3 Some Structural Characteristics of SLA ……………… (3)
  1.4 The Literature on the Theories of SLA ………………… (4)
  1.5 A Theoretical Approach Proposed by Spolsky ………… (5)
  1.6 Theoretical Applications to L2 Teaching and Learning …… (7)
  1.7 Some Distinctions in the field of SLA Research ………… (8)
      1.7.1 SLA and FLA ……………………………………… (8)
      1.7.2 Acquisition versus Learning ……………………… (9)
      1.7.3 Input versus Intake ………………………………… (10)
      1.7.4 Implicit versus Explicit Learning ………………… (11)
      1.7.5 Incidental versus Intentional Learning …………… (11)
      1.7.6 Instructed versus Non-instructed SLA …………… (12)
  1.8 Conclusion ………………………………………………… (13)
  Points for Thinking ……………………………………………… (14)
  Further Reading ………………………………………………… (15)

**Chapter 2 Views on Language, Learning and Learner** ………… (16)
  2.1 Views on the Nature of Language ……………………… (16)
      2.1.1 Phonetics and Phonology ………………………… (16)
      2.1.2 Syntax ……………………………………………… (17)
      2.1.3 Morphology ………………………………………… (18)

2.1.4　Semantics ·················································· (19)
　　　2.1.5　Pragmatics ················································· (20)
　2.2　Views of the Language Learning Process — L1 versus
　　　L2 ······························································· (20)
　　　2.2.1　Children's Acquisition of Lexicon ·················· (23)
　　　2.2.2　Children's Acquisition of Syntax ·················· (25)
　　　2.2.3　Children's Acquisition of Phonology ············· (26)
　　　2.2.4　Children's Acquisition of Semantics and
　　　　　　Pragmatics ············································· (28)
　2.3　Views of the Second Language Learner ··················· (30)
　　　2.3.1　The Learner as Language Processor ··············· (31)
　　　2.3.2　Differences between Individual Learners ········· (32)
　　　2.3.3　Cognitive Factors ········································ (32)
　　　2.3.4　Affective Factors ········································ (33)
　　　2.3.5　The Learner as Social Being ·························· (34)
　　　2.3.6　Links with Social Practice ···························· (35)
　2.4　Conclusion ······················································· (35)
　Points for Thinking ··················································· (36)
　Further Reading ······················································· (36)

## Chapter 3　An Introduction to Language Acquisition ············ (37)
　3.1　Introduction ····················································· (37)
　3.2　Developmental Patterns in L1 Acquisition ················· (37)
　　　3.2.1　A General Outline of English Acquisition
　　　　　　as L1 ······················································ (40)
　　　3.2.2　Positive and Negative Reinforcements in Children's
　　　　　　L1 Acquisition ··········································· (43)
　　　3.2.3　Beneficial Views from Children's L1
　　　　　　Acquisition ··············································· (44)
　3.3　The Controversy between Behaviorist and Mentalist
　　　Models ···························································· (45)
　3.4　Developmental Patterns in L2 Acquisition ················· (47)
　　　3.4.1　Early Stages ·············································· (47)
　　　3.4.2　Formulaic Speech ······································· (48)

         3.4.3  Structural and Semantic Simplification ............... (50)
         3.4.4  The Hypothesis of L1 & L2 Acquisition ............ (55)
  3.5  Conclusion ................................................................ (56)
  Points for Thinking ............................................................. (57)
  Further Reading .................................................................. (57)

**Chapter 4  Recent History of SLA Research** ....................... (58)
  4.1  Introduction ............................................................... (58)
  4.2  The Early Studies on Language Acquisition
        (to 1960s) ................................................................ (59)
         4.2.1  Behavioristic View of Learning — Habit
                Formation ...................................................... (60)
         4.2.2  Contrastive Analysis ..................................... (60)
         4.2.3  Behaviorism and CA for Language Teaching ...... (62)
         4.2.4  Behaviorism under Attack ............................. (63)
  4.3  The Following-up Studies in 1970s and 1980s ............ (64)
         4.3.1  The Birth of Error Analysis and
                Interlanguage ................................................. (64)
         4.3.2  Krashen and His Monitor Model ...................... (66)
         4.3.3  Schumann's Pidginization or Acculturation
                Model ............................................................. (70)
  4.4  The Recent Studies on L2A (beyond 1990s) ................ (71)
         4.4.1  The Developmental Patterns in Language
                Acquisition ..................................................... (71)
         4.4.2  Different Roles Found in Language
                Acquisition ..................................................... (72)
  4.5  Conclusion ................................................................ (73)
  Points for Thinking ............................................................. (74)
  Further Reading .................................................................. (74)

**Chapter 5  The UG Approach to Language Acquisition** ......... (75)
  5.1  Introduction ............................................................... (75)
  5.2  Universal Grammar (UG) for Language Acquisition ...... (75)
         5.2.1  Chomsky and His UG Theory ........................ (75)

   5.2.2 What Constitutes Knowledge of Language? ……… (76)
   5.2.3 How does UG Relate to Language
      Acquisition? ………………………………………… (77)
   5.2.4 How is Knowledge of Language Put to Use? …… (79)
 5.3 Arguments from First Language Acquisition ……………… (80)
   5.3.1 Characteristics of First Language Acquisition …… (80)
   5.3.2 Language Acquisition and Intelligence ……………… (81)
   5.3.3 Language Impairment and Human Brain
      Damage ……………………………………………… (82)
   5.3.4 Conclusion ………………………………………… (83)
 5.4 What Does UG Consist of? ……………………………… (83)
   5.4.1 Principles and Parameters Theory in UG ………… (83)
   5.4.2 UG Principles ……………………………………… (84)
   5.4.3 UG Parameters …………………………………… (85)
 5.5 Evaluation of UG-based Approaches to SLA …………… (86)
   5.5.1 The Scope and Achievements of the UG
      Approach …………………………………………… (87)
   5.5.2 The UG View of Language ……………………… (87)
   5.5.3 The UG View of Language Acquisition …………… (88)
   5.5.4 The UG View of the Language Learner ………… (89)
 5.6 Conclusion ………………………………………………… (89)
 Points for Thinking ……………………………………………… (90)
 Further Reading ………………………………………………… (91)

## Chapter 6 Cognitive Approaches to SLA ……………… (92)
 6.1 Introduction ………………………………………………… (92)
 6.2 Two Main Groups of Cognitive Theorists ………………… (93)
 6.3 Processing Approaches …………………………………… (94)
   6.3.1 Information-processing Models of L2
      Learning …………………………………………… (94)
   6.3.2 McLaughlin's Information-processing Model …… (94)
   6.3.3 Anderson's Active Control of Thought (ACT)
      Model ……………………………………………… (96)
   6.3.4 Application of ACT to Learning Strategies ……… (98)

　　　　6.3.5　ACT and Fluency Development in SLA ………… (100)
　6.4　Connectionism ……………………………………………… (101)
　6.5　Theories of L2 Processing ……………………………… (103)
　　　　6.5.1　Processability Theory ……………………………… (103)
　　　　6.5.2　The Teachability Hypothesis …………………… (105)
　　　　6.5.3　Perceptual Saliency ………………………………… (105)
　6.6　Evaluation of Cognitive Approaches to L2
　　　　Learning ………………………………………………………… (106)
　　　　6.6.1　Cognitivists' View of Language ………………… (106)
　　　　6.6.2　Cognitivists' View of Language Learning ……… (106)
　　　　6.6.3　Cognitivists' View of the Language Learner …… (107)
　6.7　Conclusion ………………………………………………………… (108)
　Points for Thinking ………………………………………………………… (108)
　Further Reading ……………………………………………………………… (109)

## Chapter 7　Some Other Perspectives on SLA ………………… (110)

　7.1　Introduction ……………………………………………………… (110)
　7.2　Functional Perspectives on L1 Learning and SLA ……… (110)
　　　　7.2.1　Cognitive Orientation and Textual
　　　　　　　 Orientation ……………………………………………… (111)
　　　　7.2.2　Social Orientation and Multifunctional
　　　　　　　 Orientation ……………………………………………… (112)
　7.3　Functionalist Contributions to an Understanding
　　　　of SLA …………………………………………………………… (113)
　　　　7.3.1　Functionalism and the Nature of
　　　　　　　 Interlanguage ………………………………………… (113)
　　　　7.3.2　Functionalism on Language Learning and
　　　　　　　 Development …………………………………………… (114)
　　　　7.3.3　Functionalism on the Language Learner ………… (115)
　7.4　Sociocultural Perspectives on SLA …………………………… (115)
　　　　7.4.1　Sociocultural Theory ………………………………… (115)
　　　　7.4.2　The Scope of Sociocultural Research …………… (116)
　　　　7.4.3　Mediation and the ZPD …………………………… (116)

      7.4.4 Sociocultural View of Language and Communication ……… (118)

      7.4.5 The Sociocultural View of Language Learning ……… (118)

  7.5 Sociolinguistic Perspectives on SLA ……… (119)

      7.5.1 Developmental Links between L1 and Culture ……… (120)

      7.5.2 Empirical Studies of SLA as a Situated Social Practice ……… (121)

      7.5.3 The Scope and Achievements of Sociolinguistic Enquiry ……… (123)

      7.5.4 Sociolinguistic View on Language Learning and Development ……… (123)

      7.5.5 Sociolinguistic Accounts of the L2 Learner ……… (124)

  7.6 Conclusion ……… (124)

Points for Thinking ……… (125)

Further Reading ……… (125)

## Chapter 8 Input, Interaction and Output in SLA ……… (126)

  8.1 Introduction ……… (126)

  8.2 Input and Interaction in L1 Acquisition ……… (127)

  8.3 Input and Interaction in SLA ……… (128)

      8.3.1 From Corder to Krashen's "Input Hypothesis" ……… (128)

      8.3.2 Long's Study and His "Interaction Hypothesis" ……… (129)

      8.3.3 Empirical Studies on Comprehension and Acquisition ……… (130)

      8.3.4 Rethinking the Interaction Hypothesis ……… (132)

  8.4 Output in SLA ……… (133)

  8.5 Theorizing Input, Interaction and Output Research ……… (134)

      8.5.1 Input Processing Theory ……… (135)

      8.5.2 Autonomous Induction Theory ……… (136)

  8.6 Feedback, Recasts and Negative Evidence in SLA ……… (136)

　　　　8.6.1　Feedback, Recasts and Negative Evidence
　　　　　　　in L1A ·················································· (136)
　　　　8.6.2　Negative Feedback and Recasts in the L2
　　　　　　　Classroom ············································· (137)
　　　　8.6.3　Experimental Studies of Negative Feedback ······ (138)
　　8.7　Evaluation: The Scope of Interactionist Research ········· (140)
　　　　8.7.1　Achievements of Interactionist Research ············ (140)
　　　　8.7.2　Limitations of Interactionist Research ··············· (140)
　　8.8　Conclusion ······················································ (141)
　Points for Thinking ····················································· (141)
　Further Reading ························································· (142)

**Chapter 9　Varied Perspectives on Interlanguage** ················ (143)
　　9.1　An Introduction to Interlanguage ····························· (143)
　　　　9.1.1　The Definition and Characters of
　　　　　　　Interlanguage ········································· (143)
　　　　9.1.2　The IL Concept and Research Issues ················ (143)
　　　　9.1.3　Selinker and His View of IL ························· (145)
　　9.2　Social Aspects of IL ············································ (145)
　　　　9.2.1　IL as a Stylistic Continuum ·························· (146)
　　　　9.2.2　The Acculturation Model of IL ······················ (146)
　　　　9.2.3　Social Identity and Investment in IL ··············· (147)
　　9.3　Discourse Aspects of IL ······································· (148)
　　　　9.3.1　Acquiring Discourse Rules ··························· (148)
　　　　9.3.2　The Role of Input and Interaction in IL ············ (148)
　　　　9.3.3　The Study of Foreigner Talk ························ (149)
　　　　9.3.4　The Negotiation of Meaning ························ (150)
　　　　9.3.5　The Role of Output in IL Development ············ (151)
　　9.4　Psycholinguistic Aspects of IL ································ (151)
　　　　9.4.1　Positive Transfer and Negative Transfer
　　　　　　　from L1 ················································· (152)
　　　　9.4.2　The Role of Consciousness in SLA ················· (152)
　　　　9.4.3　Processing Operations ································ (154)
　　　　9.4.4　Communication Strategies ··························· (156)

  9.4.5 Two Types of Computational Model ............ (157)
9.5 Conclusion ............................................................ (158)
Points for Thinking .................................................... (159)
Further Reading ......................................................... (159)

## Chapter 10 Researches on L2 Classroom Practice(Ⅰ) ............ (160)
 10.1 Introduction ....................................................... (160)
  10.1.1 The Necessity of the Studies on Classroom
     Practice .................................................... (160)
  10.1.2 Research-derived Theory and Classroom
     Practice .................................................... (160)
  10.1.3 The Co-work of the L2 Teachers and SLA
     Researchers .............................................. (161)
 10.2 An Introduction to the History of L2 Teaching
   Methods ............................................................ (162)
  10.2.1 L2 Teaching Methodology before the Mid of
     the 20$^{th}$ Century ...................................... (162)
  10.2.2 L2 Teaching Methodology before 1980s ........ (163)
  10.2.3 L2 Teaching Methodology from 1980s to the
     Present ..................................................... (164)
 10.3 Cross-language Competition between L1 and L2 ..... (165)
  10.3.1 Avoiding the Use of L1 in L2 Classroom ......... (165)
  10.3.2 Rethinking of Cross-language Competition ..... (166)
 10.4 Some Methods Used in L2 Classroom Research ..... (167)
  10.4.1 The Psychometric Method ............................ (167)
  10.4.2 The Interaction Analysis .............................. (168)
  10.4.3 The Discourse Analysis and Critical Discourse
     Analysis ................................................... (169)
  10.4.4 The Ethnographic Method ............................ (170)
  10.4.5 Comparative Method Studies (CMS) ............. (171)
 10.5 Data Collection and Data Analysis ........................ (172)
  10.5.1 Data Collection and Its General Dimensions ..... (172)
  10.5.2 The Naturalistic Data Collection Procedures ..... (173)

10.5.3　The Method of Data Analysis Presented by
　　　　　Gass and Selinker ……………………………… (175)
10.5.4　Some Difficulties in Data Analysis ……………… (176)
10.6　Conclusion …………………………………………… (176)
Points for Thinking ………………………………………… (176)
Further Reading …………………………………………… (177)

**Chapter 11　Researches on L2 Classroom Practice(Ⅱ)** ……… (178)
11.1　Direct Involvement of Classroom Interaction
　　　Research ………………………………………… (178)
11.2　An Introduction to Classroom Interaction ……………… (178)
　　　11.2.1　The Aspects of Classroom Interaction ………… (178)
　　　11.2.2　The Nature of L2 Classroom Interaction ……… (179)
　　　11.2.3　The Structure of Classroom Interaction ………… (180)
　　　11.2.4　The Characteristics of Classroom Interaction ……… (181)
11.3　Types of Language Use in Classroom Interaction …… (182)
11.4　Turn Taking in Classroom Discourse ………………… (184)
11.5　Differences between Classroom and Naturalistic
　　　Discourse ………………………………………… (185)
11.6　The Teacher's Role in Classroom Interaction ………… (186)
　　　11.6.1　The Teacher Talk ……………………………… (186)
　　　11.6.2　The Issues of Error Treatment in
　　　　　　　Classroom ………………………………… (187)
　　　11.6.3　The Teacher's Inconsistency in Error
　　　　　　　Treatment ………………………………… (187)
　　　11.6.4　Teachers' Questioning in Classroom
　　　　　　　Interaction ………………………………… (188)
11.7　Learner Participation ………………………………… (189)
　　　11.7.1　Quantity of Participation ……………………… (189)
　　　11.7.2　Quality of Participation ……………………… (190)
11.8　Classroom Interaction in the L2 Learning …………… (190)
　　　11.8.1　Tasks and Classroom Interaction ……………… (190)
　　　11.8.2　Group Work in Classroom Interaction ………… (191)

11.9 The Relationship between Classroom Interaction and SLA ……(192)
    11.9.1 L2 Learning in the Communicative Classroom ……(192)
    11.9.2 Effect of Classroom Interaction on L2 Learning ……(193)
11.10 Conclusion ……(194)
Points for Thinking ……(195)
Further Reading ……(195)

## Chapter 12 Conclusion ……(196)
12.1 A Brief Review of the Book ……(196)
12.2 An Integrated View of SLA Research ……(197)
12.3 Main Achievements of Recent SLA Research ……(198)
12.4 SLA Research and Language Education ……(200)
12.5 Future Directions for SLA Research ……(201)
Points for Thinking ……(204)
Further Reading ……(204)

**REFERENCES** ……(206)

# Chapter 1

# Introduction: Key Concepts and Issues in SLA

## 1.1 Language Acquisition and SLA

> *The acquisition of language" is doubtless the greatest intellectual feat any one of us is ever required to perform."*   Bloomfield, 1933

A very young child began acquiring at least one language — what linguists called as her First Language (L1) — mostly with very little conscious effort or awareness. L1 acquisition (L1A) is a complicated but relatively rapid process through which a child grows up as a competent and proficient user of her native language(s).

Every aspect of language acquisition is extremely complex. Yet young children — before the age of five — already know most of the intricate system which people have been naturally describing as the grammar of a language. Before they can add 2 plus 2, children are conjoining sentences, asking questions, using appropriate pronouns, negating sentences, forming relative clauses, and using the syntactic, phonological, morphological, and semantic rules of the grammar.

However, for those who start learning a language after childhood — for example, by enrolling in a foreign language course or emigrating to a new country — the process of learning a non-native language is far more difficult, time-consuming, and much less likely to end in a state of complete mastery or more exactly fluency.

Since the second half of the twentieth century, the world has been evolving into a time of "globalization" and the "WWW net era", when communication between people has expanded the ways beyond their local speech communities, even beyond their countries. Thus, there came into existence of the systemic study of how people acquire a second language as what Ellis described in his book:

*As never before, people have had to learn a second language, not as a pleasing pastime, but often as a means of obtaining an education or securing employment. At such a time, there is an obvious need to discover more about how second languages are learned.(1997, 3)*

SLA studies, as a field of inquiry, started in the late 1960's, lay the emphasis on empirical research based upon the interests in describing characteristics of L2, the way these characteristics change as acquisition takes place.

## 1.2 Some Definitions of SLA

SLA, as a new discipline, is still relatively young. Part of that youth is manifested in some theoretical foundation as the pendulum of beliefs has swung back and forth. However, in the 21$^{st}$ century, theoretical positions in SLA seem to be somewhat stabilizing; as to identify just what people do know about the L2 learning process.

1. A person's L1 is the language s/he learned first, as a child grows up;

2. A person's L2 (includes third, fourth) is a language learned after L1;

3. SLA is concerned with studying how people learn a second language.

Some questions raised by the people knowing more than one language include:

1) *Is learning an L2 like learning an L1?*

2) *Are children better than adults at L2 learning?*

3) *Can one speak an L2 without an accent?*

Many people use several languages in the course of a day, whether in multilingual countries such as India and Switzerland or in apparently monolingual countries such as China and England. Linguists are more

concerned with the following questions:
1) *How does L2 learning relate to Universal Grammar?*
2) *Does the language input that the learner hears make a difference?*
3) *How does one language affect the other in L2 learning process?*

These two sets of questions above are both fundamentally concerned with how one person can have two languages. SLA could be defined in both broad and narrow senses. The former refers to any language other than an L1, but the latter refers to the language playing an institutional and social role in the community. That is to say, it functions as a recognized means of communication among people speaking some other language as their L1. For example, English is learnt in Korea as an L2; Korean emigrants to the United States and Great Britain also learn English as an L2 in their new countries.

As such, the term SLA, seemingly transparent, requires careful explanation. Ellis claims (2000) that "second" can refer to any language learned subsequent to the mother tongue and it can further refer to the learning of a third or fourth language. Also, "second" is not intended to contrast with "foreign". Whether one learns a language naturally as a result of living in a country where it is spoken, or learning it through a classroom through instruction, it is customary to speak generally of L2 acquisition (L2A). Ellis then defines SLA as the study of L2A.

## 1.3  Some Structural Characteristics of SLA

SLA is a relatively new, interdisciplinary field of research. Though there were several important earlier studies, most research has been conducted since 1960 by researchers drawing heavily upon theories, research findings, and research methods in a variety of fields, including education, psychology, linguistics, anthropology, foreign languages, ESL, and applied linguistics.

Data-based SLA research is presented at a variety of conferences, and some SLA research results are published in a wide range of journals, only three of which (*Language Learning, Studies in Second Language Acquisition* and *Second Language Research*) are primarily devoted to SLA.

The brief history of SLA denotes that few issues have yet been investigated exhaustively.

On one hand, SLA research tends to be conducted cross-disciplinarily, using data collected on different subjects and on small and limited samples. The interdisciplinary research often results in defining the hypotheses, processes, findings and proposals when research methods come from different disciplines.

On the other hand, SLA research with its origins in one discipline (theoretical linguistics) often seems irrelevant to that of in another (social psychology). For example, it is difficult to relate research findings of **Universal Grammar (UG)** in adult SLA motivated by Chomsky's ideas to the results of studies of nonnative speech accommodation to an interlocutor motivated by the **Accommodation Theory.**

## 1.4 The Literature on the Theories of SLA

SLA is an immensely complex phenomenon. Millions of human beings have experience of L2A, and may have a full understanding of the activities helping them to learn or blocking them from learning. But this practical experience, together with the common knowledge, is clearly not enough to help us understand the process.

It is just necessary to understand SLA better than what we knew in the past. There are basic reasons for such an understanding of SLA. SLA research can contribute to more general understanding about the nature of language, of human learning and of intercultural communication, and thus to the human mind itself, as well as how all these are interrelated to and affect each other. SLA research can better explain the learning process and be able to account for both success and failure in L2A. If so, there will be a benefit for millions of teachers, students and self-taught learners, who are struggling with their L2A.

For a better understanding of SLA, a theory is a set of claims about the phenomena under study and the relationships between them and the processes that bring about change. SLA theory has its own aims at description and at explanation. An SLA theory will be primarily concerned with modeling the nature of the language system and will be firstly concerned with modeling the change or developmental processes of language acquisition. A particular theory for SLA may deal only with a particular stage of learning, or with the learning of a sub-aspect. This theory may propose learning mechanisms which are much more general in scope. Theories are produced collaboratively, and evolve through a process of systematic enquiry in which the claims of the theory are assessed against some kind of evidence or data. The process of theory building is a reflexive one; new developments in the theory lead to the need to collect new information and explore different phenomena and different patterns in the potentially infinite world of facts and data, which leads to new theoretical insights.

## 1.5 A Theoretical Approach Proposed by Spolsky

An example of a particular theory or "model" of L2A from Spolsky is shown here:

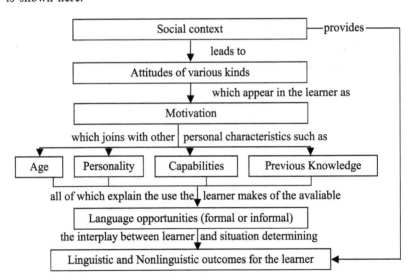

Figure 1.1 A "model" of L2A adapted from Spolsky (1989: 28)

This model depicts a "general theory of second language learning." It depicts the researcher's theoretical views on the overall relationship between contextual factors, learner differences of individuals, learning opportunities and learning outcomes.

It is thus an ambitious model in the breadth of phenomena. The rectangular boxes show the factors that are most significant for learning. Any variation can lead to differences in success or failure. The arrows connecting the various boxes show the directions of influence. The contents of the various boxes are defined at great length, as consisting of clusters of interacting "Conditions" (ibid., pp. 16-25), making language learning successful. As in Spolsky's diagram, these "conditions" summarize the results of a great variety of empirical language learning research.

How would SLA research begin to "evaluate" this or any other model to decide that this was a view of the language learning process with which experts felt comfortable and within which they intended to work?

This would depend partly on broader philosophical positions. It would also depend on the particular focus of interests, within the L2 learning process. This particular model seems well-adapted for the study of individual learners, but has relatively little to say about the social relationships in which they engage.

But whatever the focus of a theory is, it would be expected to find the following:

*1. Clear and explicit statements of the framework the theory is supposed to base on, the area to cover, and the claims to make.*

*2. Systematic procedures for confirming the theory, through data gathering and interpretation: a good theory must be testable or falsifiable in some way.*

*3. Not only descriptions of L2 phenomena, but attempts to explain why they are so, and to propose possible mechanisms for change.*

*4. Last but not the least, engagement with other theories in the field, and serious attempts to account for at least some of the phenomena that are "common ground" in ongoing public discussion.*

(Long, 1990a)

The rest of this chapter offers a brief overview of a number of SLA theoretical frameworks, researching fields and proposed claims.

## 1.6 Theoretical Applications to L2 Teaching and Learning

SLA findings and theories are critical for language teachers on the basis of the assumption that language teaching cannot take place without an explicit theory of language learning.

It first provides a body of knowledge for teachers to evaluate their own teaching practices, and then affords a learning-/learner-centered view of language pedagogy, enabling L2 teachers to examine critically the principles upon which the selection and organization of teaching materials have been based and finally the methodological procedures they have chosen to employ, presenting language features to correspond to the context in which their students acquire them.

The findings of SLA research show that L2A is a multidimensional phenomenon, with many learners and environmental variables in the learning processes and product. Consequently, theories would, lack somewhat validity when it attempts to explain L2A by some studies on single factors, such as motivation, input, interlanguage, the workings of Language Acquisition Device (LAD), output or affect variables.

The above can be considered as a sample of "accepted findings of SLA" indicated early in this chapter. The following points show a detailed illustration of a theory being either complete/adequate or incomplete/inadequate:

1. Common patterns in development in different kinds of learners under different conditions of exposure means that a theory that ignores the nature of universals in language and cognition is incomplete or, if considered complete, inadequate.

2. Systematic differences in the problems troubling L2 learners of different L1 backgrounds by certain kinds of L1/L2 comparison and by other qualitative features of the input, means that a theory that says nothing about environmental factors is incomplete or, if considered complete, inadequate.

3. Differences in rate of acquisition and the level of proficiency achievable by children and adults under comparable conditions of

exposure requires that viable theories specify either different mechanisms driving development in learners of different starting ages or differential access to the same mechanisms.

4. The subordination of affective factors to linguistic and cognitive factors means that a theory that claims to explain development solely in terms of affective factors can, at most, be an account of improving learning conditions, not an explanatory theory of language acquisition itself.

5. The need for awareness of and/or attention to language form for the learning of some aspects of an L2 means that a theory that holds all language learning to be unconscious is inadequate.

6. The impossibility of learning some L2 items from positive evidence alone means that a theory that holds that nativelike mastery of L2s can result simply from exposure to comprehensible input of that language is inadequate.

7. Studies on interlanguage development indicates a strong cognitive contribution on the learner's part and claims that environmentalist theories of L2A are inadequate.

8. A theory that assumes that change is a product of the steady accumulation of generalizations based upon the learner's perception of the frequencies of forms in the input is also incomplete.

## 1.7 Some Distinctions in the field of SLA Research

### 1.7.1 SLA and FLA

Just as the difficulty in defining a first, second or third language in such a way that it applies to all cases, it is also difficult to distinguish between the terms second and foreign language learning.

**SLA** is the study on **L2A**. According to the traditional definition, L2A typically takes place in a setting in which the language to be learned by a nonnative speaker is the language spoken in the local community. Therefore, a Chinese native learning English in England is generally defined as a L2 learner. In some definitions L2A needs to take place in either an instructed setting or a non-instructed one.

**Foreign Language Acquisition (FLA)** takes place in a setting in which the language to be learned is not the one used in the local community. So the learning of English at schools in China would be an example of FLA. In most cases, FLA takes place in a setting with formal language instruction.

The term SLA here is employed for referring to the study on both L2A and FLA because it is assumed that the underlying process is essentially similar. Wherever necessary, this coursebook will make use of the distinction between these two fields.

### 1.7.2 Acquisition versus Learning

The second tricky but also controversial distinction is the one between **Acquisition** and **Learning.** Krashen and Terrell (1983) define "acquisition" as the product of a "subconscious" process, similar to that of children in learning their L1, and learning as the product of formal teaching, which results in conscious knowledge about the language, but the distinction cannot be as simple as that.

Schmidt (1990) considers the term "subconscious" as an unlikely proposition, misleading in consciousness research, where it would imply totally without any awareness. In a non-technical sense, the term could mean "not being aware of having noticed something," which would be related to a way of learning that takes place while listening to a tape while sleeping.

Apparently, some evidence shows that people may subconsciously pick up what they already know, but there is no evidence that new information may be picked up in such a manner. It is commonly accepted that some level of attention is required to notice something, and that noticing is crucial in obtaining new information.

Krashen claimed that learning the rules could not lead to an automatic use of language as in acquisition. Probably, Krashen used the term "subconscious" in a non-technical sense, as the inability to explain what one knows. In other words, learners may use language forms correctly without being able to explain the forms.

Defined as such, acquisition is seen as a natural process of growth of knowledge and skills in a language without a level of meta-knowledge about the language, while learning is seen as an artificial process in which the "rules" of a language are learned.

In Chapter 4, the Krashen hypotheses are further discussed in detail, and the later chapters will show that there are indeed two different mental processes involved in acquisition and learning, but this does not mean that acquisition and learning cannot interact. Though not all learning necessarily leads to acquisition, learning could be the carrying out of activities that enhance the growth of knowledge.

### 1.7.3 Input versus Intake

Related to the notion of "consciousness" is the third distinction between **Input** and **Intake.** Input is everything around us we may perceive with our senses, and Intake (or Uptake) is what we pay attention to and notice.

Some level of attention is required to be able to notice something, and that noticing is crucial for taking in new information. There is a lot of information in our environment, but what and how we make use of all that information depends on our needs and interests. Most people may not be interested in the noise from the running machines, but for those who study on noise pollution it may get to be a very relevant piece of information. And at that point, they will notice. The same is true for language learning. There is little doubt that input is the main source of information for learning, but not all input leads to intake, which is necessary for teaching. It is not easy to know under what conditions input is actually helpful for learning. From experiments in consciousness, experts do know that unexpected events often arouse some attention.

In addition, expectations are important for one's perceptibility and noticeability so it is clear that teaching may have an awareness-raising effect, increasing the noticing of features in input through the establishment of expectation and comprehension.

For intake, at least some minimal level of mental processing needs to take place. There must be some awareness of new information relevant for the learning system to incorporate. Intake may refer to information that strengthens existing knowledge, or it may fill a gap in knowledge that was noticed by the learner before.

### 1.7.4 Implicit versus Explicit Learning

Related to the acquisition versus learning distinction is the fourth one on **Implicit** versus **Explicit** learning. Ellis captures its difference by using the phrase "unconscious operation" in yet another sense, namely whether general principles in language can be induced without really being able to formulate an understanding of them.

Schmidt (1990) points out that implicit learning is acquisition of knowledge about the underlying structure by a process that takes place naturally, simply and without conscious operations. Explicit learning is a more conscious operation where a learner makes and tests hypotheses in a search for structure.

According to Schmidt, there is evidence that giving learners explicit rules helped in an experimental study, and the results of larger scale studies also slightly favor an explicit focus on grammar. But there is not much evidence on which to base an evaluation of the implicit rule acquisition in L2 learning. The implicit learning issue is the most difficult to resolve. On the one hand, there is evidence for it, but there is also evidence that conscious understanding helps in the process of L2A.

In the following chapters, readers will see that there is indeed quite a lot of evidence that instruction has a positive effect on learning. Looking at Schmidt's question from a dynamic perspective, it is assumed that any kind of input, both a great deal of meaningful input and explicit instruction, will interact and affect the system.

### 1.7.5 Incidental versus Intentional Learning

The fifth related and much debated distinction in the SLA literature is the one on **Incidental** versus **Intentional** learning. A good example of intentional learning is learning words from a bilingual list in a decontextualised manner. Learning words by reading and inferring meanings from context is usually seen as incidental learning.

However, it is not easy to formulate a clear-cut distinction between incidental and intentional learning. Most of the work has focused on acquiring lexical knowledge.

While reading for pleasure a reader does not bother to look up a new word in a dictionary, but a few pages later realizes what that word means, then incidental learning is said to have taken place. If a student is instructed to read a text and find out the meanings of unknown words, then it becomes an intentional learning activity.

As what Schmidt says, the distinction of incidental versus intentional learning is related to whether noticing is required and, if so, whether such noticing is automatic or requires attention. Apparently, incidental learning without "paying attention" is both possible and effective, but only when the demands of a task focus attention on what is to be learned. However, paying attention is probably facilitative, and may be necessary if adult learners are to acquire grammatical rules that are difficult to distinguish such as the difference between *he'd* meaning *he had* or *he would*.

A good learner who is rather fluent in L2 may pay attention only to a message as a whole rather than to any particular L2 forms with which the message is expressed. In such a case, it is likely that he will learn something new from the information provided by the message, but it is unlikely that he will learn anything new about the forms of the language. Even though it is hard to resolve the issue of incidental versus intentional learning, it is much related to the role of SLA instruction. Here are some questions for thinking: what have you learned from this chapter so far:

1. Is there anything that you have learned as new information?
2. What particular language forms did you learn that were new?
3. Are there any words, for instance, in this chapter that you didn't know before?
4. Did you learn them implicitly or explicitly, intentionally or incidentally?
5. Did you just infer them from the context in which they appeared?

### 1.7.6 Instructed versus Non-instructed SLA

The sixth distinction is the most confusing one. It is not completely clear about the distinction (or interaction) between instructed and non-instructed L2 acquisition. In many cases, language acquisition takes place through a mix of instructed and non-instructed learning.

On one hand, some languages are **"learned"** mainly through formal instruction. For example, when a Chinese college student intends to learn French in China, there are not many chances for him to use French in daily life and find a French setting in which he can **"acquire"** the language. His main source of contact and input is the school library and French lessons, but he may also **pick up** some of the language through reading newspapers and books in French on his own.

On the other hand, some languages are learned mainly through informal interaction. Many migrants throughout the world move into a setting in which they have to learn the local language on their own in order to survive. In many such settings there is no formal instruction on how to learn that language, so people have to pick up the language from what they hear and see in their environment.

However, it is possible that an adult immigrant to a new country follows some language courses in a community center or he may be told what he is saying incorrectly through interaction with his friends of native speakers.

## 1.8 Conclusion

This chapter starts with some theoretical concepts and then discusses several interrelated questions that have driven research into SLA studies within the overall context of one person with two or more languages. The aim is to help the reader to get in touch with some of the issues that have been investigated, touching on areas of linguistic study of sounds, words and syntax as well as the meanings they represented. The account represents one person's route through a large maze, trying not to stray down paths less connected with linguistics. Though a comparative new discipline, SLA research is a vast and expanding one with its own annual conferences such as EUROSLA (European Second Language Association). Despite barely touching on areas such as vocabulary or phonology, Ellis (1994) makes a survey of SLA research in his 824-paged -long book. More and more new developments have been witnessed within its field of research:

1. The scope of inquiry has been broadened, from its earlier focus on linguistic (esp. grammatical) properties of language, and psycholinguistic in orientation to later work also concerned with pragmatic aspect of the

learner language, social linguistic perspective adopted and social factors influencing development considered.

2. More attention has been paid to linguistic theory, for instance, Chomsky's Universal Grammar, Halliday's functional models of language and language typology. Earlier work used to make use of simple grammatical concepts, derived from descriptive grammars, but later work makes greater use of technical concepts from a particular theory of grammar.

3. There has been much increase of theory-led research: from research-then-theory to theory-then-research in terms of methodology.

4. The awareness and reconsideration of interest in individual differences, like age, aptitude, gender, motivation and so on.

5. Emergence of other sub-fields devoted to the study of classroom L2 teaching and learning, such as the studies on the teaching methodology and those on the learning strategies and learning styles.

SLA theories intend to explain well-attested empirical findings about relationships of an input-interaction-output model (Gass, 2008) in second language development and universals, and the variance in learners and learning environments. An important component of such kind of theories will be one or more means to account for interlanguage change.

While various theories differ in scope and so often relate only to partial descriptions, they must account for generally accepted findings within their domains if they are to be credible. Identification of "accepted findings", therefore, is an important part of theory construction and evaluation.

Such findings will be the least an SLA theory needs to explain. Sample-accepted findings on learners, environments, and interlanguages are proposed along with some implications for current SLA theories.

 Points for Thinking

1. What do the definitions of SLA represent in its field of study?
2. How do we interpret the structural characteristics of SLA?
3. How does the theoretical approach by Spolsky work for language

learning?
4. What are the applications of the SLA theory to language teaching and learning?
5. What are the significances of making clear distinctions in SLA studies?

 Further Reading

Ellis, R. (1997). *Second Language Acquisition.* Oxford: Oxford University Press.

Ellis, R. (Ed.) (2000). *Learning a Second Language through Interaction.* Amsterdam: John Benjamins.

Gass, S. and Selinker, L. (2008). *Second Language Acquisition: An Introductory Course.* 3$^{rd}$ Edition. Hillsdale, NJ: Lawrence Erlbaum Associates.

Rocca, S. (2007). *Child Second Language Acquisition: A Bi-Directional Study of English and Italian Tense—Aspect Morphology.* Amsterdam: John Benjamins.

# Chapter 2

# Views on Language, Learning and Learner

## 2.1 Views on the Nature of Language

An understanding of the nature of SLA is fundamental to the understanding of what it is that needs to be learned.

Any human being is to acquire a language in the first few years of life. The knowledge acquired is largely of an unconscious sort. When a young child learns how to form particular grammatical structures, such as relative clauses, he/she may not consciously know that it is a relative clause and what it is used for. Take this sentence as an example: *I want that toy that that boy is playing with.*

A school child could utter this fully formed sentence, which includes a relative clause ("that that boy is playing with"), not knowing how to state out the function of relative clauses and how to easily divide this sentence into its component parts. *That boy is playing with that toy and I want that toy.*

The complex knowledge humans have about their native languages is largely unconscious. There are several aspects of language to be described systematically.

### 2.1.1 Phonetics and Phonology

The sound system (phonology) of all languages is complex. Minimally, it entails knowing what possible sounds are and what are not for its native speakers.

If a particular sound is studied on, it gets to the area of phonetics which describes the articulation of individual sounds. Here is an example for showing this. A native speaker of English can tell that the sound [x] in [Xi Hu] (the West Lake) is not a sound in English. The similar example can be the English consonants of [θ] & [ð] to speakers of other languages.

Phonological knowledge also involves knowing what happens to words in fast speech as opposed to more carefully articulated speech. For example, if someone wanted to say: *I am going to write a letter.* That person would undoubtedly say something like the following: *I'm gonna wriDa leDer.* Consider the following dialogue between A (a nonnative speak) and B (a native speaker):

A: *What are you going to do?*

B: *I'm gonna wriDa leDer.*

A: *What? I can't hear you.*

B: *I'm going to write a letter* (articulated slowly and clearly).

Native speakers of a language know when to combine sounds in "normal, fast" speech and when not to in slower and clearer speech. They know not only possible sounds, but also know what are possible combinations of sounds and what sounds are found in what parts of words. In English, while [b] and [n] are both sounds of English, they cannot form a "blend" in the way that [b] and [r] can: *bnick versus brain. The sound [ŋ], which is frequent in English, however, cannot appear in the beginning of words in English, although it can in other languages.

## 2.1.2 Syntax

The syntax of a language is frequently known as its grammar, referring primarily to the knowledge of word order in a sentence. There are two kinds of grammar, generally referring to Prescriptive Grammar and Descriptive Grammar.

Here are some prescriptive rules of English grammar as 1) never end a sentence with a preposition; 2) never split infinitives; 3) never begin a sentence with a conjunction; 4) never use contractions in writing; 5) use *between* only with two items and *among* only with more than two. It is about such rules generally taught in school, often ignoring the actual use of the language.

But modern linguists are concerned with descriptive grammars: the languages as they are actually used. Thus, the knowledge of syntax just refers to descriptive grammar because native speakers of English frequently violate the prescriptive rules. As with phonological knowledge, native speakers of a language know which possible sentences of their language are. For example, the sentences *The big book is on the brown table.* and *The woman whom I met yesterday is reading the same book that I read last night.* are possible English sentences, whereas *The book big brown table the on is.* and *Canceling what's but general how then the two actually.* are not possible or are ungrammatical.

So part of language is the order in which elements can and cannot occur or co-occur. Here are two English sentences *Have him to call me back.* and *That's the man that I am taller than.* For some speakers of English these are strange-sounding, for others they are perfectly acceptable. Not only do we know which sentences are acceptable in our language, we also know which sentences are grossly equivalent in terms of meaning. For example, sentences as *Tom was hit by a car.* and *A car hit Tom.* have the same general meaning in the sense that they refer to the same accident.

If someone asks *What did that car hit?* the most likely answer would be *It hit Tom* rather than *Tom was hit by it.* Thus, a native speaker not only knows what is equivalent to what, and when to use different grammatical patterns, but also knows how meaning is affected by moving elements within a sentence. English adverbs can be moved in a sentence without affecting the meaning, whereas nouns cannot. Sentences *Yesterday Sally saw Jane.* and *Sally saw Jane yesterday.* are roughly equivalent in meaning, but *Yesterday Sally saw Jane.* and *Yesterday Jane saw Sally.* do not share a common meaning.

Thus, knowing a language entails knowing a set of rules with which we can produce an infinite set of sentences. In order to see that language is rule-governed and that we can comprehend novel sentences, consider sentence *The woman wearing the green scarf ran across the street to see the gorilla that had just escaped from the zoo.* Even though such event is quite rare, people can understand what it really means.

## 2.1.3 Morphology

Morphology is the study of word formation. For example, the word *reusable* is made up of three parts: 1) *re -*, a prefix; 2) *use*, a verb; 3) *-able*, a suffix. Each part is referred to as a morpheme defined as the minimal unit of meaning. There are two classes of morphemes: bound and free. The former is one that can never be a word by itself, such as the *re* -or *-able*. A free morpheme is one that is a word in and of itself, such as *use*. Words can be created by adding morphemes, as in the following children's favorite: establish→ establish + *ment* → *dis* + establish + *ment*→*dis*+ establish + *ment* + *ari* + *an* + *ism*.

### 2.1.4 Semantics

Semantics refers to the study of meaning. It does not necessarily correspond to grammaticality because many ungrammatical sentences are meaningful as the following sentences *That woman beautiful is my mother.* and *I'll happy if I can get your paper.* These sentences by nonnative speakers of English are comprehensible, though not following the "rules" of English. The opposite is the sentence that is grammatically formed but, because of the content, is meaningless (at least without additional contextualization), as in *That bachelor is married.*

Semantics entails knowledge of the reference of words. The English word *table* refers to an object with a flat top and either three or four legs or that a *leaf* most often refers to part of a tree. But native speakers are able to distinguish between the meaning of the *leaf* of a tree and the *leaf* of a table, as in an advertisement *That table has four leaves.* The knowledge of homonyms helps to interpret the advertisement in the manner intended. For a nonnative speaker it is not so easy, as he or she might struggle to imagine *a table with four leaves.*

Additionally, it is important to note that the limits of a word are not always clear. What is the difference between a *cup* and a *glass*? For many objects it is obvious, for others it is less so. Referential meanings are clearly not the only way of expressing meaning. Native speakers of a language know that the combination of elements in sentences affects their meaning. Sentences *The man bit the dog.* and *The dog bit the man.* are totally different in meaning. Thus, the extent to which syntax and meaning are interrelate to each other.

### 2.1.5 Pragmatics

Yet another area of language as what L2 learners need to learn has to do with pragmatics, or the use of language in context. For example, when we answer the telephone and someone says *Is John there?* we know that this is a request to speak with John. It would be strange to respond *Yes* with the caller saying *Thank you* and then hanging up. Clearly, the phrase *Is X there?* in this context is a request to speak with someone and not an information question.

Similarly, the word order within a sentence (*The man bit the dog.* and *The dog bit the man.*) may have an effect on meaning in some grammatical contexts, but in others it does not. The following conversation exemplifies this:

(Setting: an ice cream store; a child, age 4)
Child:          *I want a raspberry and vanilla cone.*
Shopkeeper: *OK, one vanilla and raspberry cone coming up.*
Child:          *No, I want a raspberry and vanilla cone.*
Shopkeeper: *That's what I'm getting you.*

The child was using word order to reflect his ordering; the shopkeeper was not. In English, it does not necessarily refer to the ordering of physical objects.

## 2.2   Views of the Language Learning Process —L1 versus L2

The acquisition pattern is familiar: cries evolve to babbles, babbles are shaped into words, and words are joined to create sentences. This sequence describes the path taken by all children as the language they hear around them is taken in, internalized, and eventually developed into native-speaker competence. Although recent research has shown the immense variability in both rate and achievement for children learning their native language. But these researches of progress in themselves reveal little of the internal acquisition that is propelling the child into linguistic competence.

Experts try to understand how a child learns one language in a relatively simple cognitive and social environment, so that they have a basis for describing and interpreting a child's experience with multiple languages in complex social circumstances. The study of language acquisition began by carefully observing young children's learning to talk. Before there was a single hypothesis probing the nature of this process, researchers were recording the speech of their children and creating a database.

The most famous of these was Leopold (1939—1949) whose report remains a classic in the field. Interestingly, Leopold's daughter, the subject of the study, was being raised bilingually, although it took several decades for the study of bilingualism and L2 learning to gain a respectable position in studies of language acquisition.

Roger Brown and his students carried out the first major program of research into child language acquisition through both observation and experimental manipulation. Their eventual report and interpretation of these investigations (1973) focused only on the earliest stages of acquisition; the intention to continue the project by reporting an equally detailed analysis of the next stage was never realized.

Nonetheless, the contribution of Brown's lab research is enormous: methodologically it provided the tools for analyzing and coding speech through constructs such as Mean Length of Utterance (MLU); theoretically it presented hypotheses that were ultimately accepted, discarded, or revised, but always remained crucial in moving the field forward; and empirically it recorded the data (the utterances of Adam, Eve, and Sarah) that were the raw material upon which a generation of language researchers were bred.

The more diverse extensions of this research into language and language-related studies have been done by Brown's students. Surely, before researchers can explain why things are happening the way they do, they must know what the child is doing.

In spite of agreement among researchers that the data are essential for theory building, reliable observations based on large numbers of children have been quite difficult. The studies tend, by necessity, to be small-scale, inferential, and complicated. But even the case study of a single child, presents a difficult task to the researcher. Documenting children's utterances in the compilation of a language diary requires great efforts, but those who have persisted have gained a wealth of insights.

The challenge of empirical studies is to create indirect means of questioning, since researchers could not ask children directly to comment upon their linguistic reflections. Researchers could access children's language only through the filter of their cognition, and the two may not be equally developed. It is a wonder that research in children's language acquisition is possible at all.

Two recent initiatives from which some researchers will undoubtedly reap the benefits for years to come have provided a technical advantage to the study on children's language acquisition.

The first is the Child Language Data Exchange System (CHILDES) developed by MacWhinney in 1991, and Sokolov and Snow in 1994. This is a computerized database of transcriptions obtained by researchers over the past twenty-five years. They have reported vast amounts of children's speech collected under different conditions, examining children at different ages, and including different languages.

The database is accompanied by programs to carry out the transcription and analysis of the speech samples. The second is the large-scale investigation of 1,803 children undertaken by Fenson and others in the 1990's which provided the normative base for the MacArthur Communicative Development Inventories. The intention was to collect sufficient data on language and communicative development so that the competence of an individual child could be described with reference to this norm by means of a percentile score. The researchers assessed the language abilities of children between 8 and 30 months of age using a checklist system given to parents.

The CHILDES database is mainly a research tool in that it provides the raw data upon which hypotheses and interpretations may be tested and played out. In contrast, the MacArthur Inventories are a more practical resource, enabling its researchers and practitioners to submit the facts of language acquisition to examine under existing theories and programs. The theoretical relation between the various aspects of language, such as grammar and lexicon, is controversial, and some of the positions in this debate are described in the section outlining alternative theories of acquisition.

As children grow into the mastery of language, a brief review of children's major achievements examines their progress individually in the areas of lexicon, syntax, phonology, and pragmatics. The purpose is not to review all that is known about language acquisition but to identify some events that are either decisive in evaluating alternative theoretical interpretations or relevant to situations involving bilingualism and second language acquisition, or both.

It is not even clear that the artificial domains of language competence into which the discussion has been divided are valid. Bates and Goodman in 1997 even objected to the idea that vocabulary and syntax are separate parts of children's developing linguistic competence.

### 2.2.1 Children's Acquisition of Lexicon

Children's vocabulary acquisition needs to be described in three aspects of development: its rate and pattern, the way words are used (or even misused), and the relation between lexicon and the child's cognitive development. The normative study in 1995 reported that by sixteen months of age children could reliably understand a mean of 191 words and produce a mean of 64 words. After that point, there is the legendary production speed: by thirty months of age, the mean number of words in productive vocabulary is 534.

This period of rapid vocabulary growth during the second year of life has been called the "vocabulary burst". However, even allowing for individual variation within the pattern, the rate of vocabulary growth throughout childhood is quite astonishing. Anglin in 1993 placed this progress at about 5 words per day during the school years; Clark in 1995 estimated the rate to be 10 words per day until the age of six and only slightly fewer through to the age of seventeen; in the boldest proposal of all, Pinker in 1995 declared that children learn one word every two waking hours from about eighteen months old through adolescence.

A second salient aspect of children's early vocabulary is that early words are not always used correctly. Children make consistent, classifiable errors in their efforts to use their fledgling vocabularies. Children typically commit four types of errors while using words: overextension, underextension, overlap, and mismatch, but the greatest research attention has focused on overextension.

Overextensions occur when children apply words beyond their usual meaning, as in the famous example of using *doggie* to refer all four-legged animals, like *squirrels*. Clark in 1973 argued that these commonly observed overextensions of names in children's speech indicated that children's lexicons contained incomplete entries for the semantic features. *Dogs* and *squirrels*, for example, each contained the features "*small*", "*furry*", "*four-legged*", but lacked more specific evidence that distinguished them. Since the meaning of the word was considered to be the sum of these features, these words actually meant the same thing for children; dogs and squirrels were categorically equivalent.

In later research it became clear that children's comprehension of these two terms showed the proper respect for categorical boundaries. Children were not suffering from a conceptual confusion about biological taxonomies but were being resourceful in extending a limited system beyond its apparent limits.

The concepts to which words had been overextended usually shared some perceptual or functional feature with the actual meaning of the word, and children were attempting to label an unknown concept with a known word on the basis of analogy. What evidence was there that vocabulary development might be a part, even a highly specialized part, of children's general cognitive development?

For some portion of vocabulary, words are mapped onto cognitive structures that many researchers believe must be established before the word can be learned. For example, Tomasello and Farrar in 1984 found that children taught movement words such as *fall down* only after they succeeded in solving a task based on visible displacements.

Similarly, Gopnik and Meltzoff in 1986 found a relation between children's use of disappearance terms, like *all gone* and the completion of object permanence. Specific correspondences such as these are compelling evidence for the close association between children's developing conceptual skills and their linguistic competence.

Although the correspondences between words and concepts do not resolve questions of causality and directionality, their yoked development is an important wedge into the intractable problem of the ontological status of language in the child's mind. These associations become more detachable and amenable to scrutiny when children are learning two languages or learning languages with different semantic structures, an issue that is discussed in later chapters.

### 2.2.2 Children's Acquisition of Syntax

From the time children begin combining words to create compositional utterances, an achievement that begins to reveal itself at about eighteen months of age, there is an unmistakable respect for the word order demanded by the grammar of the adult language. More impressively, infants in the first year are able to distinguish between meanings of reversible sentences using only word order as a clue.

Hirsh-Pasek and Golinkoff from 1987 to 1996 developed a comprehension test that demonstrates these apparently precocious abilities. Infants are seated in front of two monitors, each depicting one direction of action between two agents (*cat* chases *dog*; *dog* chases *cat*), while a tape is played that describes only one of the displayed scenes (*The cat is chasing the dog*). These infants look significantly longer at the scene that matches the description than at the one that reverses the direction of action. Still, it is not clear how strongly children's responses in this task can be accepted as evidence that they are undertaking syntactic analysis.

Two aspects of syntactic development are noteworthy for general discussions of language acquisition and relevant to the extensions of these explanations into L2 acquisition. The first is the order in which the morphological system is mastered and the second is the overextension of syntactic rules.

One of the striking discoveries in the study of language acquisition by Brown and his collaborators was that there was a relatively fixed order in which fourteen grammatical morphemes [such as plural (-*s*), progressive (-*ing*), and articles] were acquired into the productive competence of the children they studied. Documenting mastery of specific linguistic units is precarious because children's early speech is so variable. Brown's decision in 1973 was to base judgments of acquisition on the criterion that children used a specific form in 90 percent of the obligatory contexts.

Comparing different criteria for determining the point of acquisition, Bates, Bretherton, and Snyder in 1988 confirmed the stability of the order of acquisition of seven of the original fourteen morphemes across a group of children. This regularity in the order of acquisition of grammatical markers is a crucial fact of language acquisition that needs to be addressed by any theory.

Across children who clearly experience different forms of input, different rates of learning, and different cognitive abilities, the stability of the acquisition order points to an explanation more intrinsic to the language itself, or to some language-learning capacity, than to the environmental input. Moreover, impressive similarities have been noted by Slobin (1985) across languages, a point to which this book will return in the later chapters.

A second characteristic of children's early syntax is the existence of a period of time, usually beginning in the third year, in which they overextend grammatical rules to irregular forms. The preeminent example of this is the overuse of *-ed* to indicate past tense on irregular verbs, creating such forms as *goed* instead of *went*. But it leads to a further question: Why do children universally and reliably commit such errors?

The observation of this pattern has been a persistent example of data invoked to distinguish between the two major competing theoretical approaches to language acquisition, formal and functional views (discussed in later chapters). It is a telling exercise in theory building that the same observation is considered central to two completely diverse interpretive positions. Nonetheless, the phenomenon is evidence of an important productive process in children's language acquisition.

### 2.2.3 Children's Acquisition of Phonology

Phonology is the only aspect of language that is clear evident from the infant's first moments of life. The newborn baby reveals virtually nothing of the particular potential that will be shaped into the ability to use structured rules of order to express intentions and concepts in socially regulated ways; the ability to vocalize these ideas, however, is manifest.

Recognizable speech is, of course, "a far cry" from the infant's first vocal outbursts, but the natural reliance on this channel of communication is evident. Equally, children born without the ability to hear begin life with hand gestures that are structurally and functionally equivalent to the vocal babbles of hearing children.

The evolution of the infant's first cries into comprehensible speech undergoes several important stages: the first linguistic sounds are discriminated at about one month old; babbling begins at about seven months of age; the first word appears by approximately twelve months and the next two or three years are spent refining the sounds and prosody to match the adult standards of the speech community. The earlier view of this development was Jakobson's claim in 1968 that there was a discontinuity between the playful babbling of infants and the emergence of words.

Three aspects of this development are important to be noted. The first is the way in which speech sounds are organized into phonemic categories; the second is the sequence of sounds incorporated into babbling and ultimately into speech; and third is the nature of the errors observed in early speech production.

The research on speech perception is the work by Eimas and others in 1971 in which they reported that infants between one and four months old could reliably discriminate between computer-generated versions of the sounds [ba] and [pa]. More importantly, the infants could make these distinctions only for sounds that carried phonemic significance; acoustic differences of equal psychophysical magnitude that were linguistically irrelevant went unnoticed.

There is a profound result: after only four weeks of life, there is evidence of a preparedness to organize heard speech into linguistic categories. Extensions of this research into the abilities of infants to distinguish between sounds for languages other than those in their environment are discussed later.

The second issue in children's developing phonological abilities is the pattern and sequence of sounds over which children gain mastery. Although it is reasonably straightforward to trace the course of phonological development across the major stages of cooing, babbling, and speaking, the qualitative shape of children's vocalizations at each of these stages is highly variable.

Third, as sounds turn into words, children consistently encounter difficulty with certain phonemes. Words take on a "baby talk" style because they lack phonemic specification and include many homonyms. Many of these errors are systematic and reflect the application of specific rules, such as devoice final consonants, substitute stops for fricatives, or reduce consonant clusters to single consonants.

Hence, these simplification processes are rules only in a restricted sense as their application is neither predictable nor assured. They may be better described as strategies adopted by children to solve problems at a moment in time. In this sense, they may share common ground with the strategies used by children to refer to objects and concepts beyond their lexical potential.

### 2.2.4 Children's Acquisition of Semantics and Pragmatics

Pragmatics is the study of language use for communication which however, includes much more than language. So any examination of the pragmatic aspects of language should be done beyond the scope of standard linguistic analysis. Communication begins well before language is evident and includes interactions that are clearly outside the child's developing linguistic competence.

As language evolves, the focus of pragmatic analysis shifts to the correspondence between the emergence of linguistic devices and their capacity to signal specific intentions and the sensitivity to socially determined rules of interaction. The mastery of these linguistic devices, and the nonverbal behaviors that precede them, are all central to children's development of pragmatic competence, and their emergence, like other more formal aspects of language, is systematic and orderly.

The pragmatic dimensions include a range of linguistic and nonlinguistic properties that contribute to the human interaction. Some are mechanical, such as the device of turn-taking; some are social, such as mutual attention to a common topic; some are cognitive, such as the speaker's communicative intentions; some are cultural, such as rules of politeness; and some are linguistic, such as the use of cohesion and coherence to connect ideas.

All these aspects of the pragmatic use of language are learned by children at the same time as they are learning the formal structure of language. Before children have mastered the formal aspects of language, however, they are capable of interacting in a conversational style and communicating their intentions. Thus, communication begins long before language is established.

How does language fit into the infant's communicative behavior? The solutions present much the same options as did the similar question regarding babbling. One view holds that language is the on-going communication by other means. Some researchers have identified specific communicative intents in infant interactions and assigned them a causal role in the subsequent development of language as a communicative tool.

A more moderate compromise position was proposed by Ninio and Snow in 1999: "Linguistic communication thus starts with words substituting for gestures, but the language system, once established, soon diverges from its nonverbal origins." The question of the continuity or discontinuity of linguistic knowledge with communicative ability is now central, not only for understanding the role of pragmatic competence in language acquisition, but also for determining a theory of linguistic structure and language acquisition.

If language is one part of a larger communicative ability and grows naturally out of children's interactions, then the burden of explanation for language structure and acquisition must begin with infant's early interactions and experiences. Language exists for communication and must be explained in those terms. Thus the function of language—communication—is primary and must be placed at the center of explanation.

Conversely, if the communication that is prior to the acquisition of linguistic structure is rudimentary, incomplete, or unsystematic, and it is only with the onset of language that intentions can be expressed reliably and systematically, then the essential aspect of language is its form, or structure. In this case, the pragmatic functions of language originate from its formal structure, and communication is a consequence of an orderly formal system.

This division marks a major difference between formal and functional theories of language acquisition, each adopting a different position regarding the primary quality of the object of study.

## 2.3 Views of the Second Language Learner

The above discussion has already made it clear the answer to the question *Who is the second language learner, and how is he or she introduced and described in current L2A research?* The infant bilingual (i. e. a child who is exposed to more than one language from birth and acquires them more or less simultaneously in the first few years of life) is not the subject of SLA. Instead, SLA research generally deals with learners who embark on the learning of an additional language, at least some years after they have started to acquire their first language.

This learning may take place formally and systematically, in a classroom setting; or it may take place through informal social contact, through work, through migration or other social forces that bring speakers of different languages into contact and make communication a necessity. So, L2 learners may be children, or adults; they may be learning the target language formally in schooling, or "picking it up" in the playground or the workplace. They may be learning a highly localized language, helping them to become insiders in a local community; or the target language may be one of wider communication relevant to their region, giving access to economic and public life.

Indeed, in the first part of the 21$^{st}$ century, the target language is highly likely to be English. It is estimated that around 375 million people speak English as their first language, another billion or so are using it as a second language, or learning to do so. Certainly it is true that much research on L2 acquisition, whether with children or adults, is concerned with the learning of English, or with a small number of other languages (French, Chinese, Spanish, German, etc.). There are many multilingual communities today where L2 involves a much wider range of languages.

However, these have been comparatively little studied.

It is possible to distinguish three main points of view among SLA researchers as far as the learner is concerned: 1) the linguistic perspective, concerning with modeling language structures and processes within the mind; 2) the social psychological perspective, concerning with modeling individual differences among learners, and their implications for eventual learning success; 3) the socio-cultural perspective, concerning with learners as social beings and members of social groups and networks. These different perspectives are briefly introduced in following sections.

### 2.3.1 The Learner as Language Processor

Linguists and psycholinguists have typically been concerned primarily with analyzing and modeling the inner mental mechanisms available to the individual learners, for processing, learning and storing new language knowledge. As far as language learning in particular is concerned, their aim is to document and explain the developmental route along which learners undergo.

Researchers are less concerned with the speed or rate of development, or indeed with the degree of ultimate second language success. Thus they tend to minimize or disregard social and contextual differences among learners; their aim is to document universal mental processes available to all normal human beings.

However, there is some controversy among researchers in this psycholinguistic tradition on the question of age. Do child and adult L2 learners learn in essentially similar ways? Or, is there a critical age that divides younger and older learners, a moment when early learning mechanisms are replaced or at least supplemented by other compensatory ways of learning?

The balance of evidence was proposed and interpreted by Long in 1990 in favor of the existence of such a cut-off point, and many other researchers agree with some version of a view by Singleton in 1999 that "younger = better in the long run". Other researchers as Birdsong in 1992 argued that this debate was far from resolved. However, explanations of why this should be are still provisional and are further discussed in Chapter 3.

### 2.3.2 Differences between Individual Learners

Real-life observation quickly tells us, however, that even if L2 learners can be shown to be following a common developmental route, they differ greatly in the degree of success that they achieve. Social psychologists have argued consistently that these differences in learning outcomes must be due to individual differences among learners, and many proposals have been made concerning the characteristics that supposedly cause these differences.

In a two-part review, Gardner and MacIntyre in 1992 and 1993 divided what they saw as the most important learner traits into two groups: 1) the cognitive and 2) the affective (emotional). Here, this chapter follows their account to summarize very briefly the factors claimed to have the most significant influence on the success of L2A. R. Ellis, and other experts have been studying this social psychological perspective on learner difference.

### 2.3.3 Cognitive Factors

There are usually three cognitive factors in SLA research:

1. Intelligence: there is clear evidence that L2 students who are above average on formal measures of intelligence or general academic attainment tend to do well in L2A, at least in formal classroom settings.

2. Language aptitude: is there really such a thing as a "gift" for language learning, distinct from general intelligence, as folk wisdom often holds? The best known formal test of language aptitude was designed in the 1950s.

This "Modern Language Aptitude Test" assesses a number of sub-skills believed to be prediction of L2A success: 1) phonetic coding ability; 2) grammatical sensitivity; 3) memory abilities; and 4) inductive language learning ability. It seems that the scores on these tests do indeed correlate with an achievement in a second language.

3. Language learning strategies: do more successful language learners set about the task in some distinctive way? Do they have some personal learning strategies? Much research has been done to describe and categorize the strategies used by learners at different levels, and to link strategy use to learning outcomes.

It is clear that more proficient learners do indeed employ strategies that are different from those used by the less proficient. Whether the strategies cause the learning, or the learning itself enables different strategies to be used, has not been fully clarified.

### 2.3.4 Affective Factors

There are usually two factors in SLA research:

1. Language attitudes: social psychologists have long been interested in the idea that a learner's attitudes towards the target language, its speakers and the learning context, may all play some part in explaining success or failure. Research on second language attitudes has largely been conducted within the framework of broader research on motivation, of which attitudes form one part.

2. Motivation: according to Gardner and MacIntyre, the motivated individual is one who wants to achieve a particular goal, devotes considerable effort to achieve this goal, and experiences satisfaction in the activities associated with achieving this goal. So, motivation is a complex construct, defined by three main components: "desire to achieve a goal, effort extended in this direction, and satisfaction with the task." (Gardner and MacIntyre, 1993:2)

They have carried out a long program of work on motivation with English Canadian school students learning French as a second language, and have developed a range of formal instruments to measure motivation. Over the years consistent relationships have been demonstrated by them between language attitudes, motivation and L2A achievement, with the strongest relationships obtained between motivation and achievement. These relationships are complex as the factors interact and influence each other.

Dornyei and Otto in 1998 recognized the dynamic and changing nature of motivation over time, in their so-called "process model" of L2 motivation. Language anxiety and willingness to communicate: the final learner characteristic that Gardner and MacIntyre consider to hold a relationship with learning success is language anxiety (and its obverse, self-confidence). They claimed in 1993 that language anxiety "is seen as a stable personality trait referring to the propensity for an individual to react in a nervous manner when speaking ... in the second language."

It is typified by self-belittling feelings of apprehension, and even bodily responses such as a faster heartbeat. The anxious learner is also less willing to speak in class, or to engage target language speakers in informal interaction. Gardner and MacIntyre cited many studies that suggest that language anxiety has a negative relationship with learning success, and some ones that suggest the opposite, for learner self-confidence.

More recently, a broad overarching construct of willingness to communicate has been proposed as a mediating factor in second-language use and L2A. This construct by MacIntyre et al. includes anxiety and confidence alongside a range of other variables which together produce "readiness" to enter into discourse at a particular time with a specific person or persons, using a second language.

## 2.3.5 The Learner as Social Being

The two perspectives on the learner highlighted so far have concentrated (a) on universal characteristics and (b) on individual characteristics. But it is also necessary to view the L2 learner as essentially a social being, taking part in structured social networks and social practices. Indeed, after some decades when psycholinguistic and individualist perspectives on L2 learners predominated, recent research is redressing the balance, as will be seen in the chapters below.

Interest in L2 learners as social beings leads to consider their relationship with the social context in which their L2 learning takes place, and the structuring of the learning opportunities that makes available. The learning process itself may also be viewed as essentially socially entangled in L2 use and interaction. Two major characteristics distinguish this social view of the learner from that of "individual differences".

First, interest in the L2 learner as a social being leads to a concern with a range of socially constructed elements in learners' identities, and their relationship with learning, so that social class, power, ethnicity and gender make their appearance as potentially significant for SLA research.

Second, the relationship between the individual learner and the social context of learning is viewed as dynamic, reflexive and constantly changing. The view of "individual differences" saw that relationship as being governed by a bundle of learner traits or characteristics (such as aptitude, anxiety, etc.), which were relatively fixed and slow to change. More socially oriented researchers view motivation, learner anxiety, etc., as being constantly reconstructed through ongoing L2 learning experience and interaction.

### 2.3.6 Links with Social Practice

SLA theory has immediate practical applications in the real world, most obviously in the second language classroom. Theorists have been and remain divided on this point. Some have argued for "pure" theory in SLA by requirements for practical application. Some others have demanded for a socially engaged perspective, where theoretical development is rooted in, and responsive to, social practice and language education, in particular. Yet others have proposed that SLA should be guided systematically by the research findings. This tension has partly been addressed by the emergence of "instructed language learning" as a distinct sub-area of research.

However, much of the theorizing and empirical evidence reviewed in this book cannot be captured within this particular sub-field. It is thought that language teachers, will themselves want to take stock of the relations between the theories, and their own beliefs and experiences in the classroom. They can make judgment on the "usefulness" of theorizing in making sense of their own experience and their practice, while not necessarily changing it.

## 2.4 Conclusion

This chapter has aimed to introduce a range of prevailing concepts in the field of SLA research. The following chapter is going to provide a narrative account of the history of SLA research, plus summary descriptions of some of the more specific language learning phenomena that any theory must explain. It then moves to a closer examination of a number of broad perspectives, or families of theories, with their distinctive views of the key questions that must be answered and the key phenomena that need to be explained.

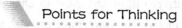 Points for Thinking

1. What are branches of modern linguistic study?
2. How do the children develop their pragmatic competence?
3. What is the significance of carrying out a study on children's L1 acquisition?
4. What are the cognitive and affective factors in SLA research?
5. What is your personal view on the significance of SLA studies?

 Further Reading

Bates, E., Bretherton, I. & Snyder, L. (1988). *From First Words to Grammar: Individual Differences and Dissociable Mechanisms.* New York: Cambridge University Press.

Bialystok, E. (2001a). *Bilingualism in Development: Language, Literacy and Cognition.* Cambridge, UK: Cambridge University Press.

Clark, E. V. (1993). *The Lexicon in Acquisition.* New York: Cambridge University Press.

Gopnik, A. and Meltzoff, A. N. (1986). "Relations between semantic and cognitive development in the one-word stage: the specificity hypothesis." *Child Development* 57: 1040-1053.

Slobin, D. (1985). "Crosslinguistic evidence for the language-making capacity." In Slobin, D. (Ed.). *The Crosslinguistic Study of Language Acquisition.* Vol. 2. Hillsdale, NJ: Lawrence Erlbaum Associates, pp.1159-1249.

# Chapter 3

# An Introduction to Language Acquisition

## 3.1 Introduction

Though language is complex in system and use, yet children of any language — before the age of five — already know most of the grammar of a language. It is obvious that children do not learn a language simply memorizing the sentences of the language and storing them in their brain. No dictionary can hold all the sentences of a language. Children in the same way as adults are creative in their use of language.

No one teaches children the rules of the grammar. Even if we remember our early years, do we remember anyone in our early years telling or teaching us how to add -s or -es to form plural? Children seem to act like competent linguists equipped with a perfect theory of language, and they use this theory to construct the grammar of the language they are exposed to.

The fact is that the child must figure out the rules of language from random input. No one tells him/her "this sentence is grammatical and that is not." Yet, somehow he/she is able to acquire and use the language of his/her speech community based on the language he/she hears around him/her. How the child acquires such a complicated system so quickly and effortlessly is the subject of this chapter.

## 3.2 Developmental Patterns in L1 Acquisition

It is a great stimulus to investigations of the acquisition of language in young children. It finds striking similarities in the language learning behavior of young children, whatever the language they are learning. It seems that children all over the world go through similar stages, use similar constructions in order to express similar meanings, and make the same kinds of errors.

The acquisition stages of children language are summarized as the followings:

| Language stage | Beginning age[①] |
| --- | --- |
| 1. Crying | Birth |
| 2. Cooing | 6 weeks |
| 3. Babbling | 6 months |
| 4. Intonation patterns | 8 months |
| 5. One-word utterances | 1 year |
| 6. Two-word utterances | 18 months |
| 7. Word inflections | 2 years |
| 8. Questions, negatives | 2 years 3 months |
| 9. Rare or complex constructions | 5 years |
| 10. Mature speech | 10 years |

These stages are not language-specific, although their actual realization obviously is. Similarly, when considering the emergence of a number of structures in English, an order of acquisition is found. Brown's (1973) "morpheme study" was probably the best-known L1 study of that time, and was to be very influential for SLA research. In a study of three children, Brown compared the development of 14 grammatical morphemes in English. He found that although the rate varied, the order of which children acquired them remained the same as listed below in a simplified form:

---

① "The ages are given as a very rough guideline only; children vary considerably both in the age of onset of a given phase, and in how fast they proceed from one phase to another."(Aitchison, 1989)

| Morphemes | Examples |
|---|---|
| 1. present progressive -*ing* | He is sitting down. |
| 2. preposition "*in*" | The mouse is in the box. |
| 3. preposition "*on*" | The book is on the table. |
| 4. plural -*s* | The dogs run away. |
| 5. past (irregular) | The boy went home. |
| 6. possessive -'*s* | The girl's dog is big. |
| 7. uncontractible copula "*be*" | Are they boys or girls? |
| 8. article "*a*"/"*the*" | He has a book. |
| 9. past regular -*ed* | He jumped the stream. |
| 10. third person regular -*s* | She runs very fast. |
| 11. third person irregular e.g. *has/does* | Does the dog bark? |
| 12. uncontractible auxiliary "*be*" | Is he running? |
| 13. contractible copula "*be*" | That's a spaniel. |
| 14. contractible copula "*be*" | They're running very slowly. |

Brown's findings show that children appear to follow a well-established pattern of language development. Nearly all the children in the researches typically begin with one-word utterances which function well in their communication with caretakers.

What is striking is that, not only do children acquire a number of grammatical morphemes in a fixed order, but they also follow rigid stages during the acquisition of a given grammar. For example, children all over the world not only acquire negatives around the same age, but they also mark the negative in similar ways in all languages, by initially attaching some negative marker to the outside of the sentence, and then gradually moving the negative marker inside the sentence, following the stages exemplified below for English:

Stage 1: Negative utterances consist of a "**nucleus**" either preceded or followed by a negator.

    e.g. **Not** *a teddy bear. Wear mitten* **no.**

Stage 2: Negators are now incorporated into affirmative clauses, include *don't* and *can't*. Negative commands appear.

    e.g. There **no** *squirrels. You* **can't** *dance.* **Don't** *bite me yet.*

Stage 3: Negators are now always getting into affirmative clauses. The "Auxiliary + not" rule has been acquired, as *don't*, etc. But some

mistakes still occur (*be* is omitted and double negatives occur):
e.g. I **don't** have a book. Paid **can't** have one. I **not** crying. **No** one **didn't** come.

Acquisition of negatives follows a regular route through stages of the learning process. These stages are not unlike the ones followed by L2 learners. Similar evidence can be found for the acquisition of interrogatives and other structures.

Findings also indicate that the acquisition of pragmatic and textual functions of the L2 also takes place in stages: the development follows a route diagrammatically as follows: assertions/requests → directives/commissives → expressives/declaration.

Children initially learn to perform assertions and requests, and only later develop the ability to express directives (such as asking, ordering, forbidding, and permitting) and commissives (such as promising). Expressives (such as thanking) and declaration (such as swearing) follow even later.

### 3.2.1 A General Outline of English Acquisition as L1

A full account of the developmental path is a necessity for describing how the learner masters the formal, functional, and semantic properties of a language: a general outline of the development of English as an L1.

| Stage | Functions | Meanings | Forms |
|---|---|---|---|
| 1 | 3 initially signaled: attention, ostension and then expressing wants; and 2 emerge later: statements and requests. | Child typically names objects initially; later, meaning relationships connected with location appear. | Early utterances limited with regard to form. Utterances consist of "operator" (e.g. "there", "look", "more", "all gone") or "operator + object" (e.g. *There mark.*) |
| 2 | Questions appear: initially "where" and "what" and yes/no question. | The child is obsessed with naming and classification. Change of location and simple attributes (e.g. "*hot*" and "*big*") appear at this stage. | Questions lack auxiliary verb—yes/no questions make use of rising intonation. Two constituent utter-ances emerge (i.e. V + O and S + O/complement). Two-word noun phrases appear (e.g. article + n. and prep. + n.). |

(续表)

| | | | |
|---|---|---|---|
| 3 | Questions firmly established and more complex expression of wants. | Change-in-state expressed (e.g. "*you dry hands*"); also mental states (e.g. "*listen*" and "*know*"), non-present time reference, aspectual state of an action, and ongoing activity. | Questions still signaled with rising intonation; three constituent utteran-ces (e.g. S+ verb + O) and three word noun phrases (e.g. prep. + article+ n.). |
| 4 | Full expression of question and negatives takes place. Several new functions appear: requesting permission, indirect requests, expla-nation, and requesting and explanation (i.e. "*why?*"). | Various modal mea-nings appear with futurity, ability, and permission. Comple-ments of psycholo-gical verbs (e.g. "*I know that you are there*") and qualifica-tion of noun phrases (e.g. "*Where's the pen what papa gave me?*") appear. | Auxiliary verb is integrated into structure of the clause. "*do*" appears early, followed by "*can*" and "*will*". Principle of recursion (one grammatical clause is embedded within the structure of another) is learnt. |
| 5 | New functions are hypothetical statements, threats, and formu-lations (i.e. offering an alternative way of getting an action performed). | More differentiated expression of time frame: reference to particular times as points of reference (i.e. "*before dinner*") and different aspectual distinctions (habitual, repetitive, and incep-tive). | Child sorts out the structure of wh-questions (i.e. S-V inversion now mastered). Variety of two-clause sentences increases. Development of various cohesive devices (pro-verb "*do*", anaphoric pronoun reference, and ellipsis). |

Another characteristic of child language that receives attention is that it is rule-governed, even if initially the rules they create do not correspond to adult ones.

As early as the two-word stage, children express relationships between elements in a sentence, such as possession, negation or location, in a consistent way. Also, it has been demonstrated convincingly that when children produce an adult-like form which is the result of the application of a rule, such as adding -*s* to *dog* in order to produce the plural form *dogs*, they are not merely imitating and repeating parrot-fashion the adult language around them.

Two kinds of evidence prove that very clearly. First, children commonly produce forms such as *sheeps or *breads, which they have never heard before and are therefore not imitating. Second, some ingenious and now famous experiments were carried out with very young children back in the 1950s, in which children were shown a picture of a strange bird-like creature and told, for example, *This is a* *wug, they were then shown a picture of two of those creatures and told *Now there is another* *wug. *There are two of them. They are two* _____.

This is a *wug*.

Now there is another *wug*.
There are two of them.
They are two _____.

The children almost invariably replied *wugs (91% of them), showing that they do not merely learn plurals by remembering each plural form they hear, but that they extract a plural rule from the language they hear, and then apply that rule to their own productions. This experiment did not only contain a series of nonsense nouns, but also nonsense verbs; for example, children were shown a picture of a person doing some strange action and told: *This person knows how to* *gling. He is* *glinging. Yesterday, he did the same thing. Yesterday, he ... ?* Children consistently answered *glinged (77% of them), again showing that they had created a rule for forming the past tense. In fact, children go through a stage, initially, of correctly supplying irregular past-tense forms, such as *took* or *went*, on the basis of having learnt these forms individually, before having created the past-tense rule. When they do so, they start producing forms such as *\*taked* and *\*goed*, which can persist for a very long time despite attempts at correction by worried parents. It is only much later that children will be able to take on board to the rules for English irregular verbs.

### 3.2.2 Positive and Negative Reinforcements in Children's L1 Acquisition

The fact that children do not seem to correct their "errors" on the basis of adult implied correction of children's utterances is well-documented in the first language acquisition literature. The following dialogue (Pinker, 1994:281) is typical of the uselessness of such attempts. One proposal is that children learn to produce correct (grammatical) sentences because they are positively reinforced when they say something right, and negatively reinforced when they say something wrong.

CHILD: *Nobody don't like me.*
MOTHER: *No, say "Nobody likes me".*
CHILD: *Nobody don't like me.*
(Dialogue was repeated eight times.)
MOTHER: *Now, listen carefully, say "Nobody likes me".*
CHILD: *Oh, nobody don't likes me.*

One kind of reinforcement is correction of "bad grammar" and reward for "good grammar". Brown and his colleagues at Harvard University studied parent-child interactions. They reported that reinforcement seldom occured, and when it did, it was usually incorrect pronunciation or incorrect reporting of facts that was corrected. They noted, for example, that the ungrammatical sentence *Her curl my hair* was not corrected because Eve's mother was in fact curling her hair. However, when Eve uttered the syntactically correct sentence: *Walt Disney comes on Tuesday,* she was corrected because the television program was shown on Wednesday.

They concluded that it was "truth value" rather than "syntactic well-formedness" that chiefly governed explicit verbal reinforcement by parents. Even if syntactic correction occurred more often than it actually did, it would not explain how or what children learned from adult responses, or how children constructed the correct rules.

In fact, attempts to correct a child's language are doomed to failure. Children do not know what they are doing wrong and are unable to make corrections even when errors are pointed out. The psycholinguist Martin Braine (1988) once tried for several weeks to correct one of his daughter's grammatical errors. Here is the story:

Child: *Want other one spoon, Daddy.*

Father: *You mean, you want THE OTHER SPOON.*

Child: *Yes, I want other one spoon, please, Daddy.*

Father: *Can you say 'the other spoon?*

Child: *Other ... one ... spoon.*

Father: *Say ... other.*

Child: *Other.*

Father: *Spoon.*

Child: *Spoon.*

Father: *Other ... spoon.*

Child: *Other ... spoon. Now give me other one spoon?*

Such conversations between parents and children do not occur often. This conversation was between a linguist who studies on child language and his child. Mothers and fathers are usually delighted that their young children are talking and consider every utterance a wonder. The "mistakes" children make are cute and repeated endlessly to anyone who will listen.

### 3.2.3 Beneficial Views from Children's L1 Acquisition

From this necessarily brief and oversimplified account of early L1 research on language acquisition, the following are concluded as the characteristics of L1A:

1. Children's language acquisition goes through several stages;
2. These stages are very similar across children for a given language, although the rate at which individual children progress through them is highly variable;

3. These stages are similar across languages;
4. Child language is rule-governed and systematic, and the rules created by the child do not necessarily correspond to adult ones;
5. Children are resistant to correction;
6. Children's mental capacity limits the number of rules they can apply at any one time, and they will revert to earlier hypotheses when two or more rules compete.

These findings seem to support Chomsky's claims that children follow some kind of pre-programmed, internal route in acquiring language. Though certain stages of acquisition can be identified, development is continuous. Children usually do not jump from one stage to the next but rather progress gradually with the result that "new" and "old" patterns of language use co-exist side by side at any one point in time.Inter-learner variability exists in L1A. This is most evident in the rate of acquisition. Individual differences may be attributable to the strategies different learners follow. Although some children with one strategy show evidence of the developmental progression, other children using different strategies typically remain silent for a longer period of time before uttering full sentences when they start to talk.

## 3.3 The Controversy between Behaviorist and Mentalist Models

Language has magic power for the child and it is a wonderful tool for the child to use to acquire whatever he/she wants. Further, children are best at imitating what around him/her by modeling their behavior. In natural settings, children learn his/her mother tongue without being aware of the language.

Behaviorist learning model claims that children acquired the L1 by trying to imitate utterances produced by people around them and by receiving negative or positive reinforcement of their attempts to do so. Language acquisition, therefore, was considered to be environmentally determined.

According to the Behaviorist theory and social learning theory, feedback, either positive or negative, comes in many forms. A smile, praise, nod, kiss, gentle touch, and even getting what the child wants through the correct use of language constitute positive feedback; and a criticism, frown, cold face, refusal and even not getting what the child wants for wrong use of language are punitive enough for the child.

The behaviorist model has been criticized on grounds that children received very little formal feedback on correctness of their utterances, many of which are uniquely created rather than imitated, and that the behaviorist model was advanced not on the basis of studies of child language but through findings from its studies of animals in laboratory settings.

Humans are different from other animals in terms of learning ability in that they are able to infer what they have not learnt from what they have learnt. A mentalist model makes itself distinctive with the following claims:

1. Language is human-specific;
2. Language exists as an independent faculty in the human mind. It is separated from the general cognitive mechanisms responsible for intellectual development;
3. The primary determinant of acquisition is the child's language acquisition device (LAD), which genetically provides the child with a general set of principles about language which can be used to discover the rules of a particular language;
4. Input data are required to trigger the process by which the LAD discovers the rules of the learned language.

It is imprudent to claim any easiness for children's language acquisition, as the mentalists hold the view that children learn their mother tongue quite easily. The process a baby learns her mother tongue will tell that it is not true. It usually takes a child years of working with language until they are able to use that language fluently. Mastery of a language means much more than the ability to speak fluently.

In general, the mentalist model is at most a plausible hypothesis which can neither be falsified nor proven. People agree that it is inappropriate to study human behavior from studies of animal behavior in laboratory settings. But the questions still remain:

*Is human behavior totally different from animal behavior?*
*Is language learning completely different from learning in general?*

Biologically, humans are different from other animals, but the existence of an independent LAD is dubious. If that is the case, language learning will be one thousand times easier than it actually is. From the perspectives of linguistics, language is made up of syntax, phonology, semantics, morphology, and pragmatics. No single part of the brain is able to be responsible for all of them. Language function in the brain is actually a network. Researchers have attempted to account for L1/L2 acquisition in terms of hypothesis testing, but it was criticized for being inefficient. Others seek to explain acquisition in terms of discovery procedures that are used to scan input data and to store noticed features. The third model is cognitive in nature. Proponents of such a model agree with the mentalists that children must make use of innate knowledge, but disagree about its nature.

Cognitive-neurological studies show that some parts of the human brain are responsible for the production and comprehension of language, but there is not enough evidence to show that language function is separate from the general cognitive mechanisms responsible for intellectual development, as the parts responsible for language also have other functions.

Cognitive psychologists argue that it consists of a general learning mechanism responsible for all forms of cognitive development, not just the language. Language acquisition has non-linguistic origins (the sensory motor stage precedes the onset of speech in children), and linguistic and cognitive knowledge develops concurrently.

## 3.4 Developmental Patterns in L2 Acquisition

### 3.4.1 Early Stages

Early stages of L2A in naturalistic settings are characterized by a silent period, the use of formulaic speech, and structural and semantic simplification. In L1A, it is necessary for children to go through a lengthy period of listening to people talk to them before they produce their first words in order that they can discover what language is and what it does. In L2A, the silent period is not obligatory because the learner already knows about language and his/her cognitive ability has been well developed, thus to lay the foundation for language. Researches show that many learners, especially children, opt for a silent period. But findings are not conclusive.

Learners, especially classroom learners, begin to talk as soon as they start learning an L2. And there is considerable individual variation in the length of the silent period, with an average of just two weeks. Even those who opted for a silent period were not completely silent, but often produced some forms of expressions right from the beginning. The reason for the silent period lies in the learner's social and cognitive orientation: outer-directed and inner-directed. The former regard language as an interpersonal social tool, with a focus on the message they wish to convey, while the latter consider language as an intrapersonal task, with a focus on the language code.

Silent period provides language learners with chances to prepare themselves for social use of the L2 by means of private speech with themselves, thus, perhaps preparing themselves for social speech later. Those who practice private speech would be good learners, whereas those who do not would not learn at all.

### 3.4.2 Formulaic Speech

L2 learners have to memorize a lot of formulaic expressions in order to communicate smoothly with native speakers. The expressions frequently embody the societal knowledge which a community shares, and are essential in dealing with daily situations, enabling the user to say the right thing at the right time in the right place.

Formulaic expressions are learnt as unanalysable wholes and employed on particular occasions, different from other samples of learner language due to their well-formedness: *No like it.* as in *I don't like it.* Each expression is closely tied to the performance of a particular function which is communicatively important to the learner. It consists of entire scripts, such as greeting sequences, which the learner can memorize because they are fixed and predictable. Formulaic speech (lexical phrases) is commonly used by both native speakers and L2 learners, which reflects the forms of language behavior. For example, *Can I help you? Could I come in? What's for dinner? What's on today?* and so on.

Achieving native-like control involves not just learning a rule system that will generate an infinite number of sentences stems.

Pattern: *NP be-tense sorry to keep-tense you waiting*
Realizations: *I'm sorry to keep you waiting.*
*I'm so sorry to have kept you waiting.*
*Mr. X was sorry to keep you waiting the other day.*

The whole utterances learned as memorized chunks as *I don't know, What's your name? How old are you?* patterns and utterances that are only partially analyzed have one or more open slots. For example, *Would you please_____?* and *Can I have ____?* So here comes another question:

*To what extent do these patterns help or hinder the acquisition of L2 grammar?*

Formulaic expressions serve as the basis for subsequent creative speech when the learner comes to realize that utterances initially understood and used as wholes consist of discrete constituents that can be combined with other constituents in a variety of rule-bound ways. For example:

*The one I don't know.*
*What's this?*
*I don't know what is this?* (Combination)
*I don't like.*
*I don't understand.* ("*don't*" came to be used in similar but different expressions.)
*I know this.* ("*know*" was eventually used without "*don't*".)
*You don't know where it is.* (Subject is replaced.)

Then, chunks are slowly memorized, releasing valuable information, which is put into the knowledge system the learner used to produce and understand creative speech. Formulaic speech and rule-created speech are unrelated. It is not easy to distinguish between formulaic and creative speech.

Language learners seem to make use of patterns that are varied to a greater or lesser extent through lexical substitution. Such speech has both formulaic and creative elements. The task the learner is facing is not just that of acquiring a rule system but also of mastering a set of lexicalized sentence patterns that will enable him/her to process language efficiently. The development of nativelike competence requires the memorization of a large set of formulaic chunks and patterns.

### 3.4.3 Structural and Semantic Simplification

The learner's early "creative" utterances are typically truncated, consisting of just one or two words, with both grammatical features and content words missing.

e.g. *Banana.* ( = *I want a banana.*)

*Clean floor.* ( = *Please give me something for cleaning floors.*)

1. Structural simplification is evident in the omission of grammatical items such as auxiliary verbs, articles and bound morphemes like plural *-s* and past *-ed*.

2. Semantic simplification involves the omission of content words — nouns, verbs, adjectives and adverbs — which would normally appear in the nativelike speech.

The reason for such simplifications is that either learners have not acquired the necessary linguistic forms or they are unable to access them in the production of specific utterances. Structural simplification can be described by means of the traditional categories of a descriptive grammar. Semantic simplification is best accounted for in terms of the descriptive categories by a case grammar. For example:

*He is hitting me.* (Agent + Action Process + Patient)
*Hitting.* (Action + Process)
*He hitting.* (Agent + Action + Process)
*Hitting me.* (Action + Process + Patient)
*He me.* (Agent + Patient)

As a matter of fact, at this stage of language development, the child frequently receives a lot of positive and negative feedback from parents and any caretaker around him/her. They are always asking him/her questions for clarification (similar to correction), but are frustrated from time to time by their misunderstanding and his/her failing to get what he/she wants. In such cases, the child is all the time struggling with the choice of words and the relations between words he/she chooses to represent his/her cognitive knowledge of the world.

### 3.4.3.1 The Acquisition of Morphemes—the Morpheme Studies

Acquisition of both morphemes and syntactic structures takes place in a number of stages, and the acquisition of a single feature also occurs across several stages. Motivated by similar studies in L1A, morpheme studies were carried out to investigate the acquisition order of English grammatical functors such as articles and inflectional features (plural -s).

Though not in complete agreement, findings indicate that some English morphemes are acquired earlier than others. Roughly speaking, their development follows the following route:

-ing / pl. / copula → aux. / art. → irregular past → regular past / $3^{rd}$ person sing. / possessive -'s.

Though the standard acquisition order is not rigidly invariant, but is remarkably similar irrespective of the language learner's L1 background, age and whether the medium is writing or speech. The studies of some world languages other than English also reveal similar acquisition order of morphemes.

### 3.4.3.2 The Acquisition of Individual Morphemes

A close look at individual morphemes shows that they are also acquired gradually and systematically through the stages. Learners do not progress from a state of non-acquisition to a state of acquisition, but through a series of stages. Take the acquisition of pronouns as an example:

| Person - $\begin{cases} I \\ he \\ you \end{cases}$ | Number - $\begin{cases} He \\ they \end{cases}$ | Gender - $\begin{cases} He \\ she \end{cases}$ | Case - $\begin{cases} He \\ me \end{cases}$ | Personal -him/her Possessive -his/her | Occasion of use: when to omit and when to use |
|---|---|---|---|---|---|

The following is a description of the stages for acquisition of English pronouns:

| Stages | Descriptions |
|---|---|
| 1 | Distinguishing just one feature, usually **person**, often just $1^{st}$ person from others. |
| 2 | Distinguishing pronouns according to **number**. |
| 3 | **Third person pronouns** added, but without gender distinction. |
| 4 | **Gender** distinguished. |

The pronoun system of a language is distinguished on the semantic dimensions and empirical studies show that English pronouns are acquired in the way quite similar to the above. Other studies with French, German and Spanish as L2s show similar pattern of language development.

So the following conclusions can be arrived at: learners with different languages as L2s experience similar problems with pronouns and solve them in similar ways. Studies show that the L1 is a factor in acquisition sequence, but there is strong evidence of universal patterns of acquisition, at least several Indo-European languages are concerned.

### 3.4.3.3 The Acquisition of Syntactic Structures

Studies conducted with English and German as L2s indicate that there exist developmental patterns in L2A.

**1. The acquisition of negatives in English**

Development of English negatives shows that the learner should follow the similar route, irrespective of the learner's L1 background (Japanese, Spanish, German, or Norwegian) and his/her age (children, adolescents, and adults):

**Firstly,** the negative particle (usually "*no*", but sometimes "*not*") is attached to a declarative nucleus. For example: *No very high. *No you watching TV.* and so on.

**Secondly,** internal negation develops; that is, the negative particle is moved inside the utterance. Negators like "*not*" and/or "*don't*" together with "*no*" are used, but at this stage, "*don't*" is still formulaic as it has not been analyzed into its components "*do*" and "*not*". For example: *Mariana not coming today. *I no can swim.* and so on.

**Thirdly,** negators are attached to model verbs, but generally occur in unanalyzed units. For example: *I can't play this one. I won't go.* and so on.

**Finally,** the L2 rule is acquired. An auxiliary system has been developed, and learners use "*not*" regularly as particle ("*no*" + verb is eliminated). Negative utterances are now marked for tense and number, but not always correctly. Here are some examples for consideration:* *He doesn't came yesterday.* *He didn't said it.* *She didn't believe two of me.* and so on.

The following table describes the stages of acquisition sequences of negation in L2 English:

| Stages | Descriptions | Examples |
| --- | --- | --- |
| 1 | External negation (i.e. "*no*" or "*not*" is at the beginning of the utterance). | *No you are playing here. |
| 2 | Internal negation (i.e. the negator "*no*", "*not*", or "*don't*" is put between the subject and the main verb). | Mariana **not** coming today. |
| 3 | Negative attachment to modal verbs. | I can't play that one. |
| 4 | Negative attachment to auxiliary verb as in target language rule. | *She didn't believe **two of me**. *He didn't **said** it. |

Learners differed from each other in the rate of development. Some could take longer than 2 years and some never traveled the whole distance. The stages are not clearly defined, but overlap considerably. Individual learners behaved differently in their choice of negative particles. Studies of the development of German negatives as L2 show markedly similar developmental patterns, although the "final state" toward which learners of English and German are different in their targets.

## 2. The acquisition of relative clauses in English

The acquisition of English relative clauses presents learners with two tasks: firstly, learners must learn that relative clauses can modify noun phrases that occur both before the verb (as subject of the main clause) and after the verb (as object or in a preposition phrase). Secondly, the learner must learn the functions that the relative pronoun can serve. Here is the table for the functions of relative pronoun in English.

| Functions | Examples |
| --- | --- |
| 1. Subject | The man **who** lives next door ... |
| 2. Direct object | The man **whom** I saw ... |
| 3. Indirect object | The man to **whom** I gave a present ... |
| 4. Object of preposition | The man about **whom** we talked ... |
| 5. Genitive | The man **whose** wife has an accident ... |
| 6. Object of comparative | The man **that** I am richer than ... |

(1) The acquisition of relative clauses with regard to the first task:

**Firstly,** learners may begin by attaching a relative clause to a noun phrase that follows the verb. Often, they retain a pronominal copy. For example:

*I know the man *who he coming.*

The relative pronoun may be functioning in a similar way to the co-coordinator "*and*", joining two main clauses. Only when learners omit the pronominal copy can they be said to have acquired the use of relative clauses. For example:

Tom is a boy *who is silly.*

**Secondly,** relative clauses modifying the subject of the main clause appear later. For example:

*The boy takes care of the dogs *who doesn't have anybody to live with.*

(2) The acquisition of relative clauses with regard to the second task:

**Firstly,** learners may begin by omitting the relative pronoun. For example:

*I got a friend speaks French.*

**Secondly,** they may use an ordinary personal pronoun. For example:

*I got a friend he speaks French.*

**Thirdly,** the relative pronoun proper is used. For example:

*I got a friend who speaks French.*

Other studies could find no clear evidence for distinguishing the order of acquisition of indirect object and genitive object of comparison. The retention of pronominal copies is also linked to the acquisition of the functions of the relative pronouns. The extent to which learners retain copies is influenced by their L1.

### 3.4.4 The Hypothesis of L1 & L2 Acquisition

The hypothesis is also called the *identity hypothesis,* which intends to answer the following two questions: *Are the universal principles that underlie L1 and L2 the same? Is LAD which mentalists claim is responsible for L1 available to L2 learners?*

SLA Research findings show that the similarities in learner language in L1 and L2 acquisition are most remarkable at the early stage of development. There is evidence of a silent period, of the use rules, and of structural and semantic simplification in both of them. And there also exists slight differences:

Many L2 learners, especially adults, do not experience a silent period. They appear to make greater use of rules and are also able to produce longer and less propositionally reduced utterances from the beginning.

Though SLA researchers disagree with each other, the morpheme acquisition order is not the same in L1 and L2 acquisition. The process by which individual morphemes are acquired display similarities and differences. The similarities between two types of acquisition are strong in syntactic structures. **L2 learners** appear to tackle the problem of learning a language in similar ways to L1 learners.

Similarities are most evident in informal learning situations when learners are attempting to engage in unplanned language use. Differences are observed in formal learning situations. Informal learning involves implicit learning, while formal learning is likely to involve at least some explicit knowledge of L2 rules. However, in general, L1 acquisition is different in many ways from FL learning which calls for more detailed observations and scientific researches.

The following table is a summary of the differences between L1 and L2 learning:

| Features | L1 acquisition | L2 acquisition |
| --- | --- | --- |
| **Overall success** | Children normally achieve perfect mastery of their L1. | Adult learners are very unlikely to achieve perfect mastery. |
| **General failure** | Success is guaranteed and failure is rare. | Complete success is very rare and failure is predictable. |

续表

| | | |
|---|---|---|
| **Variation** | There is little variation among L1 learners with regard to overall success or the path they follow. | L2 learners vary in both their degree of success, and the path they go through. Giving-up halfway frequently occurs. |
| **Goals** | The goal is a full competence and of the targeted language. | L2 learners may be content with less than target language competence and may also be more concerned with fluency than accuracy. |
| **Fossilization** | Fossilization is unknown in child language development. | L2 learners often cease to develop and also backslide (return to earlier stages of development). |
| **Intuition** | Children develop clear intuitions regarding what is a correct and incorrect sentence. | L2 learners are often unable to form clear grammaticality judgments. |
| **Instruction** | Children do not need formal lessons to learn their L1. | There is wide belief that instruction helps L2 learners in some way. |
| **Negative evidence** | Children's "errors" are not formally corrected, and correction is not necessary for acquisition. | Correction generally viewed as helpful and, by some, as necessary to L2 learners. |
| **Affective factors** | Success is not influenced by children's personality, motivation, attitudes, etc. | Affective factors play a major role in determining and enhancing proficiency of L2 learners. |

## 3.5 Conclusion

This chapter presents the studies on the acquisition of L1, moving through various stages from babbling to the creation of words to the development of complex syntax. Child second language acquisition is also considered together with the role of language transfer. L1 studies have thrown plenty of insights on the field of SLA research. There are some similarities and a lot of differences as well. In the next chapter there is an introduction to the history of SLA research.

 Points for Thinking

1. What is the significance of Aitchison's acquisition stages of children language?
2. How do the children acquire the 14 pragmatic competence English morphemes in Brown's "morpheme study"?
3. What are beneficial views obtained from the studies on children's L1 acquisition?
4. What are the differences between the Behaviorist learning model and that of Mentalist?
5. What is the significance of studies on analyzing similarities and differences between L1A and SLA?

 Further Reading

Aitchison, J. (1989). *The Articulate Mammal*. London: Routledge, as referenced in Willis, Shortall & Johns (2001:68).
Brown, H. et al. (Eds.) (1977). *On TESOL 77*. Washington D.C.: TESOL.
Brown, R.O. (1973). *Early Syntactic Development*. Cambridge, MA: MIT Press.
Chomsky, N. (1959). "Review of B. F. Skinner's Verbal Behavior." *Language* 35:26 – 58.
Chomsky, N. (2002). *On Nature and Language*. Cambridge: Cambridge University Press.
Ellis, R. (1997). *Second Language Acquisition*. Oxford: Oxford University Press.
Gass, S. and Selinker, L. (2008). *Second Language Acquisition: An Introductory Course*. 3$^{rd}$ Edition. Hillsdale, NJ: Lawrence Erlbaum Associates.
Slobin, D. (1985—1997). *The Crosslinguistic Study of Language Acquisition*. Vol. 1 – 5. Hillsdale, NJ: Lawrence Erlbaum Associates.

# Chapter 4

# Recent History of SLA Research

## 4.1 Introduction

In the previous chapter, L1A is a complicated but relatively rapid process through which children become fluent users of their native language(s). However, for those of people who start learning a language after childhood — for example, by enrolling in a foreign language (FL) course or moving to a new country — the process of learning an FL is far more difficult and much less likely to end in complete mastery or fluency.

Adult FL learners usually take years to reach a level of proficiency that most children may attain easily before their age of five, and few adults achieve native-like mastery of L2s or FLs, no matter how hard they try after they pass their childhood.

The L2 or FL learners frequently ask questions as:
1. What can explain the differences between an adult FL/L2 learner and a child L1 learner?
2. Why do some people call themselves as "the worst language learners in the world"?
3. Do adults learn L2s in the same way as children learning their L1? If not, why?
4. What kinds of instruction or learning contexts are most effective for adults?

These questions are central to the field of SLA. Though scholars have been interested in language learning for centuries, SLA research is relatively young. From the 1940s onwards, scholars began to propose a number of different theories to explain how people learn non-native languages. There is a need of an introduction to the theories of SLA — from behaviorist learning model to recent hypotheses about the input and interaction within cognitive consideration in SLA.

The kinds of research questions today are mostly rooted in earlier developments in linguistics, psychology, sociology and pedagogy. The aim of this chapter is not to present an exhaustive description of early approaches, but rather to explore the theoretical foundations of the present SLA research. The description will begin from second half of $20^{th}$ century, the time of theorizing about language learning, a period from an adjunct to language pedagogy, to an autonomous field of SLA research.

## 4.2 The Early Studies on Language Acquisition (to 1960s)

In the 1950s and early 1960s, theorizing about L2A was still very much an adjunct to the practice of language teaching. However, the idea that language teaching methods had to be justified in terms of a learning theory was well-established, since the pedagogic reform movements of the late $19^{th}$ century.

The language learning history is traced back to the 1950s and 1960s, when an impact of the "Chomskyan revolution" in linguistics came into the field of language acquisition: initially on the study of L1A and later on that of SLA. The impact on psycholinguistics in the 1970s, and its influence is still very much felt today.

As far as linguistics was concerned, "progressive" 1950s language pedagogy drew on a version of structuralism by the linguist, Palmer, in the 1920s, and subsequently by Fries and his colleagues in the 1940s. Howatt summed up this approach as follows:

*The conviction that language systems consisted of a finite set of "patterns" or "structures" which acted as models ... for the production of an infinite number of similarly constructed sentences; the belief that repetition and practice resulted in the formation of accurate and fluent foreign language habits; a methodology which set out to teach "the basics" before encouraging learners to communicate their own thoughts and ideas.*

Howatt, 1988, pp. 14–15

Howatt made clear his view that the learning theory to which language teaching experts were appealing at that time, was the general learning theory that was dominant in mainstream psychology, behaviorism.

### 4.2.1 Behavioristic View of Learning — Habit Formation

Early researchers attempted to apply behaviorist theories to the field of L1A. In the behaviorist view, language learning is seen, like any other kind of learning, as the formation of habits.

This behavioristic view of learning stems from work in psychology that described the learning of any kind based on the notions of stimulus and response. The view sees human beings as being exposed to numerous stimuli in their environment. The response they give to such stimuli will be reinforced if successful, whenever desired outcome is obtained. Through repeated reinforcement, a certain stimulus will elicit the same response time and again, which will then become a habit. Thus, the learning of any skill is seen as habit formation.

In language learning, a certain situation will call for a certain response. Meeting someone will call for a certain greeting, and the response will be reinforced if the greeting is understood. Otherwise, the response will not be reinforced, and will be abandoned. The learner will try a new one.

Behaviorist theories and the approach were widely influential in the 1950s and 1960s. Behaviorists believed that L2 learners — like children learning their L1 (or any other skill) — acquired the appropriate language behaviors (or "habits") through repetition and reinforcement. They believed that learners of English as a second language would learn the plural -s form most effectively by producing it repeatedly in their own speech.

As such, in classrooms, teachers often required learners to imitate and repeat in pattern drills (as *two cats, three dogs, five cows, seven pigs*, etc.) without necessarily paying attention to meaning. Though there is no tragedy that any students "died" from this pattern practice, the exercise of dull repetition became known as "drill and kill".

### 4.2.2 Contrastive Analysis

As language learning then was viewed as habit formation. It seemed likely that a person of one language would re-form his habits when learning an L2 and that these "old habits" would be helpful if they were similar to the new habits, but would interfere with correct learning if they were different. When a child learns an L1, the process is relatively simple: all he/she has to do is to form a set of habits as learning to respond to stimuli in his/her environment. When learning an L2, however, he/she runs into problems: he/she already has a set of well-established L1 "habits". The process of L2A therefore involves replacing those habits by a set of new ones.

An approach called Contrastive Analysis (CA) came into being for L2 learning and teaching. In order to determine which "habits" might cause interference, the structures of the two languages were systematically compared within a structuralist paradigm. If the existing L1 "habits" differed from those of L2, they could interfere with L2 development. A native speaker of Japanese, a language that has no distinction between /r/ and /l/ sounds, would tend to have problems pronouncing /r/ and /l/ in English — leading to jokes about restaurants that serve *flied lice* with the meal.

Contrastive analysis is a way of comparing languages in order to determine potential errors. As Lado pointed out in 1957, the ultimate goal was to predict areas that would be either easy or difficult for learners. Differences between the learner's L1 and the L2 were thought to be the main source of difficulty for the L2 learners. This became formally known as the Contrastive Analysis Hypothesis (CAH).

The complication is that the old L1 habits interfere with this process, either helping or inhibiting it. If structures in L2 are similar to those of L1, then learning will take place easily. Otherwise, structures are realized differently in L1 and L2, and then learning will be difficult. As such, the German structure would be much easier to learn, and the French more difficult, the English structure acting as a facilitator in one instance, and an inhibitor in the other.

There was little doubt that the learner's L1 influences the learning of L2, but researchers also found that not all errors predicted by the CAH were actually made. Moreover, quite a few errors that L2 learners made seemed to be unrelated to their L1, and L2 learners with different L1s often made similar errors.

By the early 1970s, the CAH and CA in general were criticized, not only because the hypothesis did not live up to its expectations, but even more so because the two theories—behaviorism in psychology and structuralism in linguistics—on which it was based had become outmoded and discredited. When Chomskyan hypothese came into vogue, the interest in contrasting the L1 and L2 declined because it was believed that the process of L2A was very similar to the process of L1A, which takes place without explicit attention to language forms.

### 4.2.3 Behaviorism and CA for Language Teaching

Considering language teaching, behaviorism has two-fold possible implications of its approach. Firstly, it strengthens the old saying that "practice makes perfect" in any kind of learning. In its theory, learning would take place by imitating and repeating the same structures time and again, targeting at forming a necessary habit through positive and negative reinforcement in learning. Secondly, teachers needed to focus their teaching on structures which were believed to be difficult, and these structures were different in the L1s and L2s.

The logical outcome of such beliefs about the learning process was that effective teaching would focus on areas of difference. Therefore the best teaching methods for FL teachers was a sound knowledge of those areas. Researchers embarked on the huge task of comparing pairs of languages in order to pinpoint areas of difference, therefore of difficulty. The term CA can be traced back to Fries, who wrote in the introduction to his book *Teaching and Learning English as a Foreign Language*.

The language teaching for two decades was based on a behaviorist view of language which is basically a system of habits. Learning takes place by producing a response to a stimulus and receiving either positive or negative reinforcement. It claims that if one receives enough positive reinforcement for a certain response it will become a habit. It should be clear that language teaching should involve a lot of pattern drills, for forming proper habits in the learner, similar to learning to drive.

### 4.2.4  Behaviorism under Attack

Both linguists and psychologists witnessed major developments in the 1950s and in the 1960s. Linguistics saw a shift from structural linguistics, based on the description of the surface structure, to generative linguistics that emphasized the rule-governed and creative nature of human language.

In the field of psychology, behaviorism in shaping the child's learning and behavior was losing ground in favor of more developmentalist views of learning, such as Piaget's cognitive developmental theory. The clash of views about the way of language learning came to a head at the end of the 1950s with two publications. They were Skinner's *Verbal Behavior* in 1957 and Chomsky's review of Skinner's book, in 1959, which was a fierce critique of Skinner's views.

Chomsky's criticisms centered on a number of issues: children do not learn and reproduce a large set of sentences, but they routinely create new sentences that they have never learnt before. This is only possible because they internalize rules rather than strings of words; extremely common examples of utterances such as *it *breaked* or *Mummy *goed* show clearly that children are not copying the language around them but applying rules.

Chomsky was also incensed by the idea that people could compare the behavior of rats in a laboratory, learning to perform simple tasks, to the behavior of children learning language without direct teaching, a fundamentally different task because of its sheer complexity and abstractness.

Furthermore, children have been shown not to be usually corrected on the form of their utterances but rather on their truth values. When correction does take place, it seems to have very little effect on the development of language structure.

For the above reasons, Chomsky claimed that children have an innate faculty that guides them in their learning of language. Given a body of speech, children are programmed to discover its rules, and are guided in doing that by an innate knowledge of what the rules should look like. There is to be a detailed discussion of Chomsky's ideas in later chapters. Suffice it to say for now in this chapter that this revolutionary approach to the study of language gave a great stimulus to the field of psycholinguistics, and especially to the study of L1A and L2A.

## 4.3 The Following-up Studies in 1970s and 1980s

There was a move in 1970s away from behaviorist theories and to approaches that focused on the various learner-internal mechanisms involved in L2A. It consequently led to the emergence of new theories of SLA. Thus, there came a wealth of studies in L2 learners that seemed to show convincingly that it is systematic, that it is largely independent of the L1 of the learner, and that it presents many similarities with L1A, even though there are differences. These were empirical findings that overturned the contemporary beliefs about how L2s are acquired.

### 4.3.1 The Birth of Error Analysis and Interlanguage

The findings soon came to the attention of researchers and teachers interested in SLA. They noticed that the predictions made by Contrastive Analysis did not seem to be effective in practice. Teachers were finding out that differences in pairs of languages were not necessarily difficult, and similarities in two languages not easy.

Contrastive Analysis predicted that all errors would be caused by interference from L1, which was shown to be unfounded. L2A studies showed convincingly that the most of errors could not be traced to L1. Such studies became common, and a book-length treatment of the topic appeared in 1974 by Richards who proposed Error Analysis (EA) as a replacement for Contrastive Analysis.

The L2 produced by learners began to be seen as a linguistic system in its own right, worthy of description. Corder in 1967 began to focus attention on studying learners' errors, as they evidently did not all originate in L1 by any means. EA showed clearly that most of the errors made by L2 learners did not come from their L1.

SLA researchers started to classify errors and to compare them with those made by children learning their L1. Child language was seen as an object of study in its own right, rather than as an approximation of adult language. In SLA research, coupled with the interest in understanding learner-internal errors, interest in the overall character of the L2 system was also growing. It could not be denied that the first language did have an influence on the L2, but not as starting point to predict L2 errors. The learner's language, or rather "Interlanguage" (IL), a term by Selinker in 1972, became the starting point for analyzing L2 learner's errors.

IL refers to the language that the L2 learner produced, both as a system which can be described at any one point in time as resulting from systematic rules and systems that characterize learner progression. In other words, the IL concept relies on two fundamental notions: the language produced by the learner is a system in its own right; and it is a dynamic system, evolving over time. IL studies thus moved one step beyond EA, by focusing on the learner system, rather than only on its errors.

Some of the L2 learner's errors could be traced back to "cross-linguistic influence", going from L1 to L2 and vice versa, or to "language transfer" that not only errors are transferred (negative transfer) from L1 to L2, but also things that were similar between L1 and L2 can be helpful in acquiring the L2 (positive transfer). Many L2 errors do occur in a learner's L2, traceable to the L1 or not. It is much in line with thinking in terms of Dynamic Systems Theory. As was previously mentioned, errors and a great deal of variability are parts of an individual's L2 learning process.

In the following five sentences, each with a clear L2 error, two are clearly related to the L1, the others are not (from James, 1998:147).

1. *Can I *become* (rather than *get*; from German *bekommen*) a beefsteak.
2. *He wanted to *cancel* (rather than *conceal*) his guilt.
3. *I think Senhor is *constipated* (rather than *caught a cold*; from Portuguese *constipado*).
4. *It was a *genius* (rather than *genuine*) diamond.
5. *She listened to his *speak* (rather than *speech*).

At one point EA developed two totally different goals. Firstly, through addressing those errors clearly influenced by the L1, the applied linguists such as Corder and James could improve the teaching process. Secondly, applied linguists such as Gass and Selinker wanted to study the learner's IL in its own right, not so much to discover the ways to teach but to discover in a more abstract manner how L2 is learned.

A somewhat confused picture thus emerges from the empirical characteristics of the 1970s and the 1980s. Researches have tried to address some of the L2A issues. But before we turn to the 1990s, we need to review a highly influential attempt to conceptualize these issues in a comprehensive model by Krashen's Monitor Model.

### 4.3.2 Krashen and His Monitor Model

Krashen's theory evolved in the late 1970s in a series of articles, as a result of L2A findings. Krashen thereafter refined and expanded his ideas in the early 1980s in a series of books and based his general theory around a set of five basic hypotheses: 1) the Acquisition-Learning hypothesis; 2) the Monitor hypothesis; 3) the Natural Order hypothesis; 4) the Input hypothesis and 5) the Affective Filter hypothesis.

#### 4.3.2.1 The Acquisition-Learning Hypothesis

This hypothesis has been highly influential, and still remains the source of much debate today. It claims that Acquisition and Learning are separate processes. Acquisition refers to the "subconscious process identical in all important ways to the process children utilize in acquiring their first language" and learning refers to the "conscious process" those results in "knowing about" language (Krashen, 1985:1).

Acquisition is the result of natural interaction with the language via meaningful communication, and learning is the result of classroom experience, in which the learner is made to focus on form and to learn about the rules of L2s. In Krashen's terminology, learners would have learnt the rule, but not acquired it.

Krashen has been criticized for his vague definition of what constitutes conscious versus subconscious processes, as they are very difficult to test in practice. Nonetheless, this contrast between acquisition and learning has been very influential, especially among FL teachers who saw it as an explanation of the lack of correspondence between error correction and direct teaching, on one hand, and their students' accuracy of performance, on the other.

What is problematic in this distinction is Krashen's claim that learning cannot turn into acquisition, that is, that language knowledge acquired or learnt by these different routes cannot eventually become integrated into a unified whole. The debate about whether different kinds of knowledge interact or remain separate is still alive today, even though the terms used might differ.

#### 4.3.2.2 The Monitor Hypothesis

The Monitor Hypothesis states that acquisition "initiates" the speaker's utterances and is responsible for fluency, and "learning has only one function as a Monitor or editor" and that "learning comes into play" only to "make changes" in the form of utterance, after it has been "produced" by the acquired system. The Monitor is thought to alter the output of the acquired system before or after the utterance is actually spoken out, but the utterance is initiated entirely by the acquired system.

The concept of the Monitor explains individual differences in learners. It is clear that the Monitor does not operate all the time. When learners need the grammatical rules, they might make use of the Monitor to consciously modify the output produced by the acquired system. Needless to say, the pressures and demands of conversing in the L2 in real time do not often allow for such monitoring to take place.

There are three groups of Monitor users. Monitor "over-users" attempt to avoid making mistakes and are constantly checking the conscious stock of rules they possess. Their speech is consequently very halting and non-fluent. Then Monitor "under-users" seem not to care much about the errors they make, because speed and fluency are more important for them. They rely closely on the acquired system and do not seem able or willing to consciously apply what they have learnt to their output. In between the two are the supposed "optimal Monitor users", who use the Monitor hypothesis when it is appropriate and does not interfere with communication.

Monitor hypothesis has been criticized for the fact that they are for the time being impossible to test and prove empirically in the researches.

#### 4.3.2.3 The Natural Order Hypothesis

The Natural Order hypothesis is undoubtedly supported by the kind of empirical evidence on L2 acquisition. The learners acquire the rules of language in a predictable order, some rules tending to come early and others late. The order does not appear to be determined solely by formal simplicity and there is evidence that it is independent of the order in which rules are taught in language classes.

Although there is evidently some truth in its claims, this hypothesis has been criticized for being too strong. It ignores well-documented cases of language transfer, or of individual variability. Not only are such cases ignored; there is no place for them in Krashen's theory.

The hypothesis has also been criticized for being based almost exclusively on the morpheme studies which, in any case, reflect accuracy of production rather than acquisition sequences. However, Krashen provides little help in understanding why this should be the case.

#### 4.3.2.4 The Input Hypothesis

The Input hypothesis is linked to the Natural Order hypothesis in that it claims a move along the developmental continuum by receiving comprehensible input. Comprehensible input is defined as L2 input just beyond the learner's current L2 competence, in terms of its syntactic complexity. If a learner's current competence is $i$ then comprehensible input is $i+1$, the next step in the developmental sequence. Input which is either too simple ($i+i$) or too complex ($i+2/3/4$ ...) will not be useful for acquisition. Krashen views the Input hypothesis as central to his model of SLA.

He argues that speaking is a result of acquisition and not its cause. Speech cannot be taught directly but "emerges" on its own as a result of building competence via comprehensible input. If input is understood, and there is enough of it, the necessary grammar is naturally provided. The language teacher need not attempt deliberately to teach the next structure along the Natural Order — it will be provided in just the right quantities and automatically reviewed if the student receives a sufficient amount of comprehensible input.

Krashen's Input hypothesis has been frequently criticized for being vague and imprecise for determining the level $i$, and level $i+1$. This vital point has never been made clear. Moreover, his claim is somewhat circular: acquisition takes place if the learner receives comprehensible input, and comprehensible input has been provided if acquisition takes place.

The theory becomes impossible to verify, as no independently testable definitions are given of what comprehensible input actually consists of, and therefore of how it might relate to acquisition. Nor does the theory specify the internal workings of the "LAD" where acquisition actually takes place — this remains an opaque black box.

### 4.3.2.5 The Affective Filter Hypothesis

Krashen believes that learners need to receive comprehensible input for language acquisition. This is not sufficient. Learners also need to "let that input in", as it were. This is the role of the so-called Affective Filter, which supposedly determines how receptive to comprehensible input a learner is going to be. This Hypothesis captures the relationship between affective variables and the process of SLA by positing that acquirers vary with respect to the strength or level of their affective filters.

Those whose attitudes are not optimal for SLA will not only tend to seek less input, but also have a high or strong affective filter — even if they understand the message, the input will not reach that part of the brain responsible for language acquisition, or the LAD. Those with attitudes more conducive to SLA will not only seek and obtain more input; they will also have a lower or weaker filter. They will be more open to the input, and it will strike "deeper".

Although both researchers and teachers would agree that affective variables play an important role in SLA, Krashen's Affective Filter remains vague and atheoretical. Many self-conscious adolescents suffer from low self-esteem and therefore presumably have a "high" filter, so:

1. Are they therefore all bad language learners?
2. Are all the confident and extrovert adults (with a "low" filter) good language learners?

Clearly, they are not. All these issues remain vague and unexplored.

### 4.3.2.6 The Summary of Krashen's Monitor Model

This brief account has described criticisms of Krashen's five hypotheses and of his overall model, which have been current almost since Krashen first advanced them. It remains true that Krashen's ideas have been highly influential in shaping many research projects, and considerably advancing a better understanding of SLA. The Input hypothesis, for example, has stimulated a major ongoing tradition of theorizing and empirical research on input and interaction for most of SLA theorists in the field.

Krashen's overall weakness was the presentation of what were just hypotheses that remained to be tested, as a comprehensive model that had empirical validity. He used his hypotheses prematurely as a basis for drawing pedagogical implications.

As for a conclusion to the discussion and analysis on Krashen's Monitor Model, although there is criticism on the five hypotheses that Krashen put forth and on their validity as overall explanatory theory of SLA, it is nonetheless necessary to acknowledge the significant contribution this research agenda has made in the field of numerous research projects and has taken the field many steps forward, in particular by focusing attention on unexplored areas. However, there is reason to be skeptical of the substance of these hypotheses proposed by Krashen and his followers and the power attributed to them.

### 4.3.3 Schumann's Pidginization or Acculturation Model

Other models appeared in the 1970s, which attempted similarly to theorize SLA findings. One model, as it views SLA from a radically different angle, also remained influential during subsequent decades. Schumann first proposed his "Pidginization or Acculturation Model" in the late 1970s. On the basis of naturalistic studies of untutored learners, he noticed that early interlanguage resembled pidgin languages with characteristic features such as fixed word order and lack of inflections.

L2A was compared to the complexification of pidgins, and this process was linked to degree of acculturation of the learners. The closer they feel to the speech community of L2, the better learners will "acculturate", and the more successful their L2A will be. The more alienated from that L2 speech community they perceive themselves to be, the more pidgin-like their L2 will remain.

This model was influential in opening up alternative lines of research comparing L2A with pidginization and creolization, and in bringing to the social psychological variables and their role in L2A. For a substantial period, Schumann's proposals were the most theoretically ambitious claims about L2A, which drew on sociolinguistic thinking. The later chapters will resume this model, briefly, alongside other newer sociolinguistic approaches.

## 4.4 The Recent Studies on L2A (beyond 1990s)

By the mid-1980s, SLA research was no longer subordinate to the immediate practical requirements of curriculum development and education pedagogy for language teaching. Instead, it had matured itself into a more independent and autonomous field of inquiry, which encompasses a number of substantial programmes of SLA issues, with their distinctive theoretical orientations and methodologies.

### 4.4.1 The Developmental Patterns in Language Acquisition

The links of SLA research with other related disciplines have by no means disappeared, and many new links have developed ever since. SLA research into the structure of language(s) and its use continues to be extensively drawn upon, and so is research into language variation and change. There are a number of ways for researchers to set about identifying the developmental patterns in SLA — the orders and sequences. There are some methods and approaches to do the study:

The first method is to examine whether learners' errors change over time. But errors are not the total of learner language, and error analysis has not succeeded in providing clear and conclusive evidence of developmental patterns.

The second method is to examine samples and data of learner language (IL) collected over a period of time in order to identify when specific linguistic features emerge. According to this approach, "acquisition" is defined as "first occurrence". It is widely applied in L1 acquisition, but not so common in L2 acquisition researches.

The third method is obligatory occasion analysis, a common way for identifying and describing developmental patterns. The procedure is as follows:

1) collecting the samples of naturally occurring learner language;
2) identifying occasions for the use of specific L2 features;

3) calculating the percentage of accurate use of the feature;

4) providing an operational definition of whether a feature has been acquired.

The fourth method is native-like analysis. It is an extension of obligatory occasion analysis. It is designed to take into account the incorrect use of specific grammatical features in contexts.

The fifth method is frequency analysis, method of SLA research involving identifying the variants of a given feature and examining the frequency of the occurrence of each variant. For example, a learner may make negative utterances using a) "*no*" + verb, b) "*don't*"+ verb, and c) auxiliary + verb.

The sixth method is to infer the order of development from data of cross-sectional studies by using a number of statistical procedures. For example, the accuracy order with which different features were performed corresponded to the acquisition order.

The seventh method is called implicational scaling. It seeks to exploit the inter-learner variability in order to establish which features different learners have acquired and whether the features can be arranged into a hierarchy according to whether the acquisition of one feature implies the acquisition of one or more other features for each learner.

### 4.4.2 Different Roles Found in Language Acquisition

New links have emerged with cognitive science (the development of fluency; the role of awareness or consciousness while learning), with neuro-psychology (connectionist models; modularity of the brain) and with socio-cultural frameworks (Vygotskyan learning theory) that have greatly enriched both the perception and conception of the many facets of L2 acquisition. But the SLA research program continues to have its own focus on a number of fundamental SLA research issues carried forward from the 1970s. The following roles can be identified in SLA.

#### 4.4.2.1 The role of internal mechanisms

Firstly, it is language-specific as (1) how similar are the L1 and L2 acquisition processes, and how far are the similarities caused by language-specific mechanisms still being activated? (2) If language-specific mechanisms are important, how can they best be modeled? (3) How relevant is the current Chomskyan conception of Universal Grammar?

Secondly, it is cognitive as in what respects are L2 learning and processing which can be similar to the learning and processing of one's L1 and any other complex skill?

### 4.4.2.2 The role of the first language

It is clear that cross-linguistic influences from one's L1 and other languages are operating in SLA, but it is also clear that such language transfer is selective: some L1 properties transfer and others do not. An important aspect of today's research issue is still to understand better the phenomenon of transfer.

### 4.4.2.3 The role of psychological variables

These variables require the studies on the affective force of individual characteristics of the L2 learner, such as age, gender motivation, personality, language aptitude, educational background, etc., in his/her L2 learning process.

### 4.4.2.4 The role of social and environmental factors

These factors demand researches on the similarities of L2A to the creation of pidgins and Creoles, and on the overall socialization of the L2 learner is related to the language learning process.

### 4.4.2.5 The role of the input

Input plays an important role in shaping or speeding up L2A process. There exists a close relationship between the comprehensible input and internal learning mechanisms. Therefore, classroom interaction patterns do facilitate the L2 learning.

## 4.5 Conclusion

We will now turn to examine how these issues have been tackled across the range of current perspectives on SLA, starting in Chapter 3 with linguistics-inspired attempts to model the contents of the "black box" of the LAD, left largely unexplored in the proposals of Krashen, who says nothing about learning, only acquisition.

Points for Thinking

1. What is the main concern of the Behaviorist theory?
2. How does Contrastive Analysis carry out its study on L2 learning?
3. What are the differences of Error Analysis from Contrastive Analysis?
4. What are the significance and weaknesses of Krashen's Monitor Model?
5. What are the roles played by Input Hypothesis and Affective Filter Hypothesis?

 Further Reading

Ellis, R. (1997). *Second Language Acquisition.* Oxford: Oxford University Press.

Ellis, R. (Ed.) (2000). *Learning a Second Language through Interaction.* Amsterdam:John Benjamins.

Howatt, A.P.R. (1984). *A history of English Language Teaching.* Oxford: Oxford Uni. Press.

Howatt, A.P.R. (1988). "From structure to communicative." *Annual Review of Applied Linguistics* 8:14 – 29.

Krashen, S. (1985). *The Input Hypothesis: Issues and Implications.* New York:Longman.

Schumann, J. (1978b). "The acculturation model for second language acquisition." In R. Gingras (Ed.). *Second Language Acquisition and Foreign Language Teaching.* Arlington, VA: Center for Aplied Linguistics, pp.27 – 50.

# Chapter 5

# The UG Approach to Language Acquisition

## 5.1 Introduction

SLA research relatively young has been influenced in its formation by other disciplines. In turn, SLA has also exerted some influence on these source disciplines. At present, some would conceptualize SLA as an independent field with its own research agenda and with a multidisciplinary focus, whereas others would conceptualize it as a sub-discipline of one source discipline or another.

With regard to the influence, each of these disciplines has on SLA, the difference can be found in the general emphasis: 1) linguistics focuses on the products of acquisition; 2) psychology focuses on the process by which those systems are created and 3) sociolinguistics focuses on social factors that influence the linguistic product of acquisition.

In this chapter, we focus our discussion of that relationship on the area of research that has dominated the theoretical study of SLA over the years, Universal Grammar.

## 5.2 Universal Grammar (UG) for Language Acquisition

### 5.2.1 Chomsky and His UG Theory

The UG approach was developed by the American linguist, Noam Chomsky, and numerous followers over the last few decades. Linguistic theory is not primarily concerned with SLA. This particular linguistic approach has been much the strongest linguistic influence on L2 acquisition research in recent years and has inspired a great wealth of studies, articles and books on SLA, both empirical and theoretical.

Its main goals are to answer three basic questions about human language: 1) What constitutes knowledge of language? 2) How is knowledge of language acquired? 3) How is knowledge of language put to use? Here, "knowledge of language" is an ambiguous term. It means the subconscious mental representation of language that underlies all language use.

The UG approach to SLA begins from the perspective of "learnability". The theory underlying UG assumes that language consists of a set of abstract principles that characterize core grammars of all natural languages. In addition to invariable principles are parameters that vary across languages.

UG is therefore a property theory that attempts to characterize the underlying linguistic knowledge in L2 learners' minds. In contrast, a detailed examination of the learning process itself will be the main concern of the cognitive approaches that will be described in the later chapters.

## 5.2.2 What Constitutes Knowledge of Language?

Linguistic theory aims to define what all human languages have in common, as well as the distinctive characteristics that make human language different from other systems of communication. It also needs to describe in what way individual human languages can differ from one another.

Although all human languages have a great deal in common, it is equally obvious that they are also different from one another. The UG approach claims that all human beings inherit a universal set of principles and parameters that control the shape human languages can take, and which are what make human languages similar to one another.

It is obvious that English speakers' ability to form *yes/no* questions does not depend merely on knowledge that a word in a sentence must be moved to the front.

To form the question: *Will the letter arrive tomorrow*? one needs to move the third word in the sentence: *The letter will arrive tomorrow.* While to form the question: *Is this a dagger I see before me*? one needs to move the second word of the sentence: *This is a dagger I see before me.*

What is crucial in question formation is knowledge of syntactic categories: to be able to form English questions, it is necessary to recognize the class of auxiliary verbs, and to know that items of this class are put first in questions.

More examples will be given later in this chapter. More recently, in his Minimalist Program, Chomsky argues that the core of human language is the lexicon, which can be characterized as follows:

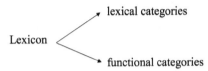

Basically, lexical categories include "content" words, such as verbs, nouns, adjectives and adverbs; and then functional categories include "grammatical" words such as determiners or auxiliaries, as well as abstract grammatical features such as Tense, Aspect or Agreement, which may be realized morphologically.

One of the main interests of the UG approach for SLA research is that it provides a detailed descriptive framework which enables researchers to formulate well-defined hypotheses about the task facing the learner, and to analyze learner language in a more focused manner.

### 5.2.3 How does UG Relate to Language Acquisition?

UG is thought as an innate language facility that limits the extent to which languages can vary. The task for learning is greatly reduced if one is equipped with an innate mechanism that constrains possible grammar formation. Before relating the question of UG to SLA, we turn briefly to issues from child language acquisition: *How does the child create the mental construct that is language?*

Chomsky first resorted to the concept of UG because he believes that children could not learn their first language so quickly and effortlessly without the help of an innate language faculty to guide them. If there is a biologically endowed UG, this would make the task facing children much easier. This would also explain why the different languages of the world are strikingly similar in many respects.

If children have to learn a complex set of rules, there must be something other than the language input to which they are exposed that enables them to learn language with relative ease and speed. The theoretical need for an innate language faculty is based on a negative argument. The claim is that, on the basis of language input alone, children cannot attain the complexities of adult grammars.

It is not merely an anti-behaviorist notion that argues against an input/output scheme. Rather, it is based on the fact that children come to know certain properties of grammar that are not obviously learnable from input, as illustrated by the following examples from English discussed by White (1989):

(1) *I want to go.*
(2) *I wanna go.*
(3) *John wants to go but we don't want to.*
(4) *John wants to go but we don't wanna.*
(5) *Do you want to look at the chickens?*
(6) *Do you wanna look at the chickens?*
(7) *Who do you want to see?*
(8) *Who do you wanna see?*

Examples 1 to 8 show the range of possibilities for changing *want to* to *wanna*. However, there are many times in English where the sequence *want to* cannot be replaced by the informal *wanna*, as in 9 to 10 and 11 to 12:

(9) *Who do you want to feed the dog?*
(10) * *Who do you wanna feed the dog?*
(11) *Who do you want to win the race?*
(12) * *Who do you wanna win the race?*

Without prior information to guide learners, it would be difficult to determine the correct use of *want to* versus *wanna* in informal English. The input does not provide sufficiently specific information about where to use *wanna* and where not to use it.

However, in most instances, the language-learning environment does not provide information to the child concerning the well-formedness of an utterance. Furthermore, as it was discussed in Chapter 3, even with explicit correction, children's grammars are often impervious to change.

### 5.2.4 How is Knowledge of Language Put to Use?

The UG approach to language is concerned with knowledge of language which human beings possess as Linguistic Competence. It is not about Linguistic Performance, which gets into the domain of language use.

Innateness is chosen as an explanation because Chomskians see the study of language as a means of exploring the human mind. It is justified as an explanation for universals on the grounds that the evidence children have available through the language they hear around them is insufficient for them to develop the complex, abstract grammar which underlies any language.

Theoretically, there are two kinds of evidence available to learners as they make hypotheses about correct and incorrect language forms: positive evidence and negative evidence.

Positive evidence comes from the speech learners hear and thus is composed of a limited set of well-formed utterances of the language being learned. Negative evidence, on the other hand, is composed of information to a learner that his or her utterance is deviant with regard to the norms of the language being learned.

Since UG has tried to account for the acquisition of any language, its principles tend to be very abstract. And while the fact of their existence is predicted by the theory, syntactic analysis is required to establish what the universals are, so that the nature or existence of any one particular universal may be questioned if the accuracy of the syntactic analysis from which it is derived is questioned.

UG is the system of principles, conditions and rules that are elements or properties of all human languages. It is taken to be a characterization of the child's prelinguistic state. Thus, the necessity of positing an innate language faculty is due to the inadequate input, in terms of quantity and quality, to which a learner is exposed. Learning is mediated by UG and by the L1.

## 5.3 Arguments from First Language Acquisition

### 5.3.1 Characteristics of First Language Acquisition

As a theory of the human capacity for language, UG is a characterization of those innate, biologically determined principles that constitute one component of the human mind—the language faculty. A review in some more details needs to be done over the arguments that support the existence of an innate language faculty in children.

As suggested by Chomsky, the child is innately or biologically programmed to attend to certain aspects of possible language variation in the input to which he or she is exposed. The child sets the values of these dimensions of language organization when he or she is exposed to the relevant language data, and on the basis of his or her being thus exposed, a number of different facts of the organization of a particular language can be derived deductively. As such, the principles and parameters approach to language proposes a very strong theory of L1A.

To summarize briefly, the essential claim of the theory of UG within the principles and parameters framework is that it constrains the language learner's hypotheses about which dimensions of language variation are significant in the possible grammars for a language. It constrains these hypotheses by providing a restricted range of possible values (preferably two) for a given dimension of language variation (that is, for a parameter) and it provides multiple consequences for grammar construction. It thus places heavy constraints on the hypothesis space.

The discussion on the brief outline of L1A, the main characteristics of which are summarized in 3.2.1 of this text, as children's processing language acquisition through developmental stages. So it could be somewhat concluded from the evidence that there could have been a specific mechanism in the human brain.

The device could be attributed to the more general cognitive make-up of human beings which leads them to process information, whether linguistic or not, in the way and process they do. Children learning maths or learning to play the piano also go through fairly well-defined stages, though not at such a young age, and not necessarily so successfully.

### 5.3.2 Language Acquisition and Intelligence

However, another striking L1A feature is that it does not seem to be linked in any clear way to intelligence. In fact, children vary greatly in the age at which they go through each developmental stage, and in how fast they go through each stage. By age three or four, though, individual differences have largely disappeared, and the late starter has usually caught up with the precocious child. Moreover, early onset of language is not linked to intelligence; Steinberg states that "many very famous people, including Albert Einstein, are reputed to have been slow to talk" (1993).

Not only is language development not directly linked to intelligence, but it is also one of the most complex and abstract pieces of knowledge children have to cope with at such an early age, perhaps even during the entire course of their life. To give an example of the complexities of language which children have to go through, just consider the following reflexive sentences, some of which are grammatical and others not. The nouns and the pronouns that refer to the same person are printed in italics:

(a) *John* saw *himself*.

(b) \* *Himself* saw *John*.

(c) Looking after *himself* bores *John*.

(d) John said that *Fred* liked *himself*.

(e) \* *John* said that Fred liked *himself*.

(f) John told *Bill* to wash *himself*.

(g) \* *John* told Bill to wash *himself*.

(h) *John* promised Bill to wash *himself*.

(i) *John* believes *himself* to be intelligent.

(j) \* *John* believes that *himself* is intelligent.

(k) *John* showed *Bill* a picture of *himself*.

(White, 1989, cited in Lightbown and Spada, 1993: 9 - 10)

Now imagine you are the child trying to work out what the relationship between the reflexive pronoun and its antecedent is; you might conclude from (a) and (b) that the reflexive pronoun must follow the noun it refers to, but (c) disproves this. Sentences (d), (e), (f) and (g) might lead you to believe that the closest noun is the antecedent, but (h) shows that this cannot be right either. It is also evident from (h) that the reflexive and its antecedent do not have to be in the same clause. Furthermore, the reflexive can be in subject position in (i), an untensed clause, but not in (j), a tensed clause. Moreover, the reflexive can sometimes have two possible antecedents, as in (k) that *himself* can refer to either *John* or *Bill*.

This group of samples should be enough to convince anyone of the magnitude of the task facing children; how can they make sense of this, and invariably arrive at the correct rule?

### 5.3.3 Language Impairment and Human Brain Damage

In support of the view that language is not linked to intelligence, there is also a large body of evidence from children with cognitive deficits who develop language normally. These children show dissociation between language development and the kind of supposed cognitive prerequisites that Piaget and his followers would argue are necessary for language development. Fluent use of language with complex syntax and adult-like vocabulary is found in individuals whose overall mental development is otherwise very slow and remains below that of a seven-year-old.

Evidence of the opposite is also found: children who are cognitively "normal", but whose language is impaired, sometimes severely. This condition, known as "specific language impairment", is characterized by language being deficient in specific ways. Further evidence has been found in brain-damaged adults that language is separate from other kinds of cognitive faculties. And it is the left hemisphere that controls language. Damage to the region in front of and just above the left ear (Broca's area) usually results in effortful, hesitant and very non-fluent speech, with no grammatical structure in evidence, consisting largely of specific nouns with few verbs, and poorly articulated. The comprehension of speech, in contrast, usually remains good. This condition is called Broca's aphasia, and is the mirror image of Wernicke's aphasia.

Wernicke's aphasia usually results from an injury to the region of the brain around and under the left ear (Wernicke's area). The patients produce fluent and rapid speech, generally grammatically complex and well-structured, but lacking in content words with specific meaning; they produce general nouns and verbs, such as *something, sniff, got, put* or *did,* and the speech is so vague that it is usually incomprehensible. In this condition, the comprehension of speech is severely impaired.

### 5.3.4 Conclusion

The outlined picture of the relationship between brain and language is necessarily very oversimplified. Nonetheless, it shows clearly that specific areas of the brain deal with specific aspects of language, and that suffering from a language deficit does not necessarily mean having lost language completely, but usually means having problems with one or more aspects of language.

After having reviewed the kind of argumentation used by universalists in order to propose the existence of a language-specific module in the brain, which allows the child to learn language so easily and effortlessly, let us now turn to the question of what this so-called language faculty or UG might be like.

## 5.4 What Does UG Consist of?

Generative linguistics has changed considerably since the last 50 years or so, from the early phase of phrase structure rules to the recent development. The search for "descriptive adequacy" has attempted to account for the details of increasing numbers of typologically unrelated languages, while the search for "explanatory adequacy" has aimed to make effective cross-language generalizations.

It is impossible to give a full account of UG and its principles and parameters, but it is necessary to know how it has been applied to the study of language acquisition.

### 5.4.1 Principles and Parameters Theory in UG

The principles and parameters framework has a dual aim: to characterize the Native Speaker's (NS) knowledge of language, or linguistic competence, and to explain how the acquisition of such competence is possible. Linguists argue that the input alone is simply insufficient to allow the child to attain full adult competence.

Linguistic competence extends beyond the input in various ways: for instance, children and adults can understand and produce sentences that they have never heard before. They know, without being explicitly taught, that certain structures are not possible and that others are ambiguous.

All acquisition is assumed to proceed on in this UG framework. The input data intrigue the properties of UG. That is, they cause UG parameters to be set without learning having to take place. Negative evidence (information about ungrammaticality) plays a minimal role.

### 5.4.2 UG Principles

Language learning is highly constrained in advance, thus making the task for the child much more manageable. The universal principle is the principle of structure-dependency, which states that language is organized in such a way that it crucially depends on the structural relationships between elements in a sentence (such as words, morphemes, etc.). Consider the following sentences:

(a) *She* bought a new car yesterday.

(b) *My friend* bought a new car yesterday.

(c) *The friend that I met in Australia last year* bought a new car yesterday.

(d) *The friend I am closest to and who was so supportive when I lost my job two years ago* bought a new car yesterday.

The phrases in italics in (b), (c) and (d) are the same kind of groupings and perform the same role in the sentences, and refer to one single individual. Moreover, the speaker could carry on adding details about this friend more or less by using devices such as *and, that, which,* etc., running the risk of boring the listener to tears! It is obvious that the crucial word in these groupings is *friend* or *she*.

This kind of structural grouping is called a **Phrase**, and in the previous examples, the main or central element (the head) of this phrase is a noun (or pronoun). In fact, all languages in the world are structured in this way, and are made up of sentences which consist of at least a **Noun-Phrase (NP)** and a **Verb-Phrase (VP)**.

This knowledge — that languages are structure-dependent — is a crucial aspect of all human languages that has many implications; it is a principle of UG which explains many of the language procession. The basic concept behind this principle is that linguistic principles operate on

syntactic (or structural) units. Consider the following sentences:
(1) The boy who is standing over there is happy.
(2) Is the boy who is standing over there __ happy?
(3) * Is the boy who __ standing over there is happy?

The rule for question formation makes reference to the subject, which in the cases of (1) and (2) is a complex subject consisting of a noun phrase (*the boy*) and a relative clause (*who is standing over there*). The rule does not make reference to a nonstructural unit, such as the first verb. Thus, yes/no questions are formed by moving the main verb to the front of the sentence, not by moving the first verb in the sentence to the front as in (3).

In general, the results of this study support the notion that learners' grammars are constrained by principles, or structure-dependent principle. Thus, with regard to UG principles, there is conflicting evidence as to whether L2 learners 1) have the direct access to UG, 2) have access to UG through his L1 or 3) have no access to UG at all.

### 5.4.3 UG Parameters

As well as abstract principles and structural relationships, UG contains its parameters, which are principles that differ in the way they work or function from language to language. That is to say there are certain linguistic features that vary across languages. These are expressed through the concept of linguistic parameters.

Parameters have limited values. In learning an L1, the data a child is exposed to will determine which setting of a parameter that the child will select. The idea is that parameters give the child advance knowledge of what the possibilities will be, that is, they limit the range of hypotheses that have to be considered. Parameter settings are fixed on the basis of input from the language being acquired.

The issue for SLA is to determine whether and how a given linguistic parameter can be reset. One of the most interesting aspects related to the concept of parameters is that they involve the clustering of properties. Once a parameter is set in a particular way, all related properties are affected.

An example is provided by certain differences between English and French. The two languages behave differently regarding negative placement, as can be seen by comparing (1a) and (1b), question formation, as in (2a) versus (2b), adverb placement, as in (3a) and (3c) versus (3b) and (3d), and quantifier positions, as in (4a) and (4c) versus (4b) and (4d):

(1) a. * John likes not Mary.

    b. *Jean n' aime pas Marie.*

(2) a. * Likes she John?

    b. *Aime -t -elle -Jean?*

(3) a. * John watches often television.

    b. *Jean regarde souvent la télèvision.*

    c. Mary often watches television.

    d.* *Marie souvent regarde la télèvision.*

(4) a. * My friends like all Mary.

    b. *Mes amis aiment tous Marie.*

    c. My friends all like Mary.

    d. * *Mes amis tous aiment Marie.*

In English, verb-raising is prohibited, accounting for the impossibility of postverbal negation in (1a), for the lack of inversion with main verbs in (2a), and for the placement of adverbs and quantifiers immediately to the left of the verb, as in (3c) and (4c). The parameter thus accounts for a cluster of properties; the properties do not have to be learned separately by the L1 learner.

Indeed, the child does not have to learn about verb movement at all. Rather, the possibility is built in as part of UG, and there is enough evidence from simple sentences to trigger the acquisition of the appropriate setting. For example, the position of the negative *pas* in French indicates that the verb has moved, whereas the position of *not* in English indicates that it has not. From such evidence, the parameter is "set" and the cluster of properties associated with verb movement emerges.

## 5.5 Evaluation of UG-based Approaches to SLA

UG is a well-established theory of language, which has been highly influential in many areas of linguistic research, including language acquisition research.

### 5.5.1 The Scope and Achievements of the UG Approach

It is important to note that UG approach aims to describe and explain human language. As such, even if its prime concern is not SLA, it is nonetheless directly relevant to the study of L2s, which are assumed to be natural languages.

SLA researchers, in order to understand the interlanguage (IL) system, need to understand what constrains formal language systems generally. UG, however, is a linguistic theory, with its own aims and objectives, and not a learning theory. Although one of Chomsky's stated objectives is to understand how knowledge of language is acquired, and how knowledge of language is put to use, most of the work to date has focused on his first question: what constitutes knowledge of language?

The UG descriptive framework and language acquisition data, both first and second, has been hugely influential in helping researchers to draw up hypotheses about a range of issues which are central to our understanding of SLA, such as the exact nature of the language system.

As a general theory of language therefore, the scope of UG is potentially very broad. It would be fair to say, however, that UG research has been primarily concerned with the description and explanation of the formal system underlying language. Moreover, its focus has been primarily morphosyntax, and other aspects of the linguistic system have received much less attention. The UG contribution to our understanding of the acquisition of morphosyntactic properties in SLA has been outstanding, and will no doubt feed into a comprehensive SLA theory.

### 5.5.2 The UG View of Language

The UG view of language has been very influential since the 1950s, but not uncontroversial. The UG theory views language as a mental framework, underlying all human languages. It focuses on some aspects of language and not others. Until very recently, syntax was the privileged object of study. UG is only concerned with the sentence and its internal structure, rather than any larger unit of language.

Work at the level of smaller units (words, morphemes, phonemes) has also been primarily concerned with structure and how different elements relate to one another. This is one of the major criticisms of work in UG tradition. It studies language somewhat, in a vacuum, as a mental object rather than a social or psychological one. Moreover, it separates language knowledge and language use rigidly, and some linguists disagree with this division.

However, tapping the underlying linguistic representations of L2 learners is even more difficult than in the case of native speakers, as L2 representations are less stable. L2 learners' intuitions are much more likely to be unstable, and therefore less reliable. Grammaticality judgment tests have often been relied on in SLA studies, as without them it can be very difficult to get evidence about hidden grammatical properties, which might not be present in learners' spontaneous output.

Despite of these criticisms, UG has been highly influential as a theory of language, and is probably the most sophisticated tool available for analyzing language today, whether L1 or L2s.

### 5.5.3 The UG View of Language Acquisition

When applied specifically to the context of SLA, how successful can the UG theory claim to be? UG-based approaches to SLA have been criticized for exactly the same reasons as the theory itself. It has left untouched a number of areas that are central to our understanding of the L2 learning process.

First, linguistically, this approach has in the past been almost exclusively concerned with syntax. Even if recent interest in phonology, morphology and the lexicon should redress the balance somewhat, semantics, pragmatics and discourse are excluded.

Second, the UG approach has been exclusively concerned with documenting and explaining the nature of the L2 linguistic system.

Third, the social and psychological variables that affect the rate of the learning process are beyond its scope of research and therefore ignored.

Bearing the above in mind, there is little doubt that the UG approach to research into SLA has been highly influential and fruitful, and has generated a wealth of studies that have greatly enhanced our understanding of L2 morphosyntactic development. It has been very useful as a tool for linguistic analysis, enabling researchers to formulate well-defined and focused hypotheses that could even be tested in empirical work.

This powerful linguistic tool has been useful in describing not only the language produced by L2 learners, but also the language to be acquired as L1. The work carried out by SLA researchers within this framework is also feeding into our more general understanding of human language.

This approach has also been useful, not only in establishing some of the facts about SLA, but also meeting with some success in explaining those facts. For example, it has enabled L2 researchers to draw up a principled view of language transfer or cross-linguistic influence, in terms of principles and parameters.

### 5.5.4 The UG View of the Language Learner

The UG approach is only interested in the learner as the possessor of a mind that contains language; the assumption is that all human beings are endowed with such a mind, and variations between individuals are of little concern to UG theorists. The emphasis is very much on language as the object of study, rather than on the speaker or learner as a social being, and the focus is on what is universal within this mind.

Overall, there is little doubt that the UG approach to SLA research meets the criteria for a good theory by making clear and explicit statements of the ground it aims to cover and the claims it makes, by having systematic procedures for theory-evaluation, by attempting to explain as well as describe at least some L2A phenomena, and finally by engaging increasingly with other theories in the field.

As one of the most active and developing theories, it can be expected to continue to make highly valuable contributions to the field.

## 5.6 Conclusion

UG is a theory relevant to the issue of linguistic competence. Although UG provides constraints on possible grammars in the course of acquisition, it is not, of itself, a theory of acquisition. This point is often misunderstood, perhaps because of terms like LAD, which many people in the past would equate with UG. It would be more accurate to think of UG as a component within an LAD or as part of a language faculty.

A number of researchers have pointed out that theories of acquisition must explain both the problem of what L2 learners come to know and that of how they attain this knowledge. Most research looking at the operation of UG in SLA has focused on the nature of the L2 learner's grammar, looking for evidence for or against the involvement of UG principles and parameters, and exploring the nature of the initial state and subsequent grammars.

Even if one looks for UG-based properties in learner grammars at various points in time, this is a question of representation rather than development. We should bear in mind that UG itself is not a learning theory; it can only interact with other theories that try to explain learning development.

To account for grammar change (i.e., development), one needs a theory of

1) how the L2 input interacts with the existing grammar;

2) what properties of the input act as triggers for change;

3) what properties force changes to the current representation, and

4) what might drive stages of acquisition.

Some L2 learnability work has looked into these kinds of issue as

1) the role of positive and negative evidence;

2) learning principles;

3) proposals that grammar change is failure-driven and

4) possible triggers in the input.

However, this is an area where much work remains to be done.

## Points for Thinking

1. How does the UG describe the knowledge of human language?
2. How are the UG theory and its framework related to the field of SLA?
3. What are the main characteristics and stages of children's L1A?
4. What are the principles and parameters in the framework of UG?
5. What are the significances and weak points of the UG theory for language learning?

Further Reading

Chomsky, N. (2002). *On Nature and Language*. Cambridge: Cambridge University Press.

Gass, S. and Selinker, L. (2008). *Second Language Acquisition: An Introductory Course*. 3$^{rd}$ Edition. Hillsdale, NJ: Lawrence Erlbaum.

Lightbown, P. M., Spada, N. & White, L. (Eds.) (1993). "The role of instruction in second language acquisition." [Thematic issue]*Studies in Second Language Acquisition 15*(2).

Steinberg, L. (1993). *Adolescence*. (3$^{rd}$ Edition). New York: McGraw-Hill.

Sternberg, R. J. (1997). *Thinking Styles*. New York: Cambridge University Press.

# Chapter 6

# Cognitive Approaches to SLA

## 6.1 Introduction

There is in Chapter 5 an outline of the work by SLA researchers who are interested in the development of L2 grammars from a purely linguistic viewpoint. Thus, L2A is seen as different from other kinds of learning, and a description of the linguistic systems (the L1, the L2 or the IL) is crucial to an understanding of the L2 learning.

Since the last decade there has been increasing interest in the part of cognitive psychologists and psycholinguists in characterizing the cognitive processes that support SLA research.

One focus is to understand how cognitive systems are constrained by the context and timing of acquisition and to identify the source of these constraint. A second one concerns the cognitive consequences of having two languages active in early childhood. A third one addresses the representations, processes, and strategies that are used when skilled adult bilinguals read and speak words and process sentences in each of their two languages.

The third focus becomes the focus on cognitive approaches to L2 learning. The SLA researchers put more emphasis on the learning component of L2A. These researchers view L2 learning as just one example of learning among many others, and they believe that people can understand the L2A process better by understanding how the human brain processes and learns new information.

The focus here is still very much on the learner as an individual, different from the work of social theorists, and also different from UG theorists who draw their hypotheses from the study of linguistic systems. Cognitive theorists are centrally concerned with how learners access this linguistic knowledge in real time, or in the strategies they might employ when their incomplete linguistic system lets them down, or why some individuals are doing better than others at learning other languages.

## 6.2 Two Main Groups of Cognitive Theorists

Some researchers believe that there is a language-specific module for L1A, and that L2 learning is different and relies on general cognitive mechanisms. There are also some researchers who believe that, even for L1A, some learning aspects are innate and other aspects not. And some others would like to leave the question open.

Even within frameworks concentrating firmly on the processing component of language learning, the possibility of an innate linguistic module is not directly rejected. The approaches are increasingly seen as complementary rather than conflictual. Consequently, cognitive theorists fall into two main groups:

1. Some theorists believe that language knowledge might be "special" in some way, but are concerned to develop their theories to complement the theories such as UG or Lexical Functional Grammar.
2. Other theorists believe that they can explain both the nature of language knowledge and how it is processed through general cognitive principles. In fact, they do not generally make the distinction between competence and performance. In this view, the learner is seen as operating a complex processing system that deals with linguistic information in similar ways to other kinds of information.

It is concluded that the first group of linguists belong to the Processing Approaches, and the second group to the Emergentist or Constructionist Approaches.

The first group investigates the work of psycholinguists who have analyzed the SLA of procedural skills from a range of perspectives. This chapter will mainly focus on Information-processing Approaches, and

Processability Theory (Picnemann,1998).

The second group investigates approaches that study the acquisition of language from the emergentist or constructionist point of view. In this school, L2A is done through usage, by extracting patterns and rules from the input, and building stronger associations in the brain. The focus is particularly on the Connectionist Approach.

Before moving on, it is necessary to stress that the field of cognitive linguistics is vast and expanding fast, and this book has only focused on what is generally perceived as the approaches applied to investigate the process of SLA.

## 6.3 Processing Approaches

The approaches have in common the fact that they are interested in the way in which the human brain's processing mechanisms deal with the language acquisition.

The **Information-processing Approach** investigates how different memory stores (short-term memory and long-term memory) deal with new L2 information, and how this L2 information is automatized and restructured through repeated activation.

The **Processability Theory** looks specifically at the processing demands made by various aspects of L2, and the implications for the L2/FL learnability and teachability.

### 6.3.1 Information-processing Models of L2 Learning

The discussion originates from information-processing models developed by cognitive psychologists. Firstly, it comes to McLaughlin's information-processing model. Second, the attention will be turned to Anderson's Active Control of Thought (ACT) model, and pay particular attention to O'Malley and Chamot's application of the model in learner strategies and to Towell and Hawkins' application to the development of fluency.

### 6.3.2 McLaughlin's Information-processing Model

McLaughlin says " that the basic notion of the information-processing approach to psychological inquiry is that complex behavior builds on simple processes" (1996). Moreover, these processes are modular and can therefore be studied independently of one another. Table 6.1 summarizes the main characteristics of such an approach (McLaughlin, 1996: 214).

| | Characteristics of the Information-processing Approach |
|---|---|
| 1 | Humans are viewed as autonomous and active. |
| 2 | The mind is a general-purposed, symbol-processing system. |
| 3 | Complex behavior is composed of simpler processes; these processes are modular. |
| 4 | Component processes can be isolated and studied independently of other processes. |
| 5 | Processes take time; therefore, predictions about reaction time can be made. |
| 6 | The mind is a limited-capacity processor. |

Automatization is a notion based on the work of psychologists (Shiffrin and Schneider, 1977), who claim that the way in which people process information may be either controlled or automatic, and that learning involves a shift from controlled towards automatic processing.

Learners first resort to controlled processing in L2. This processing under control involves the temporary activation of a selection of information in the memory. Such processing requires lots of attentional control on the part of the subject, and is constrained by the limitations of the short-term memory.

Through repeated activation, sequences first produced by controlled processing become automatic. The sequences are stored as units in the long-term memory, which means that they can be made available very rapidly whenever the situation requires it, with minimal attentional control on the part of the subject. As a result, automatic processes can work in parallel, activating clusters of complex cognitive skills simultaneously.

Once a learner has activated the sequence *Good morning, how are you?* a number of times, it becomes automatic and does not require attentional control. So, learning in this view is seen as the movement from controlled to automatic processing via practice (repeated activation). However, once acquired, such automatized skills are difficult to delete or modify.

It is necessary for simple sub-skills and routines to become automatic before more complex ones can be tackled. Once our learner has automatized *Good morning, how are you?* he or she is free to deal with the learning of more complex language. This continuing movement from controlled to automatic processing results in a constant restructuring of the linguistic system of the L2 learner.

This may explain some characteristics of interlanguage. Restructuring destabilizes some structures in the interlanguage, which seemed to have been previously acquired, and hence leads to the temporary reappearance of L2 errors. Restructuring is also the result of exemplar-based representations becoming rule-based.

This account is especially convincing in its explanation of the annoying issue of fossilization which refers to the fact that L2 learners, unlike L1 learners, sometimes seem unable to get rid of non-native-like structures in their L2 despite of abundant linguistic input over many years.

Fossilization in this model would arise as a result of a controlled process becoming automatic prematurely, before it is native-like. Thus they are likely to remain in the learner's interlanguage, giving rise to a stable but erroneous construction. However, this general idea does not explain why some structures seem much more likely to fossilize than others.

### 6.3.3 Anderson's Active Control of Thought (ACT) Model

Anderson's ACT model is not dissimilar from McLaughlin's. It is more wide-ranging with different terms, but the practice leading to automatization also plays a central role. It enables declarative knowledge (i.e. knowledge of what to know) to become procedural knowledge (i.e. knowledge of how to do something).

One of the major differences is that Anderson posits three kinds of memory: a working memory, similar to McLaughlin's short-term memory, and two kinds of long-term memory — a declarative long-term memory and a procedural long-term memory. Anderson believes that declarative and procedural knowledge are different kinds of knowledge that are stored differently.

A simple example shows what is meant by declarative and procedural knowledge.

If one is learning to drive, he will be told that if the engine is revving too much, he needs to change to a higher gear; he will also learn how to change gear. In the early stages, knowing that (declarative knowledge) he has to do this does not necessarily mean that he knows how (procedural knowledge) to do it quickly and successfully.

In other words, he goes through a declarative stage before acquiring the procedural knowledge linked with this situation. With practice, however, the mere noise of the engine getting louder will trigger his gear changing, without even having to think about it. This is how learning takes place in this view: by declarative knowledge becoming procedural and automatized.

Anderson's (1983) application of his model to L1 acquisition has been criticized for insisting that all knowledge starts out in declarative form. Considering language learning, Anderson does not claim that all knowledge needs to start as declarative knowledge any longer. However, other applications, such as to the learning of algebra, geometry or computer programming, have been very successful.

According to Anderson, the move from declarative to procedural knowledge takes place in the following table of three stages:

|   | Stages | the Knowledge from Declarative to Procedural |
|---|---|---|
| 1 | The cognitive stage | A description of the procedure is learnt. |
| 2 | The associative stage | A method for performing the skill is worked out. |
| 3 | The autonomous stage | The skill becomes more and more rapid and automatic. |

Similar to McLaughlin's, ACT model would explain the step-by-step nature of learning. When tasks become proceduralized, they are accessed automatically, without having to resort to the working memory. Therefore, new declarative knowledge can be attended to and then proceed through the associative and eventually autonomous stages.

It suggests that the learner's speech becomes more fluent as more knowledge becomes proceduralized, and is then accessed more quickly and efficiently. However, most contemporary theorists of SLA, from whatever perspective, would not agree with the implied position taken by Anderson. Some information-processing theorists have responded by suggesting that the "declarative knowledge" component can be subdivided into conscious and unconscious parts. Others have argued that these processing models are most helpful in explaining some related studies in L2A.

In the following sections we will see how Anderson's model has been applied to two such related studies: to the application of learning strategies to the L2A problem, and to the development of L2 fluency.

### 6.3.4 Application of ACT to Learning Strategies

Learning strategies must not be confused with communication strategies, although there is some overlap; their focus is on facilitating learning, whereas communication strategies are used in order to overcome a specific communicative problem. Learning strategies can be classified into three categories, as exemplified in the following table (Source: O'Malley and Chamot, 1990: 43):

| Generic strategy classification | Representative strategies | Definitions |
| --- | --- | --- |
| Metacognitive strategies | Selective attention | focusing on special aspects of learning tasks, as in planning to listen to key words or phrases. |
| | Planning | planning for organizing either written or spoken discourse. |
| | Monitoring | reviewing attention to a task, comprehension of information that should be remembered, or production while it is occurring. |
| | Evaluation | checking comprehension after completing a receptive language activity, or evaluating language production after it is done. |

| | | |
|---|---|---|
| Cognitive strategies | Rehearsal | repeating the names of items or objects to be remembered. |
| | Organization | grouping and classifying words, terminology, or concepts according to their semantic or syntactic attributes. |
| | Inferencing | using information in text to guess meanings or new linguistic items, predict outcomes or complete missing parts. |
| | Summarizing | intermittently synthesizing what one has heard to ensure the information has been retained. |
| | Deducing | applying rules to the understanding of language. |
| | Imagery | using visual images (either generated or actual) to understand and remember new verbal information. |
| | Transfer | using known linguistic information to facilitate a new task. |
| | Elaboration | linking ideas contained in new information or integrating new ideas with known information. |
| Social or affective strategies | Co-operation | working with peers to solve a problem, pool information, check notes or get feedback on one of learning activities. |
| | Questioning for clarification | eliciting from a teacher or peer additional explanation, rephrasing or examples. |
| | Self-talk | using redirection of thinking to assure oneself that a learning activity will be successful or to reduce anxiety about a task. |

Thus, strategies have to be learnt in exactly the same way as other complex cognitive skills. A good language learner will be a learner who has proceduralized the strategies described in the table. An obvious pedagogical implication of such a view is that L2 learners would benefit from being taught learning strategies. If learning strategies are skills, then they can be taught, with the advantage that they will become proceduralized more quickly, therefore freeing working memory space for other aspects of learning.

A problem raised by O'Malley and Chamot is that the teaching of strategies will involve considerable time and effort. Learning is an active and dynamic process in which learners make use of a variety of information and processing strategies.

- Language use is a complex cognitive skill that has properties in common with other complex skills in terms of how information is stored and learnt.
- Language learning entails a progression from initial awareness to processing information, and consequently to automaticity in language use.
- Learning strategies parallel theoretically derived cognitive processes and have the potential to influence learning outcomes in a positive manner.

They made it clear, however, that such an approach did not concern itself with the language learning route followed by learners. It dealt exclusively with the rate of learning and how learning strategies can influence it.

### 6.3.5 ACT and Fluency Development in SLA

Towell and Hawkins (1994) applied psychological models and incorporated aspects of the ACT model into their overall model of SLA, in order to account for fluency development. They rejected the idea that Anderson's model could account for all aspects of SLA, and adopted models of Natural Language Processing (NLP), to explain how grammatical knowledge is transformed into fluent performance in the L2s.

Their model attempts to integrate how learners learn the L2 system with how they learn to use the system. In order to explain why certain grammatical structures appear before others, and why learners go through fairly rigid stages in their acquisition of L2s, they resort to a UG approach.

In order to understand how learners use this grammatical knowledge in increasingly efficient ways, they appeal to an information-processing account. In the first stage, a hypothesis will be stored in the declarative long-term memory. In their account, declarative knowledge may be implicit or explicit, and the learner will not normally have any conscious analyzed knowledge of such Universal Grammar-derived hypotheses.

This model allows them to make a number of specific claims concerning different kinds of learning: "Internally derived hypotheses about L2 structure, if confirmed by external data, will give rise to a production which will be stored in procedural memory, first in associative form and eventually in autonomous form." (ibid., p.250)

Learning strategies facilitate the proceduralization of mechanisms for faster processing of linguistic input. They are incorporated in the information-processing part of the model, without having to interact with internal hypotheses.

This model attempts to reconcile internal, UG-derived hypotheses about L2 structure with what actually happens to these hypotheses during the processes of language learning and language use. It thus represents an ambitious attempt to link together linguistic and cognitive approaches to the study of SLA.

## 6.4 Connectionism

The Connectionist (previously known as Associationist) Approach to learning has been around for some time, but advances in computer technology have given it a new breath of life. Since the mid-1980s especially, there has been a growing number of studies applying a connectionist framework to the general study of memory and learning. More recently, connectionism has been applied to SLA.

Connectionism, or parallel distributed processing compares the brain to a computer that would consist of neural networks: complex clusters of links between information nodes. These links or connections become strengthened or weakened through activation or non-activation, respectively.

Learning in this view occurs on the basis of associative processes, rather than the construction of abstract rules. In other words, the human mind is predisposed to look for associations between elements and create links between them. These links become stronger as these associations keep recurring, and they also become part of larger networks as connections between elements become more numerous. When applied to the learning of language, connectionism claims that learners are sensitive to regularities in the language input and extract possible patterns on the basis of these regularities. Learning occurs as these patterns become strengthened by repeated activation.

An illustrative example of a connectionist network which consists of several modules is shown in the figure on the right and the arrows indicate the direction of flow of excitation or inhibition.

The Connectionist Approach differs strikingly from the accounts presented so far, as it does not believe that the learning of rules underlies the construction of linguistic knowledge, but rather that this happens through the associative processes.

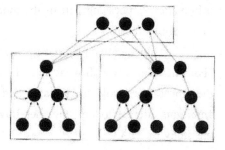

(Source: Elman et al., 1996: 51)

This goes against much the linguists', belief in, namely that language is a set of modules (syntax, morphology, phonology) with an accompanying lexicon, and that the task facing language learners is to extract rules from the language around them in order to build up their own mental set of those rules, as well as learning the lexicon which will then fit into the slots made available by the grammar.

Connectionism claims that learning is not rule-governed, but is based on the construction of associative patterns. It is a fundamental departure from most currently held views. Connectionism is seen as an alternative to symbolic accounts of language acquisition: rule-like behavior does not imply rule-governed behavior.

Connectionism is thus the computer modeling of the constructivist or emergentist views of language learning. It is a transition theory that aims to explain how these associative patterns emerge in learners. Language learning is all about the building of billions of associations and the extraction of patterns resulting in rule-like behavior.

Connectionism provides the computational tools for exploring the conditions under which emergent properties arise.

## 6.5 Theories of L2 Processing

The next two approaches focus on the factors controlling the way in which L2 learners process the linguistic input. The first one is **Processability Theory** and the second is **Perceptual Saliency Approach.**

### 6.5.1 Processability Theory

Like Towell and Hawkins, the processability theory outlined by Pienemann and others also claims the need to use both a theory of grammar and a processing component in order to understand SLA. However, the processability theory focuses on the acquisition of the procedural skills required for processing the formal properties of second languages.

The theory of grammar, titled as **Lexical Functional Grammar** (LFG) by Kaplan in 1982, also differs from the Chomskyan theory, which is exclusively a theory of linguistic knowledge. LFG is a theory of grammar that attempts to represent both linguistic knowledge and language processing within the same framework. It has its aims to be psychologically plausible, that is to say, it is to be in line with the cognitive features of language processing models.

Processability theory aims to clarify how learners acquire the computational mechanisms that operate on the linguistic knowledge they construct. Pienemann believes that language acquisition itself is the gradual acquisition of these computational mechanisms, as the procedural skills necessary for language processing.

Pienemann describes LFG as " the unification of lexical features, which is one of the main characteristics of LFG, captures a psychologically plausible process that involves 1) the identification of grammatical information in the lexical entry; 2) the temporary storage of that information and 3) its utilization at another point in the constituent structure" (1998: 73). The L2 learners have to make it sure that a verb and its subject have the same number feature, or that a noun and its article have the same gender, number and case features, in languages where this is appropriate.

Consider the following sentence: *Peter walk a dogs*. It is ungrammatical because in English the verb *walk* and its subject *Peter* do not have the same person and number feature (third person singular), and the article *a* and the noun *dogs* in its plural form also do not share the same number feature.

In SLA, the ability to match features across elements in a sentence usually develops step by step. The basic logic behind processability theory is that language learners cannot access hypotheses about the L2 that they cannot process by themselves. The language learners are claimed to have a Hypothesis Space in learning, which develops gradually over time.

So, Pienemann (1998) proposed a proceduralized process for L2A: "a word needs to be added to the L2 lexicon before its grammatical category can be assigned. The grammatical category of a lemma is needed before a category procedure can be called." And he added: "1) only if the grammatical category of the Head phrase is assigned can the phrasal procedure be called; 2) only if a phrasal procedure has been completed and its value is returned can Appointment Rules determine the function of the phrase, and 3) only if the function of the phrase has been determined can it be attached to the S-node and sentential information be stored in the S-holder."

What this means in practice is that learners will be able to share information across elements in a sentence in gradually less local domains. Initially, they will not be able to produce any structures that require the matching of L2 grammatical information using syntactic procedures: For example, learners will mark both nouns and articles within a noun-phrase as +*feminine* or to match person in subject and verb.

This notion of perceptual saliency has also been used by others. Before the topic is touched upon, however, there is a need to outline one further aspect of Pienemann's theory. It has attracted a great deal of interest from different SLA studies because of its potentially pedagogical implications in the field of language teaching and learning: that is his well-known **Teachability Hypothesis.**

### 6.5.2 The Teachability Hypothesis

Pienemann developed his processability theory in order to explain the well-documented observation that L2 learners follow a fairly rigid route in their acquisition of grammatical structures. This notion implies that structures only become "learnable" when the previous steps on this acquisitional path have been acquired.

For Pienemann learners, at any time, can only operate within their Hypothesis Space, which is constrained by the processing resources they have available to them at that time. This has led him to develop his teachability hypothesis, in which he considers the pedagogical implications of the learnability or processability model, and draws precise conclusions about how some structures should be taught.

The predictions of the teachability hypothesis are: 1) the step by step stages of acquisition cannot be skipped through formal instruction; and 2) the instruction will be most beneficial if it focuses on structures from "the next stage".

But possibly the most interesting aspect is the attempt to establish a link between learning and teaching. It pays attention not only to the language learning stages, but also to the beneficial instructions on structures. This is a refreshing trend, as SLA researchers rarely attempt to assess the pedagogical implications of their research.

### 6.5.3 Perceptual Saliency

Cognitivists would like to lay their stress on the significance of perceptual salience. The perceptual saliency approach is largely based on the work of Slobin in the 1970s and 1980s. He was culminating with the publication of a cross-linguistic collection of child language development studies starting in 1985.

Slobin argues that the similarity in linguistic development across children and across languages is because human beings are programmed to perceive and organize information in certain ways. It is this perceptual saliency that drives the learning process, rather than an innate language-specific module.

Slobin has devised, added to and refined over the years a number of operating principles which guide children in their processing of the linguistic strings they encounter. His operating principles have been adapted to L2A by Andersen. Piencmann's processibility or teachability theory also draws on the notion of perceptual saliency.

## 6.6 Evaluation of Cognitive Approaches to L2 Learning

### 6.6.1 Cognitivists' View of Language

There is no doubt that most recent researchers have gained much help from cognitive approaches about the role of processing mechanisms in SLA. It helped us to understand better the development of human cognitive mechanisms over time the difficulties in eradicating fossilized structures even if we do not understand yet why some structures fossilize and not others.

The scope of cognitivists' research varies widely, from the application of general models of language processing, to studies using computers in order to simulate the acquisition of discrete grammatical phenomena.

Some cognitivists see their field of enquiry as being specifically the processing mechanisms and how they develop in L2A. They believe that we also need a property theory in order to understand the linguistic system, which will complement the transition theory they are developing.

Others, adopting an emergentist or connectionist view of learning, see their field of enquiry as the whole process of language learning. They do not separate the development of processing from the development of the linguistic system.

Processing theorists do not say much about the nature of language itself; they focus on the study of the processing constraints operating in SLA. It does not mean that they do not incorporate a linguistic theory in their overall model of SLA, such as LFG in the case of Pienemann, or UG in the case of Towell and Hawkins.

### 6.6.2 Cognitivists' View of Language Learning

Cognitivists investigate mainly the development of processing in L2 learners. In order to do that, psychologists make use of laboratory techniques to measure accurately performance indicators such as length of pauses, priming effects. Linguists, apply linguistic analysis techniques to study L2 learners' productions or intuitions. They tend to consider language outside of the mechanisms underlying its use.

Both methodologies have their advantages and disadvantages. Earlier laboratory studies have the benefit of being able to control in a precise way the variables under study. This very fact can also be seen as a disadvantage, as it assumes one can study aspects of language or its rules in isolation, without taking account of the necessary interaction between the different language modules.

Cognitive approaches have also been able to enlighten us on what processes are involved in the speeding up of the acquisition process. The ultimate goal of any SLA model has been much enriched by studies of the cognitive processes involved. Our understanding of how L2 learners use and process language has greatly increased, and the development of fluency has received well-deserved attention. The connectionist approach is an exciting and promising new avenue for research. Especially within the field of L1A, there have been important developments recently.

A lot more will be heard about processing approaches to SLA. Recent models have made well-developed proposals for integrating linguistic and cognitive dimensions, even if much research remains to be done. Both linguistic theories and cognitive ones will surely feed into a comprehensive model of SLA study, encompassing both linguistic and cognitive development in the process of language learning.

### 6.6.3 Cognitivists' View of the Language Learner

Cognitivists, like the linguists, are concerned primarily with the individuals and individual learning strategies. They do not view the learner as a social being. But they are interested in the learner's mind, as an information processor rather than in the specificity of the linguistic information it contains.

Additionally, a distinctive feature of connectionist approaches lies in the links they attempt to build with neurology and even neurobiology. Connectionists believe that language learning should be studied within the actual architecture of the brain, and make use of neurological information.

Researchers recently have investigated in some detail the psychological constraints underlying L2A, such as the role of memory, of noticing and attention, of implicit or explicit learning and of individual differences (e. g. motivation, aptitude, intelligence, etc.), and their pedagogical implications.

## 6.7 Conclusion

The models, applied to the study of L2 acquisition have tended to be concerned with the acquisition of relatively simple and artificial data, somewhat removed from the richness and complexity of natural languages and language learning contexts, and much more research needs to take place before connectionist simulations of L2A give us a more comprehensive picture of the processes involved in real learning contexts.

At present, a wealth of L2 studies have been carried out recently from the angle of cognitive psychology. The methods used as well as the questions asked differ substantially from more traditional SLA studies which stem directly from the field of linguistics, or from a more functional-, socio-cultural- and sociolinguistic-oriented approaches which are the topics of Chapter 7.

Points for Thinking

1. What are the two main groups of cognitive theory concerning language learning?
2. How do we interpret the characteristics of the Information-processing Approach?
3. What is the contribution made by Anderson's ACT theory?
4. What are the significances of theory by O'Malley and Chamot to language teaching and learning?
5. What are the Processability Theory and Teachability in the SLA research?

**Further Reading**

Bresnan, J. (Ed.) (1982a). *The Mental Representation of Grammatical Relations*. Cambridge, Massachusetts: MIT Press.

Ellis, R. (Ed.) (2000). *Learning a Second Language through Interaction*. Amsterdam: John Benjamins.

Gass, S. and Selinker, L. (2008). *Second Language Acquisition: An Introductory Course*. 3$^{rd}$ Edition. Hillsdale, NJ: Lawrence Erlbaum.

Kaplan, R. M., Bresnan, J. (1982). "Lexical-functional grammar: a formal system for grammatical representation." In Bresnan (Ed.). *The Mental Representation of Grammatical Relations*. Cambridge, Massachusetts: MIT Press, pp. 173 – 281.

O'Malley, J. M. and Chamot, A. U. (1990). *Learing Strategies in Second Language Acquisition*. Cambridge: Cambridge Uni. Press.

# Chapter 7

# Some Other Perspectives on SLA

## 7.1 Introduction

As a discipline, the study of L2A is newer and less developed than that of L1A. In part this is probably because unlike L1A research, the study of L2A has grown out of practical or applied concerns, such as language teaching. SLA study has largely concentrated on modeling the language development within the individual learner, in response to an environment defined narrowly as a source of linguistic information.

Some researchers adopt a broadly functional or pragmatic approach to the study of learners' interlanguage development and are centrally concerned with the ways in which L2 learners set about making meaning, and achieving their personal communicative goals. However, it is clear that some sustained programmes of empirical research are now developing, in which sociolinguistic ideas are viewed as much more central to the understanding of SLA.

## 7.2 Functional Perspectives on L1 Learning and SLA

The term "functional" here is different from the one in the UG theory. Here, functionalism in linguistics is the explication of grammatical structure in which semantic and pragmatic constructs are integral. Theoretical linguists who have adopted this perspective in varying degrees include Halliday and other functionalists.

A functional approach to L2A attempts to explain facts about the acquisition of an L2, either by an adult, or by a child. Researchers studying child language have been interested in the meanings that children are trying to convey. The table of two-word utterances is drawn from one of the child language studies by Brown in 1973:

|   | Relation | Example |    | Relation | Example |
|---|---|---|---|---|---|
| 1 | Attributive | big house | 7 | Recurrence | more ball |
| 2 | Agent-Action | Daddy hit* | 8 | Non-existence | All-gone ball |
| 3 | Action-Object | hit ball | 9 | possessive | Daddy's chair |
| 4 | Agent-Object | Daddy ball | 10 | Entity-Locative | book table |
| 5 | Nominative | that ball | 11 | Action-Locative | go store |
| 6 | Demonstrative | there ball |   |   |   |

These utterances are interpreted as expressing a range of semantic relations. The utterance "*Daddy hit*" is interpreted not as an expression of the formal syntactic relationship: Subject+ Verb, but as a combination of semantic categories of "Agent+ Action". It shows that the child's language at this point is lacking in function words and overt morphological markers of case, tense, number, etc.

Some researchers in this tradition have argued essentially that "syntactic categories develop as prototypes based on semantic information." Others believe that formal syntactic categories have an independent origin and that interactions between syntactic, semantic and pragmatic information are vital in driving forward L1A.

Budwig (1995) produced a survey of broadly functionalist approaches to the study of child language growth, and divided them into four main "orientations": cognitive orientation, textual orientation, social orientation and multifunctional orientation.

### 7.2.1 Cognitive Orientation and Textual Orientation

Cognitive orientation can be exemplified by the work of Slobin who proposed the existence of a "basic child grammar". Budwig described it by saying that "one of the opening wedges for grammar is the linguistic encoding of a scene in which an agent brings about a change of state in an object." At the level of discourse, functional linguists are interested in how both vocabulary and grammar (connectives as *and/but/whereas,* deictic elements as *this/that*) are deployed to create textual cohesion across sequences of clauses and sentences.

In child language studies, functional researches have examined the systems used by older children to establish cohesion in their narratives. The following example is drawn from a particular study of children's gradual acquisition of the different discourse functions of English determiners (Karmiloff-Smith, 1979: 222 – 223, translated from original French):

| |
|---|
| Time 1 C: Isabelle gave a talk about her rabbit and Alexia will give a talk about the tortoise<br>E: About which tortoise?<br>C: ...*the* tort... well, *hers,* and well... not only *hers* ... well ... *the* tortoises, about *all the* tortoises. |
| Time 2 E: You remember that Isabelle gave a talk about her rabbit and Alexia gave one about the tortoise?<br>C: Yes.<br>E: About which tortoise?<br>C: About *the* animal, *the* tortoise (shrugs shoulders as if it were quite obvious). |

At Time 1, when Child C is just aged 7 years 9 months, she has difficulty in distinguishing the deictic and generic functions of the definite article; by Time 2, when she is aged 9 years 2 months, generic functions are used without any difficulty.

### 7.2.2 Social Orientation and Multifunctional Orientation

Functionalist research with a social orientation is interested in relationships between the development of children's formal language system, and aspects of their social world. Some of this work examined the speech acts that children perform, and their relationships with lexical or grammatical choices.

Budwig re-analyzed some of the data gathered by Brown, arguing that expressions involving first-person possessive determiners (*my* pencil) consistently expressed different speech acts from expressions involving the child's own name (*Adam* pencil) — the first group were indicative (That's *my* pencil), whereas the second group were volitional (*I, Adam,* want a pencil).

In her research, Budwig examined the self-reference forms (*I, me, my, Own Name,* etc.) used by a group of two-year-old children to express the semantic notions of agentivity and control, and also sought to explain variability in usage in terms of the different pragmatic functions that were being expressed.

Megan at 20 months used the three forms *I, my* and *Meggie* for self-reference: *my* was seen as expressing high agentivity (***my** open that*), while *Meggie* expressed mid or low agentivity (***Meggie** swinging*) and *I* was used typically for mental state verbs (***I** wanna wear that*). The differences in usage could be related to pragmatic function, as *my* typically appeared in disputes over control of objects: ***My*** cups! said as Megan grabs cups from another child. Over time, Megan extended the use of *I* to perform a wider range of functions and her use of *my* and *Own Name* became more target-like.

Budwig's study is typical of recent research on form-function relationships in child language. She reviews possible factors that may drive children forward to continually reorganize their systems of form-function relationships along the documented developmental path: linguistic maturation; cognitive development; encounters with target input; and communicative need.

## 7.3 Functionalist Contributions to an Understanding of SLA

The functionalist view claims that language development is driven by pragmatic communicative needs, and that the formal resources of language are elaborated in order to express more complex patterns of meaning. Its research typically takes the case studies of individuals or groups of learners, usually adults in the early stages of L2A, who are acquiring the language in informal environments rather than in the classroom. These studies have offered us rich accounts of both the rate and route of naturalistic L2A, at least in the early stages.

### 7.3.1 Functionalism and the Nature of Interlanguage

The functionalist tradition has added an understanding of

interlanguage (IL) communication, and has made interesting suggestions about the interactions of formal and functional development.

Functionalist researchers have demonstrated the wide range of devices (lexical and pragmatic as well as formal) which IL users adopted in order to convey meaning. The hypothesis has suggested how learners may use overlaps in word meaning and morphological form as an entry point into formal subsystems of their target language.

A continuing limitation on functionalists' characterization of IL is that most attention has been paid to the earliest stages of development. The IL of more advanced learners has been explored thoroughly in some areas only, such as the development of reference to past time and the use of past-tense verb morphology (Bardovi-Harlig, 2000). The range of target languages investigated is also not very wide (most research has been done with Germanic or Romance languages) and the extent of influence of learners' L1 on post-basic varieties is not clear.

### 7.3.2 Functionalism on Language Learning and Development

Functionalist researchers insist universally on the gradual nature of L2 development and syntacticization, with learners working actively on only part of the system at any one time, but with possible reorganizational consequences that may spread widely through the system. At the same time, most functionalist researchers have so far adopted a "patch" approach, working on overall utterance structure, or alternatively exploring development within semantic and formal sub-systems.

Functionalist research has also focused largely on the analysis of learners' L2 output, and has paid relatively less attention to input and even to interaction. Bardovi-Harlig has noted the frequency in input of adverbial forms, and appeals to input processing theory by VanPatten (2002) in suggesting that learners may therefore not need to notice or process verb morphology in the language that they hear.

Conversely, Andersen makes claims in respect to frequency patterns in input, when commenting on the acquisitional patterns associated with the aspect hypothesis. As far as the European Science Foundation research is concerned, however, the main research team paid little attention to the details of input and interaction in which their subjects were engaged. They have not paid detailed or systematic attention to the emergence within interaction of new linguistic forms.

### 7.3.3  Functionalism on the Language Learner

Much functionalist research has concerned itself with naturalistic adult learners, acquiring a socially dominant L2 in the workplace and other non-domestic settings. The driving forces promoting SLA for such learners have been explained as: a) immediate communicative need, and b) a longer-term and more variable desire for social integration within the L2 community.

Functionalists have conducted extensive comparative cross-language research, but have been mainly interested in the discovery of universal rather than language specific characteristics of the learning process. Functionalist research on the emergence of L2 morphology has, however, concerned itself with instructed learners, who are seen as more successful in acquiring L2 morphology.

However it is not clear from a functionalist perspective why classroom learners should be more successful than uninstructed learners. It is possible that classroom discourse forces L2 learners to attend to the communicative value of formal items (tense and aspect morphology), which are communicatively redundant in daily discourse. But this idea has not been followed up systematically by any of the research groups.

## 7.4  Sociocultural Perspectives on SLA

### 7.4.1  Sociocultural Theory

Lev Semeonovich Vygotsky, born in 1896 in Orsha, in the Russian Empire (today in Belarus), was a researcher and theorist of child development. He was active in Moscow between 1925 and his early death in 1934. His *Thought and Language* in English appeared in 1962.

His views on child development have become increasingly influential, having been taken up and promoted by psychologists and child development theorists and applied in classroom studies by many educational researchers. Parts of his wide-ranging writings remain untranslated, and contemporary interpretations and modifications to

Vygotsky's original ideas mean that current sociocultural theory is best described as "neo-Vygotskyan". A number of key ideas current in contemporary interpretations or discussions of Vygotsky have recently been taken up by SLA theorists.

### 7.4.2 The Scope of Sociocultural Research

Researchers working in a socio-cultural framework are making an attempt to apply a theory of cognition and of development that has been influential in other domains of social and educational research, to the language-learning problem. Learning is seen as a social and inter-mental activity, taking place in the Zone of Proximal Development (ZPD), which precedes individual development (view as the internalization or appropriation of socially constructed knowledge).

The empirical research has used a varied range of socio-cultural constructs, such as private speech, activity theory, scaffolding the ZPD to address a variety of aspects of SLA, from the acquisition of lexis and grammar, to meta-cognition and the development of learning strategies, via the development of skills such as L2 writing.

This commitment to ethnographic research techniques is in line with the tenets of activity theory about the unique and holistic character of interaction within the individual ZPD. The students studied by Aljaafreh and Lantolf (1994) improved the accuracy of their written English.

Up to now, the strongest sociocultural claims about the relationship between interaction and learning have been made on a local scale, with reference to discrete elements of language. Their potential as a general account of language learning has not yet been demonstrated.

### 7.4.3 Mediation and the ZPD

#### 7.4.3.1 Mediation and Mediated Learning

The sociocultural view believes in the centrality of language as a "tool for thought", or a means of mediation, in mental activity. In turn, it is claimed that the nature of our available mental tools can itself shape our thinking to some extent.

From this view, learning is also a mediated process. It is mediated partly through learners' developing use and control of mental tools (languages, the central tool for learning). Importantly, learning is also seen as socially mediated, dependent on face-to-face interaction and shared processes, as joint problem solving and discussion.

A mature, skilled individual is capable of autonomous functioning, that is of self-regulation. However, the child or the unskilled individual learns by carrying out tasks and activities under the guidance of other more skilled individuals, such as caretakers or teachers. The child or the learner is inducted into a shared understanding of how to do things through collaborative talk, until eventually they take over (or appropriate) new knowledge or skills into their own individual consciousness.

So, successful learning involves a shift from collaborative inter-mental activity to autonomous intra-mental activity. The process of supportive dialogue which directs the attention of the learner to key features of the environment, and which prompts them through successive steps of a problem, has come to be known as scaffolding.

### 7.4.3.2 The ZPD by Vygotsky

The ZPD was defined as "the difference between the child's developmental level as determined by independent problem solving and the higher level of potential development as determined through problem solving under adult guidance or in collaboration with more capable peers" (Vygotsky, 1978: 85).

For the entire human race, as well as for the individual infant, learning is seen as first social, then individual. Consciousness and conceptual development are seen firstly as inter-mental phenomena, shared between individuals; later, individuals develop their own consciousness, which becomes an intra-mental phenomenon.

Donato (1994) claims that "scaffolded performance is a dialogically constituted interpsychological mechanism that promotes the novice's internalization of knowledge co-constructed in shared activity." The metaphor of scaffolding has been developed in neo-Vygotskyan discussions to capture the qualities of the type of other-regulation within the ZPD which is supposedly most helpful for the learning or appropriation of new concepts.

Scaffolded help has the following functions: 1) recruiting interest in the task; 2) simplifying the task; 3) maintaining pursuit of the goal; 4) marking critical features and discrepancies between what has been; 5) producing the ideal solution; 6) controlling frustration during problem solving; and 7) demonstrating an idealized version of the act to be performed.

For human beings, and even for the individual infant, language is the prime symbolic mediating tool for the development of consciousness. Throughout their life, human beings remain capable of learning; and the local learning process for more mature individuals acquiring new knowledge or skills is viewed as essentially the same. New concepts continue to be acquired through social or interactional means.

### 7.4.4 Sociocultural View of Language and Communication

Sociocultural theory views language as a "tool for thought". It is therefore critical theories of communication, which present language primarily as an instrument for the passage back and forth of predetermined messages and meanings. Communication is seen as central to the joint construction of knowledge (including that of language forms), which is first developed inter-mentally, and then internalized by individuals.

Similarly, private speech, meta-statement, etc., are valued positively as instruments for self-regulation, as the development of autonomous control over new knowledge. However, sociocultural theorists of SLA do not offer in its place any thorough or detailed view of the nature of language as a system.

Indeed, most of the studies on language development within the ZPD have focused on individual lexical items or morphsyntactic features as defined in traditional descriptive grammars. This limitation is recognized by researchers in the field. Aljaafreh and Lantolf (1994) point out if this tradition is to realize its ambitions to transform SLA research, it will need to locate itself more explicitly with respect to linguistic theory.

### 7.4.5 The Sociocultural View of Language Learning

Sociocultural theorists assume that the same general learning mechanisms will apply to language, as to other forms of knowledge and skill. However, all learning is seen as first social, then individual; first inter-mental, then intra-mental. Learners are seen as active constructors of their own learning environment. So, all this can be related to ideas of automatization and proceduralization of new knowledge.

Ohta (2001) has developed a very full account of language learning that integrates a range of sociocultural concepts with cognitive ideas about learning processes. She sees private speech as giving rich opportunities for repetition and rehearsal of new language items, hypothesis testing, and the manipulation of target structures during language play and the private rehearsal of interactional routines prior to use.

Similarly, she sees peer interaction and co-construction as providing learners with increased opportunities for noticing, selective attention to different aspects of target language production and increasing the capacity of working memory. Her classroom data provide rich exemplification in support of these detailed claims.

But while sociocultural theorists are ready to claim that ZPD-supported intentional learning can precede development, they have not seriously addressed the empirical question as to whether intervention in the ZPD simply scaffolds people more rapidly along the common routes of interlanguage development, or whether language learning can bypass or alter these routes, by skilled co-construction.

The preoccupation of sociocultural theorists with classroom learning should be noted. This reflects current enthusiasm among educators generally for Vygotsky's ideas. Concepts of ZPD, scaffolding and activity theory provide appealing alternative interpretations of the SLA and developmental opportunities afforded by classroom basics such as teacher-student interaction, problem-solving and communicative tasks, learner strategy training, focus on form and corrective feedback.

This ensures that sociocultural theory will receive continuing attention, despite of its apparent "incommensurability" with the vision of language as an autonomous and abstract system acquired through specialized mechanisms, which predominates in SLA research and has inspired most of the empirical work.

## 7.5 Sociolinguistic Perspectives on SLA

Sociolinguistics is itself a diverse field with multiple theoretical perspectives. Considering this fact, the following section will necessarily be selective, identifying the theoretical strands within contemporary sociolinguistics and anthropological linguistics that are having the clearest impact on the field of SLA.

The successive section will therefore deal with: 1) variability in L2 use; 2) L2 socialization; 3) communities of practice and situated SLA; 4) SLA and the (re)construction of identity; and 5) affect and emotion in SLA.

### 7.5.1 Developmental Links between L1 and Culture

The strand of sociolinguistic research is mainly concerned with language learning and development: the study of language socialization. The research has its roots in anthropological linguistics, and focuses on ethnographic studies of children learning to talk, to read and to write their L1, in varied societies. Researchers in the language socialization tradition believe that language and culture are not separable, but are acquired together, with each providing support for the development of the other.

Ochs and Schieffelin (1984; 1995) examined talks to children and by children in a variety of societies, and showed that these practices were themselves culturally organized. In the well-studied white middle class communities of North America, infants were viewed as conversational partners almost from birth, with caretakers interacting with them extensively one-to-one, and compensating for their conversational limitations by imputing meaning to their utterances, and engaging in clarification routines (e.g. by use of comprehension checks and recasts).

In Samoa, a small islandic country in South Pacific Ocean, infants are not viewed as conversational partners at all for the first few months. Then, they are encouraged to get involved in different types of interaction, for example being taught explicitly to call out the names of passers-by on the village road. Among the Kaluli, there is much direct teaching of interactional routines; however, in both communities, children's unintelligible utterances are seldom clarified or recast.

Ochs (1988) examined Samoan children's early utterances, and provided examples of links between linguistic development and socialization into particular roles and routines. Ochs documented instances of Samoan infants' early vocalizations being interpreted in this way. In all these cultural settings, children learn successfully to talk, leading them to conclude that: "grammatical development per se can not be accounted for in terms of any single set of speech practices involving children."

A language socialization perspective, in contrast, aims to take systematic account of the wider frameworks and socially recognized situations within which speech acts are performed. In summary, a language socialization perspective predicts that there will be a structured strategic relationship between language development and "culturally organized situations of use".

### 7.5.2 Empirical Studies of SLA as a Situated Social Practice

The L1 socialization perspective has proved appealing to SLA researchers who are concerned to develop a more integrated perspective on language learning, viewed as both a cognitive and a social process. One of the first L2 researchers to use this perspective was Poole, who conducted an ethnographic study of adult English L2 classrooms, claiming that "a teacher's language behavior is culturally motivated to an extent not generally acknowledged in most L2 literature" (1992: 593).

Poole showed that the teachers in her study scaffolded their learners extensively, and led and directed whole class tasks as group activities. However, in the closing stages of these same tasks, the teachers praised the students as if they alone had accomplished them. This was reflected in the teachers' **pronoun** usage; thus one teacher introduced a task with *"Describe the picture and see if we can make a story out of it."* Then, at the end, the teacher praised the class: *"Good work* **you** *guys!"* *" That's hard!"* *"***you** *-***you** *did a good job."* *"I'm impressed!"* (1992: 605).

The ideas of socially situated learning which takes place through participation in the activities of one or more communities of practice, have been used to study L2 development among both children and adults.

One obvious application is to view the classroom as a community of practice, as Toohey (2000) has done in a study of a group of six young English as L2 learners. Over a three-year period, the study tracked the children's developing identities and patterns of participation as they progressed from kindergarten to second grade of primary school. He showed that some were more successful than others in establishing themselves as legitimate peripheral participants in the classroom community.

Another study that adopted the same overall view of language learning as a social practice, located in communities of practice, is that of Norton in 2000. This study was conducted with five adult women from diverse language backgrounds, all of them recent immigrants to Canada, who were attending classes of English as L2 but also using English to different degrees at home and in a variety of workplaces. The women participants completed questionnaires and diaries, and were also interviewed at intervals, over a space of two years.

One participant in the study was a Polish girl called Eva, who was living with a Polish partner, and hoped eventually to study at university. She was working at a restaurant called Munchies, where at first she could not approach her co-workers or engage them in conversation: "When I see that I have to do everything and nobody cares about me because — then how can I talk to them? I hear they *doesn't* care about me and I don't feel to go and smile at them." (2000)

As time passed, however, she gained enough confidence to find conversational openings, joining in conversations about holidays with her own experiences of holidays in Europe. Thus, she gained acceptance as a "legitimate speaker", and correspondingly developed her opportunities for using English.

However, she paid close attention to how her fellow workers did this, appropriated their utterances during routines such as ordering meals, and took the initiative to start serving customers directly. In this way Eva widened her participation in the linguistic practices of the restaurant, and further increased her own language learning opportunities as a result.

Toohey and Norton (2001) argued that the qualities that made Eva successful L2 learners have to do only partly with her own actions and interventions. Critical to her success was the fact that she gained more and more access to the social and verbal activities of the target language community of practice.

In the case, Eva experienced attempts to subordinate or isolate her;

however, she could and did draw on both social and intellectual resources to overcome these difficulties. So, the learners' success in being accepted was central to access to language learning opportunity; and this success derived partly from their own actions, partly from their respective communities' willingness to adapt and to accept them as legitimate participants.

### 7.5.3 The Scope and Achievements of Sociolinguistic Enquiry

This chapter has introduced different strands of sociolinguistic theorizing about L2 use and L2 development. Among them, sociolinguistic factors play a role of increasing importance as learners become more advanced, but it is clear that much variability must be attributed primarily to psycholinguistic influences.

The remaining strands deal with SLA in a broad way, embedded in its social context. It frequently involves case studies of individuals or groups of learners; great attention is paid to the personal qualities and ambitions of the learners, and their own social contribution to the learning context. Valuable concepts such as the "community of practice" have been introduced to this field in recent work, which have been helpful for theorizing SLA as a social practice, in an integrative way.

On the other hand, it is still rare to find in sociolinguistic work, any close attention being paid to the linguistic detail of the learning path being followed, or the cognitive processes involved as mentioned by Watson-Gegeo and Nielsen (2003).

### 7.5.4 Sociolinguistic View on Language Learning and Development

As far as language learning is concerned, sociolinguistically oriented research has provided rich descriptions of the context for language learning, and the speech events (daily encounters or classroom lessons) through which it is presumed to take place. Like the Vygotskyan theorists, they believe that learning is a collaborative affair, and language knowledge is socially constructed through interaction. But they pay less attention than the sociocultural theorists to the linguistic detail of interaction.

There is no real parallel in L2 socialization studies to the detailed work of Ochs (1988) on linguistic development in L1 socialization. While Ochs offers evidence to support her claim that the L1 development can be influenced by the nature and quality of interactions in which the child becomes engaged, this idea has not yet seriously been investigated for L2 development, from a "socialization" perspective.

So current ethnographies of L2 communication and of L2 socialization offer a great deal of evidence to show that the learning context, and the learner's evolving style of engagement with it, may affect the rate of SLA. The patterning of learning opportunities, through communities of practice with structured and sometimes very unequal power relationships, has been invoked to explain learners' differential success even though motivation is high.

### 7.5.5 Sociolinguistic Accounts of the L2 Learner

L2 ethnographies take an interest in various L2 learners, from the youngest pupils to adult migrants. They take a more rounded view of the learner as a social being, than other perspectives. Dimensions such as gender and ethnicity are seen as significant for language learning success. Most striking, though, is the emphasis placed by contemporary ethnographic researchers on the dynamic and alterable nature of learners' identity and engagement with the task of SLA.

Self-esteem, motivation are believed to be both constructed and reconstructed in the course of L2 interaction, with significant consequences for the rate of learning and ultimate level of success.

## 7.6 Conclusion

It is clear that a wealth of L2 studies have been carried out recently from the angles of functional, sociocultural and sociolinguistic perspectives. However their theories and models which have been applied to the SLA study have concerned with the acquisition of collected or empirical data, somewhat not so closely related to the richness and complexity of natural languages and language learning mechanisms.

The modern researches, different substantially from traditional SLA study, are focusing on Input, Interaction and Output which are the topics of Chapter 8.

## Points for Thinking

1. What are the functionalist views on first and second language acquisition?
2. How do we interpret the contributions of the Sociocultural Theory to language and language learning?
3. What is the relationship between ZPD and the mediated learning of language?
4. What do the sociolinguistic theorists contribute to the study of language learning?
5. What are the significances of empirical studies done by sociolinguistic theorists?

## Further Reading

Budwig, N. (1995). *A Developmental-functionalist Approach to Child Language*. Mahwah, NJ: Lawrence Erlbaum.

Karmiloff-Smith, A. (1979). "A functional approach to child language." *A Study of Determiners and Reference*. Cambridge: Cambridge University Press.

Poole, D. (1992). "Language socialization in the second language classroom." *Language Learning* 42: 593 – 616.

Toohey, K. (2000). *Learning English at School: Identity, Social Relations and Classroom Practice*. Clevdon: Multilingual Matters.

Toohey, K. and Norton, B. (2001). "Changing perspectives on good language learners." *TESOL Quarterly* 35: 307 – 322.

Vygotsky, L. S. (1978). *Mind in Society: The Development of Higher Psychological Processes*. Cambridge, MA: Harvard University Press.

# Chapter 8

# Input, Interaction and Output in SLA

## 8.1 Introduction

It is commonly believed that learning an L2 involves learning the rules of its grammar along with vocabulary items and rules of pronunciation. Putting those rules to use in the context of conversation is then construed as a natural extension of grammar acquisition.

The original inspiration from the Input Hypothesis was advanced by Stephen Krashen since the 1980s. The Input Hypothesis claims that the availability of input which is comprehensible to the learner is the only necessary condition for language learning to take place. This claim sparked off a number of traditions of empirical research into the environmental conditions for learning, which are still highly active today.

Michael Long advanced the argument that in order to understand more fully the nature of input for SLA, greater attention should be paid to the interactions in which learners were engaged. This view has become known as the Interaction Hypothesis.

A second challenge to Krashen was put forward by Merrill Swain, whose work with immersion students in Canadian schools had led her to question the claim that comprehensible L2 input was sufficient to ensure all-round interlanguage development. Swain advanced another set of claims about the relationship between language use and language learning, the so-called Output Hypothesis.

These theoretical claims have led to extensive empirical work, examining the detail of L2 Input-Interaction-Output involving L2 learners, and seeking to explain its relationship with interlanguage development.

## 8.2　Input and Interaction in L1 Acquisition

It will be helpful to recap briefly on current understandings of the role of input and interaction in L1A. It is well known that adults and other caretakers commonly use "special" speech styles when talking with young children, and terms such as baby talk are commonly used to refer to this. This empirical research tradition of investigating **Child-directed Speech** (CDS) has remained very active. CDS has demonstrated its solid contributions to language acquisition. Some findings from this tradition are potentially relevant for SLA:

1.CDS has mostly been studied in English-speaking contexts and most usually in a middle-class family setting. In CDS contexts, explicit formal corrections of the child's productions are unusual, but recasts are common.

  CHILD:  *Fix Lily*

  MOTHER: *Oh ... Lily will fix it*

2.There seems to be a relationship between the caretaker's use of inverted yes-no questions: *Have you been sleeping?* and children's developing control of verbal auxiliaries in English as an L1.

3. Despite of the potential usefulness of CDS as input data, it is clear that caretakers are not typically motivated by any prime language-teaching goal, nor is their speech in general specially adapted so as to model the target grammar.

4. Cross-cultural studies of interaction with young children have made it clear that styles of CDS found in middle-class societies are far from universal, and that societies can be found where infants are not seen as conversation partners (Lieven, 1994).

CDS researchers in this field seem generally to agree 1) that multi-dimensional models are necessary, covering a range of components as parental input, learning mechanisms and procedures and linguistic constraints built into the child; and 2) that the way forward lies in close, detailed studies of relationships between the features of the input, and of related features in the child's linguistic knowledge.

The CDS studies remain hopeful that it will eventually demonstrate exactly how it is that environmental linguistic evidence interacts with and constrains the linguistic hypotheses under development by the child learner.

## 8.3 Input and Interaction in SLA

### 8.3.1 From Corder to Krashen's "Input Hypothesis"

The early L2 conceptualizations were based on a behaviorist view. The major driving force of language learning was the language to which learners were exposed. Corder in 1967 made an important distinction between two L2 terms: Input and Intake. Input refers to what is available to the learner, whereas intake refers to what is actually internalized (or in Corder's terms, "taken in") by the learner.

It has always been clear that comprehensible and contextualized data are necessary for L2A to take place. The precise developmental contribution of the language used to address L2 learners first attracted serious attention from psycholinguists and L2 researchers in the light of the Input Hypothesis proposed by Krashen.

The Input Hypothesis claims that exposure to comprehensible input is both necessary and sufficient for SLA to take place. The hypothesis states that: "Humans acquire language in only one way — by understanding messages, or by receiving 'comprehensible input'... We move from i, our current level, to $i+1$, the next level along the natural order, by understanding input containing $i+1$." Linked to the hypothesis are two further ideas (Krashen, 1985).

Krashen proposed three stages in turning Input into Intake: 1) understanding an $i+1$ form; 2) noticing a gap between the $i+1$ form and the interlanguage rule which the learner currently controls; and 3) the reappearance of the $i+1$ form with minimal frequency.

The concepts of "understanding" and "noticing a gap" are not clearly operationalized, and it is not quite clear how the state of "$i$" is to be characterized, or whether the "$i+1$" formula is intended to apply to all aspects of language, including vocabulary, phonology and syntax. But numerous critics have pointed out that the Input Hypothesis is supported by little empirical evidence, and is not easily testable.

Krashen's proposals encouraged others to examine more closely the characteristics of the language input available to L2 learners. It was grammatically regular, but often simplified linguistically by comparison with talk between native speakers (e.g. using shorter utterances and a narrower range of vocabulary or less complex grammar).

Long (1985) argued that the degree of simplification reported in many descriptive studies was puzzlingly variable. He proposed a more systematic approach to linking features of environmental language and learners' L2 development. Therefore, Long shifted his attention towards more interactive aspects of Foreigner Talk Discourse.

### 8.3.2 Long's Study and His "Interaction Hypothesis"

Long went on to propose his Interaction Hypothesis as an extension of Krashen's original Input Hypothesis. Long conducted a study of two pairs of speakers: one consisting of 16 natives speakers (NS) and the other of 16 native speaker—non-native speaker (NS—NNS), carrying out the same set of face-to-face oral tasks.

Long showed that there was little linguistic difference between the talk produced by NS pairs and NS—NNS pairs, as shown on measures of grammatical complexity. There were important differences between the two sets of conversations when these were analyzed from the point of view of conversational management and language functions performed.

Specifically, for solving ongoing communication difficulties, the NS—NNS pairs were more likely to use conversational tactics such as repetitions, confirmation checks, comprehension checks or clarification requests. Native speakers apparently resort to these tactics in order to solve communication problems when talking with less fluent non-native speakers, and not with any conscious motive to teach grammar. The following is an example of interactional modifications in NS—NNS conversations.

| NS | NNS |
|---|---|
| And right on the top of the truck place the duck. The duck. *Duck.* | I to lake it? *Dog?* *Duck.* |
| It's yellow and it's a small animal. It has two feet. | |
| You take the *duck* and put it on top of the *truck.* | I put where it? |
| Do you see the *duck?* | *Duck?* |
| Yeah. *Quack, quack, quack.* That one. The one that makes that sound. | |
| Ah yes, I see in the -in the head of him. | Put what? |
| OK. See? OK. Put him on top of the *truck.* | Truck? |
| The bus. Where the boy is. | Ah yes. |

From the view of the **Interaction Hypothesis,** such collaborative efforts should be very useful for language learning. As they struggle to maximize comprehension, and negotiate their way through trouble spots. They are collaborating to ensure that the learner is receiving $i+1$ rather than $i+3$, or indeed, $i+0$.

On the whole, these studies have taught us a good deal about the types of task that are likely to promote extensive negotiation of meaning, inside and outside the classroom. They have also demonstrated that negotiation of meaning occurs between non-native speaker peers, as well as between more fluent and less fluent speakers, given the right task conditions.

As Long points out, these studies have mostly been undertaken in Western educational institutions, and little is known yet about the kinds of negotiation and repair that may typify L2 interactions in other contexts. Also, many early interaction studies did not go beyond the first descriptive steps of establishing the existence and general patterning of conversational repair.

### 8.3.3 Empirical Studies on Comprehension and Acquisition

One of the first studies that attempted to establish a link between interactional modifications and increased comprehension was conducted by

Pica in 1987.

Groups of L2 learners listened to different versions of a script instructing them to place colored cutouts on a landscape picture, and tried to complete the task. One group heard a linguistically simplified version of the script, but individuals were not allowed to ask any questions as they carried out the instructions. The second group heard an authentic version, but individuals were encouraged to ask for clarifications, etc., from the person reading the script.

Pica was nonetheless able to show that the learners allowed to negotiate the meaning of an unmodified script were more successful on the task than those who simply heard the simplified script, and argued that this shows increased comprehension because of interactional modifications of the input. This study seems to show that interactional adjustments are more effective in promoting comprehension of input than are linguistic adjustments alone.

In another study, Gass (1994) asked NS—NNS pairs to undertake a game of problem-solving communication. This involved placing figures in particular locations on a landscape scene. The "game" was run twice, first of all with the NS participants issuing instructions to their NNS interlocutors, and second, the other way around.

When the NS participants gave instructions on the first occasion, half were asked to follow a linguistically pre-modified script, and the other half followed an unmodified script. For each script, half the NS subjects were instructed to allow negotiation about meaning, and the other half were not. In this study, both the modified script without interaction, and the unmodified script with interaction, seemed to increase NNS comprehension (as measured by success on the task), compared with those who heard the unmodified script and could not negotiate around it.

A somewhat different kind of development did take place for the "negotiation" group however. It turned out that those NNS subjects, who had been allowed to interact with their interlocutor during Trial 1, were significantly better at giving directions during Trial 2, than those who had not. Gass and Varonis consider the possibility that the NNSs might have learnt a larger number of useful vocabulary items during their interactive experience of Trial 1, only to reject it. Instead, they argue that the Trial 2 data show evidence of NNS having internalized various useful communicative strategies, as exemplified below(Gass and Varonis, 1994: 296):

Trial 1

JANE: All right now, above the sun place the squirrel. He's right on top of the sun.

HIROSHI: What is ... the word?

JANE: OK. The sun.

HIROSHI: Yeah, sun, but...

JANE: Do you know what the sun is?

HIROSHI: Yeah, of course. Wh-what's the

JANE: Squirrel. Do you know what a squirrel is?

HIROSHI: No.

JANE: OK. You've seen them running around on campus. They're little furry animals. They're short and brown and they eat nuts like crazy.

Trial 2

HIROSHI: The second will be ... put here. This place is ... small animal which eat nuts.

JANE: Oh, squirrel?

HIROSHI: Yeah (laughter).

Using the data from the examples above, the researchers point out that the subject Hiroshi seems to have learnt, not the lexical item *squirrel* but a strategy for defining it, using more basic vocabulary.

The somewhat contradictory findings of these studies call for stronger theoretical models to clarify the links between interaction and acquisition. Some researchers also criticized the earlier interactionist research as being too one-sidedly preoccupied with functional aspects of L2 interaction and of neglecting linguistic theory.

### 8.3.4 Rethinking the Interaction Hypothesis

L2 input or interaction researchers have shown themselves quite responsive to the ongoing development of both linguistic and information processing theory within SLA studies. This is evident in Long's eventual reformulation of the Interaction Hypothesis, which places much more emphasis on linking features of input and the linguistic environment with "learner-internal factors", and explaining how such linkages may facilitate subsequent language development.

The new version highlights the contribution to L2 learning of negative evidence as to the structure of the target language. It also highlights the attempt to clarify the processes by which input becomes intake, through introducing the notion of selective attention. These concepts are also repeatedly referred to, in current discussions of output and its contribution to language development.

## 8.4 Output in SLA

Most researchers agree that output is necessary to increase fluency, as learners must practise producing L2 utterances if they are to learn to use their interlanguage system confidently and routinely. However, the Output Hypothesis advanced by Swain (1995) makes a number of claims which go beyond this "practice function of output, and which have to do with the development of the interlanguage system, and not only increased efficiency in using it."

Swain (1998) proposes three functions for learners' output: 1) the "noticing/triggering" function, or what might be referred to as the consciousness-raising role; 2) the hypothesis-testing function; and 3) the metalinguistic function, or what might be referred to as its "reflective role". In her own research, Swain has concentrated largely on the "reflective" role of output, and especially the possible contribution of metalinguistic talk between peers to L2 development.

Other researchers have conducted research that tries to link learners' opportunities for output more directly to L2 development. Nobuyoshi and Ellis (1993) conducted a small-scale study of the role of output in the development of English past tense. They tried to encourage English L2 learners to modify their output by means of clarification requests, as in the following example(Nobuyoshi and Ellis, 1993: 205):

Learner: *Last weekend, a man painting, painting "Beware of the* dog".

Teacher: *Sorry?*

Learner: *A man painted, painted, painted on the wall "Beware of the dog".*

Of the three students who had received this treatment, two maintained the resulting increased accuracy in using past tense forms.

Larger studies by Izumi (1999; 2000) explored the potential of pushed output to promote English L2 students' learning of the counterfactual condition in English:

e.g. *If Ann had travelled to Spain in 1992, she would have seen the Olympics.*

Experimental groups were given different kinds of texts including rich examples of the structure, and had to generate similar texts (in an essay writing). Control groups meanwhile received the same textual inputs, but did other activities (answered questions). The writings of the experimental groups showed improvement during the experimental treatment, but on the final post-tests, focusing on the L2 grammar, the control groups performed just as well. Thus it seemed that rich input combined with a variety of "noticing" activities, may have been enough in this case to lead to grammar learning, without any added benefit being derived from the output requirement.

So, it seems that the benefits of "pushed output" remain somewhat elusive and hard to demonstrate, at least as far as L2 grammar development is concerned.

## 8.5 Theorizing Input, Interaction and Output Research

The survey of input, interaction and output research has shown that a good deal of the research carried out has been descriptive in nature, and attempts to link different types of L2 use with SLA have so far produced only mixed results. It seems that stronger theorizing is required, for interaction studies to progress.

Clearly, interactionist researchers themselves are increasingly interested in modeling internal linguistic and psycholinguistic factors.

However, no very full or detailed models of language processing have been proposed by any of the interactionist researchers. The following section presents an introduction to two models that have been advanced so far: the Input Processing Theory and the Autonomous Induction Theory.

### 8.5.1 Input Processing Theory

Input Processing Theory (IPT) has been developed over the last decade by VanPatten (1996). It has become well known largely because of an associated research program on language pedagogy and it is concerned to explain how environmental L2 input becomes converted into intake.

The IPT does not offer a complete model of these processes. Instead, it offers a set of principles that seem designed primarily to explain the apparent failure of L2 learners to process completely the linguistic forms encountered in L2 input, and hence to explain their impoverished intake which in turn restricts the development of grammatical form.

The principles assume that learners have preferences for semantic processing over morphological processing. In a sentence, *we travelled to London by train yesterday,* past time is signaled twice, by the *-ed* verb inflection, and by the adverb *yesterday.* According to Input Processing Theory, learners are likely to parse a sentence like this only incompletely, extracting temporal information from the adverb and ignoring the "redundant" verb inflection.

The approach has led to a series of pedagogical experiments that have tried to force L2 classroom learners to parse input morphology more fully. For example, they may be exposed to input in which verb inflections are the only available clues that provide temporal information, or in which prepositional phrases are the only available clues for location; see various studies reviewed in VanPatten (2002).

However, the IPT is primarily focused on explaining the shortcuts and restricted processing strategies which learners seem to use. It clearly does not offer a complete model of normal or successful processing of input. It also does not offer any extended explanation of how intake is processed further and becomes integrated more permanently in some way into the progressive interlanguage system.

### 8.5.2 Autonomous Induction Theory

A much more complete and ambitious model of these processes is Autonomous Induction Theory (AIT) offered by Carroll (2000), who accepts that human mental representations of language involve a number of distinct modules with limited interconnections. She proposes a version of Inductive Learning (I-learning), which is initiated when learners fail to parse incoming language stimuli adequately using their existing mental representations and analysis procedures.

Carroll argues that the I-learning of AIT differs from other inductive language learning theories because it is constrained by the preexisting mental representations of language, which are strongly resistant to change.

Although Carroll's model is complex, it is relevant to SLA study because she also presents a well-developed critique of interactionist research. Carroll challenges a commonplace among interactionist researchers, who claim that increased L2 comprehension can lead to identification and acquisition of language form, in a sequential manner.

"I-learning" is the term applied to learning by generalization from examples. It has been commonly criticized as inadequate with reference to language learning, because it fails to explain why learners processing the environmental language around them are so successful at working out the complexities of natural language, and in particular, why they never produce so-called "wild grammars".

## 8.6 Feedback, Recasts and Negative Evidence in SLA

This section will look more closely at recent researches on the role of feedback in L2 interaction, and its particular contribution to interlanguage development.

### 8.6.1 Feedback, Recasts and Negative Evidence in L1A

Some theorists argue for a strongly innatist model of language learning. They have claimed that language is simply not learnable from the normal type of input, which provides mostly positive evidence of the structure of the target language, and lacks negative evidence in the form of, for example, grammar corrections studied. They put forward a question as "*In the absence of negative evidence, how are learners to discover the limits and boundaries of the language system they are learning?*"

For nativists, the existence of some form of UG is needed to eliminate many possible generalizations about language structure that are compatible with the input received, but are actually incorrect. Other Researchers (Bohannon, 1990; Farrar, 1992) assert that negative evidence is much more prevalent in child-directed speech than was previously thought, in particular by claiming that caretakers' recasts of poorly formed child utterances offer the implicit negative evidence about children's interim grammatical hypotheses.

There is controversy among child language researchers on this issue, particularly concerning the standards to be applied to evidence supporting claims that recasts promote grammatical development. Long (1996) concludes that L1A researchers have generally succeeded in demonstrating that (implicit) negative evidence: a) is regularly available in child-directed speech; b) exists in usable form; and c) is picked up and used by child learners, at least in the short term.

Whether negative evidence is necessary for the acquisition of core aspects of language still remains less clear, however.

### 8.6.2 Negative Feedback and Recasts in the L2 Classroom

Further observational studies have examined the occurrence, and apparent effects, of negative feedback in the L2 classroom. They are variants on a quite longstanding tradition of research into classroom error correction, which had already suggested some benefits from active correction strategies. Chaudron (1988) typically evaluated the usefulness of recasts as compared with other types of negative feedback, as reflected in student uptake in immediately following interaction sequences.

The studies by Lyster (1998) illustrate this type of classroom investigation. A study in a Canadian immersion context looked at different types of error feedback offered by teachers. They noted that recasts were much the most common type of feedback (60%) compared with negotiation of form (34%) and explicit meta-linguistic corrections (6%). However, recasts were much less likely to lead to immediate self-correction by the students than were other feedback types.

A further analysis of the same recorded lessons (Lyster, 1998) showed that the kind of negative feedback provided by the teachers varied according to the type of error that had been made. The teachers were much more likely to respond to lexical errors with some kind of negotiation (e.g. clarification requests), while they typically responded to both grammatical and phonological errors with recasts.

As far as the phonological errors were concerned, recasting seemed an effective teacher strategy, as the students later repaired more than 60% of these mistakes. However, recasting was much less effective for repair of grammar mistakes; only 22% of all spoken grammar mistakes were corrected, and the majority of these grammar repairs happened when the teachers adopted the (less usual) strategy of negotiation.

Similar evidence is offered by a study of a communicatively oriented adult English L2 classroom. Panova and Lyster (2002) interpret the findings as showing that while recasts may offer valuable negative evidence, students are not necessarily under pressure to attend to them, at least in communicatively oriented classroom settings. They suggest that interactive feedback modes may thus be more effective in pushing classroom learners to adjust their hypotheses about L2 grammar and vocabulary.

### 8.6.3 Experimental Studies of Negative Feedback

The studies seem to claim that improved performance in immediately succeeding utterances can be taken seriously as evidence of learning, but the researchers doing these descriptive studies are generally aware that it is not always the fact.

It is possible that the corrections which are produced by learners immediately after negative feedback are quickly forgotten, and do not affect their underlying interlanguage system; it is also possible that recasts can function as effective input and lead to learning, without any explicit repair being produced.

For these reasons, a number of researchers have tried to design more focused experimental studies of its effect on SLA. An example is the study (Mackey and Philp, 1998) of the use of recasts, and their impact on the learning of English as L2 question forms. Thirty five adult learners took part in a specially designed program of information-gap tasks, pushing them towards production of English as L2 questions.

The students carried out the tasks with a native speaker interlocutor, and also completed a series of pre-and post-tests that identified their level on the developmental scale for English questions. Some in the study received intensive recasting from the NS interlocutor whenever they made an error in question formation. Others did the same tasks, but without receiving the recasting "treatment", whereas a control group did the pre- and post-tests only.

However, the post-tests showed that most of the learners, who experienced recasting, progressed by at least one stage further. No other group made similar progress. The researchers interpreted these results as showing that recasting was beneficial for learners who were developmentally ready, in spite of the lack of overt uptake while interaction was actually in progress.

Nicholas (2001) points out the findings to date for "negative feedback" research are still somewhat inconclusive and difficult to interpret. One increasingly recognized problem is that very little is known about 1) how much attention learners pay to the feedback they receive, or 2) how they interpret it.

Some researchers are now trying to use a variety of introspection techniques. Mackey (2000) made video-recordings of interactions, and played them back to the learners concerned, asking them to recall their thinking during selected correction episodes, as these were replayed to them.

The recall showed that learners had been aware of lexical and phonological correction episodes, which they could identify and comment on. But they were less likely to have noticed grammatical episodes, or to identify them correctly if they did notice them, as the learner's comment on the following episode shows (Mackey et al., 2000: 486):

NNS (on video): *It have mixed colors.*
NS: *It has mixed colors.*
NNS: *Mixed colors.*
NNS (subsequent recall): *Uh, I was thinking ... nothing, she just*

*repeat what I said.*

Here, the learner made a mistake during the video interaction, which was recast by the NS interlocutor. However, her comments during the recall activity showed her awareness that her message was repeated, and had not noticed the correction in the recast.

## 8.7 Evaluation: The Scope of Interactionist Research

### 8.7.1 Achievements of Interactionist Research

The achievements to date of research in the Input or Interaction tradition may be summarized as follows:

It has been shown that NS and NNS interlocutors can work actively to achieve mutual understanding, at least when undertaking a wide range of problem-solving tasks. It has been shown that these negotiations involve both linguistic and interactional modifications, which together offer repeated opportunities to "notice" aspects of L2 form, whether from positive or negative evidence.

It has been shown that NNS participants in "negotiations for meaning" can attend to, take up and use language items made available to them by their NS interlocutors. It has also been shown that learners receiving negative feedback, relating to particular L2 structures, can in some contexts be significantly advantaged when later tested on those structures.

### 8.7.2 Limitations of Interactionist Research

The achievements of this tradition are still constrained by some limitations. Work on interaction has been carried out almost entirely within a Western educational setting; and more cross-cultural studies of L2 interaction will be needed.

All researchers in the Input or Interactionist tradition seem to accept that SLA must be the result of interaction between environmental stimuli, a learner-internal language system, and some language-specific learning capabilities. Attempts at modeling this interaction are mostly still very fragmentary and incomplete.

It is still far from the most productive research about the role of interaction in learning. There are still not many studies that focus on particular language structures, tracking them through processes of instruction, negotiation, output or recasting, and documenting learners' subsequent use and control of these particular items.

It is clear that negotiation, recasts, etc., can vary in their usefulness for acquisition, and it seems that this variation is related to the developmental stage of the learner, as well as to different areas of the target language system (lexis, phonology, syntax, etc.).

## 8.8 Conclusion

The Input, Output and Interaction hypotheses have led to very active strands of empirical research. A first phase of research leaned heavily towards documenting the phenomenon of meaning negotiation. If it could be shown that negotiation increased comprehensibility of target language input, it was assumed that this would also enhance SLA.

Attempts such as those of VanPatten and of Carroll remain relatively unusual and have not been fully integrated with the empirical traditions of interactionist research. However, one thing is clear, while Input or Interaction research remains highly active, it cannot solve these difficulties alone. Its future is intertwined with the development of more comprehensive models of the learner-internal L2 learning process.

 Points for Thinking

1. What does the child-directed speech contribute to the SLA study?
2. What are the findings of empirical studies on comprehension and acquisition?
3. What is the difference between the study on output in L1A and that of in SLA?
4. What are the significances of Input Processing Theory and Autonomous Induction Theory?
5. What are the differences between feedback in L1A and that of in SLA?

Further Reading

Carroll, S. (2000). *Input and Evidence: The Raw Material of Second Language Acquisition.* Amsterdam: John Benjamins.

Corder, S. P. (1981). *Error Analysis in Interlanguage.* Oxford: Oxford University Press.

Krashen, S. (1981). *Second Language Acquisition and Second Langauge Learning.* Oxford: Pergamon.

Long, M. H. (1980). *Input, Interaction and Second Language Acquisition.* Los Angeles: University of California, PhD dissertation.

Swain, M. (2000). "The output hypothesis and beyond: mediating acquisition through collaborative dialogue." In Lantolf, J. (Ed.). *Sociocultural Theory and Second Language Learning.* Oxford: Oxford Uni. Press, pp.97 – 114.

# Chapter 9

# Varied Perspectives on Interlanguage

## 9.1 An Introduction to Interlanguage

### 9.1.1 The Definition and Characters of Interlanguage

The term Interlanguage (IL) was coined by Selinker, in the fact that an L2 learner constructs a linguistic system that draws partly on his L1 but is also different from the target language. That is, IL refers to the systematic knowledge of an L2, independent of both the learner's L1 and the target language. A learner's IL refers to 1) the IL Continuum: the interconnected systems which characterize learners' progress over time; 2) an IL: the system observed at a single stage of development; and 3) particular L1 and L2 combination.

There are two views concerning the nature of the IL continuum: 1) restructuring continuum in which the learner is gradually replacing features of his L1 as he acquires features of L2; 2) recreation continuum in which the learner is slowly creating the rule system of L2 in a manner very similar to the child's acquisition of his L1.

An IL is generally characterized by being systematic and dynamic. It is systematic because learners behave "grammatically" on the rules they have internalized, and it is also dynamic as the language learners' mental grammars are always in a state of change.

### 9.1.2 The IL Concept and Research Issues

This concept of IL offers a general account of how SLA takes place. It incorporates elements from mentalist theories of linguistics (the notion of a language acquisition device) and elements from cognitive psychology (learning strategies). It involves the following premises about the L2 learner in SLA:

1. His system of **abstract linguistic rules** underlying comprehension and production of the L2. It is viewed as an IL and a "mental grammar".
2. His **permeable** grammar which is open to influence from both the outside (input) and the inside (the overgeneralization, and transfer errors, etc.).
3. His **transitional** grammar which changes from time to time by adding rules, deleting rules, and restructuring the whole system.
4. His systems of **variable rules.** Some researchers argue that learners are likely to have competing rules at any one stage of development. And others see variability as an aspect of performance rather than competence.
5. His employmemt of **various learning strategies** to develop his ILs. The various kinds of learners' errors reflect different learning strategies.
6. His grammar fossilization. The prevalence of backsliding (i.e. the production of errors representing an early stage of development) is typical of fossilization, which does not occur in L1 acquisition and thus is unique to L2 grammars.

The study of IL does not offer a very precise explanation of what takes place. In fact it is, perhaps, more useful for the questions it raises than the answers it provides.

(a) When does input work for acquisition and when does it not?
(b) Why do learners sometimes employ an L1 transfer strategy and sometimes an overgeneralization strategy?
(c) What makes learner language so variable?
(d) What causes learners to restructure their ILs?
(e) Why does IL restructuring result in clearly identifiable sequences of acquisition?
(f) Why do most learners fossilize?

Clearly, the concept of IL needs to be elaborated to address the above issues.

### 9.1.3 Selinker and His View of IL

As in EA and L1 studies since the 1960s, Selinker (1972) and others considered the development of the IL to be a creative process, driven by inner forces in interaction with outside factors, and influenced both by IL and by input from L2.

Selinker stresses that there are differences between IL development in SLA and L1 acquisition by children, including different cognitive processes involved either: 1) language transfer from L1 to L2; 2) transfer of training, or how the L2 is taught; 3) strategies of L2 learning, or how learners approach the L2 materials and the task of L2 learning; 4) strategies of L2 communicative, or ways that learners try to communicate with others in the L2; and 5) overgeneralization of the L2 linguistic material, in which L2 rules that are learned are applied too broadly.

The concept of an IL as a system of learner language which is at least partially independent of L1 and L2 has been highly productive in the study of SLA. It is generally taken for granted now, although controversies remain concerning its specific nature and whether "progress" should be measured against native-speaker norms by Selinker and other scholars.

## 9.2 Social Aspects of IL

The prevailing perspective on IL is psycholinguistic, as reflected in the metaphor of the computer. Researchers have been primarily concerned with identifying the internal mechanisms. However, SLA has originally acknowledged the importance of social factors. Three different approaches to incorporating a social angle on the study of SLA can be identified as the following three views:

1. regarding IL as consisting of different "styles" which learners call upon under different conditions of language use.
2. concerning how social factors determine the input that learners use to construct their IL.
3. considering how the social identities that learners negotiate in their interactions with native speakers shape their opportunities to speak and, thus, to learn an L2.

### 9.2.1 IL as a Stylistic Continuum

Considering variability in learner language, Tarone (1983) has proposed that IL involves **a stylistic continuum**. She argues that learners develop a capability for using the L2 and that this underlies "all regular language behavior". This capability, constituting "an abstract linguistic system", is comprised of a number of different "styles" which learners access in accordance with a variety of factors.

At one end is the **careful style**, and at the other is the **vernacular style**. Tarone's idea of IL is attractive in a number of ways. It first explains why learner language is variable; and then suggests that an IL grammar is constructed according to the same principles as NSs; and last relates language use to language learning.

In short, Tarone's theory seems to relate more to psycholinguistic rather than social factors in variation. As Tarone has acknowledged, the model also has a number of problems. The research has shown that learners are not always most accurate in their careful style and least accurate in their vernacular style. And the role of social factors remains unclear on whether the concept of "social group" is applicable to classroom L2 / FL learners.

Another theory on the idea of stylistic variation is Giles's **Accommodation Theory** (1979), which seeks to explain how a learner's social group influences the course of SLA. He suggests that when people interact with each other they emphasize either social cohesiveness (a process of **convergence**) or social distinctiveness (a process of **divergence**).

According to Giles's theory, then, social factors influence IL development via the impact they have on the attitudes that determine the kinds of language use learners engage in. Accommodation theory suggests that social factors, mediated through the interactions that learners take part in, influence both how quickly they learn and the actual route that they follow.

### 9.2.2 The Acculturation Model of IL

Another perspective on social factors can be found in Schumann's **Acculturation Model** (1978), which has been influential, and built around the metaphor of **distance**.

Schumann investigated in a case study, a thirty-three-year-old Costa Rican named Alberto, who was acquiring English in the United States. He found very little evidence of any linguistic development over a ten-month period in Alberto who used a "reduced and simplified form of English" throughout. In short, Alberto appeared to have fossilized, or as Schumann's "pidginized", at an early stage of development.

Schumann entertained a number of possible reasons—intelligence and age—and dismissed all of them. This led him to consider the formation of a Pidgin in SLA. Schumann proposed that Pidginization resulted when learners failed to acculturate to the L2 group, when they were unable or unwilling to adapt to a new culture. The main reason for learners failing to acculturate is **Social Distance.**

Schumann recognizes that social distance is sometimes indeterminate. He suggests psychological distance becomes important and identifies a further set of psychological factors, such as language shock and motivation. And social factors determine the amount of contact with the L2 individual learners' experience and thereby how successful they are in learning.

There are two problems with such a model. It fails to acknowledge 1) that factors like integration pattern and attitude are not fixed and static but, potentially, variable and dynamic, and 2) that learners are not just subject to social conditions but can also become the subject of them; they can help to construct the social context of their own learning.

### 9.2.3  Social Identity and Investment in IL

The notion of social identity is central to the theory Peirce advances (1995). She argues that language learners have complex social identities in terms of the power relations that shape social structures. Learning is successful when learners are able to construct an identity that enables them to be heard and become the subject of the discourse. It requires investment, which learners have to make if they believe their efforts will increase the value of their "cultural capital".

Peirce's social theory of SLA affords a different set of metaphors. SLA involves a "struggle" and "investment". Learners are not computers who process input data but combatants and investors who expect a good return on their efforts.

Sociocultural models of SLA are intended to account for learner's relative success or failure in learning. They seek to explain the speed of learning and the ultimate level of proficiency of different groups of learners. But sociocultural models may be less relevant to FL settings where learners' principal contact with the FL is in a classroom.

## 9.3 Discourse Aspects of IL

The study of learner discourse in SLA has been informed by two rather different goals. Firstly, there are attempts to discover how L2 learners acquire the L2 "rules" of discourse. Secondly, a number of researchers have sought to show how interaction shapes IL development.

### 9.3.1 Acquiring Discourse Rules

There are rules in the ways in which NSs communicate with each other. An English compliment usually calls for a response and failure to provide one can be considered a sociolinguistic error. Furthermore, in American English compliment responses are usually quite elaborate, involving some attempt on the part of the speaker to play down the compliment by making some unfavorable comment.

There is a growing body of research investigating learner discourse. This shows that the acquisition of discourse rules, like the acquisition of grammatical rules, is **systematic**, reflecting both distinct types of errors and developmental sequences.

However, more work is needed to demonstrate which aspects are universal and which are language specific as it is already clear that many aspects of learner discourse are influenced by the rules of discourse in the learner's L1. There will be a discussion on how learners transfer discourse features from their L1 to the L2.

### 9.3.2 The Role of Input and Interaction in IL

The bulk of the research on learner discourse has been concerned with whether and how input and interaction affect SLA.

A behaviorist view treats language learning as environmentally determined from the outside stimuli and the reinforcement they receive. Mentalist theories emphasize the importance of the learners' brains which are equipped to learn language. Interactionist theories acknowledge the importance of both input and internal language processing.

In short, learning takes place as a result of a complex interaction between the linguistic environment and the learner's internal mechanisms. If learner discourse can be shown to have special properties it is possible that these contribute to acquisition in some way. Just as caretakers modify the way they speak to children learning their L1, so do NSs modify their speech when communicating with L2 learners. These modifications are evident in both input and interaction.

### 9.3.3 The Study of Foreigner Talk

Ferguson (1975) began his investigations of special registers, such as **"baby talk"** and **"foreigner talk"**. His work was primarily descriptive and input modifications have been investigated through the study of foreigner talk.

Foreigner talk can be identified both 1) ungrammatical and 2) grammatical. The former is characterized by the deletion of certain grammatical features such as copula *be*, modal verbs and articles, the use of the past tense form, and the use of special constructions such as "*no +* verb". These are shown in the following example:

NS: You *won't* forget *to buy* some bread on your way home, *will you*?

NNS: *No* forget *buying* bread, eh?

NS: Yes, some bread. ...You *will not* forget *to buy* it ...on your way home. ... Get it when you *are coming* back home. ...All right?

In the above NS—NNS dialogue, various types of modification can be identified. So, the talk is usually delivered at a slower and repeated pace, and the input is often simplified. The talk is sometimes regularized, consisting of elaborated expressions, such as using *when you are coming home* to replace *on your way home*.

Some L2 learners receive formal instruction and some do not. Perhaps the L2 equivalent to motherese, "foreigner talk" or "teacher talk" has been made the object of an immense amount of study. It is based presumably on the hope that there is a causal connection between simplified L2 input and successful L2 learning.

### 9.3.4 The Negotiation of Meaning

Input modifications of these kinds originate in the person addressing a learner. However, there are times when learners still fail to understand. When this happens they pretend they have understood. Research shows that learners sometimes do this.

Alternatively, learners can signal that they have not understood. This results in interactional modifications as the participants in the discourse engage in the negotiation of meaning. The extract below is an example of an exchange between two learners, Lzumi and Hiroko. As a result of this negotiation both learners end up correcting their own errors. There is plenty of evidence to suggest that modified interaction of this kind is common in learner discourse.

>Hiroko: *A man is uh. drinking c-coffee or tea with uh the saucer of the uh uh coffee set is uh in his uh knee.*
>Lzumi: *in him knee.*
>Hiroko: *uh on his knee.*
>Lzumi: *yeah.*
>Hiroko: *on his knee.*
>Lzumi: *so sorry, on his knee.* (Gass & Varonis 1989: 80 – 81)

There is still only limited empirical evidence that these modifications do assist IL development. Success is achieved by using the situational context to make messages clear and through the kinds of input modifications found in foreigner talk. According to Krashen's theory, then, L2 acquisition depends on comprehensible input.

Michael Long's interaction hypothesis also emphasizes the importance of comprehensible input but claims that it is most effective when it is modified through the negotiation of meaning. Thus, L2 learners receive input relevant to aspects of grammar that they have not yet fully mastered.

Another perspective on the relationship between discourse and SLA is provided by Evelyn Hatch. Hatch (1978) emphasizes the collaborative endeavors of the learners and their interlocutors in constructing discourse.

One way in which this can occur is through **scaffolding**, which is common in the early stages of L2A and may account for some of the early transitional structures that have been observed in IL.

Other SLA theorists have drawn on the theories of Vygotsky. The two key constructs, based on Vygotsky's theory, are **motive** and **internalization**. The former concerns the active way in which individuals define the goals of an activity by deciding what to attend to and what not to. The latter concerns how a novice comes to solve a problem with the assistance of an "expert", and then internalizes the solution. In this respect, the notion of the ZPD is important.

### 9.3.5 The Role of Output in IL Development

After all, discourse supplies L2 learners with the opportunity to produce language as well as hear it. Krashen (1985) argues that "speaking is the result of acquisition not its cause." He claims that learners can learn from their output by treating it as auto-input. In effect, Krashen is refuting the cherished belief of many teachers that languages are learned by practising them.

In contrast, Swain (1995) has argued that comprehensible output also plays a part in SLA. She suggests that learners can learn from their own output. Output can serve a consciousness-raising function by helping learners to notice gaps in their ILs. Output helps learners to try out a rule and see whether it leads to successful communication. Sometimes, learners talk about their own output, identifying problems with it and discussing ways to put them right.

In particular, there are metaphors that suggest that SLA is a distinctively human and social activity of negotiation and collaboration. And the next part is to examine some of the mental mechanisms of SLA.

## 9.4 Psycholinguistic Aspects of IL

Psycholinguistics is the study of the mental structures and processes involved in the acquisition and use of language. The study of psycholinguistic aspects of SLA has given rise to many acquisition models, such as L1 transfer, the role of consciousness, processing operations, and communication strategies.

### 9.4.1 Positive Transfer and Negative Transfer from L1

L1 transfer refers to the influence that the learner's L1 exerts over the acquisition of an L2. This influence is apparent in a number of ways.

First, it is noted in error analysis, that the learner's L1 is one of the sources of error in learner language. This influence is referred to as negative transfer. However, in some cases, the learner's L1 can facilitate SLA. SVO syntactic structures are common in Chinese and English, so Chinese learners are much less likely to make syntactic errors than are Japanese learners. This type of effect is known as positive transfer.

L1 transfer may be reflected in the overuse of some forms. Some Chinese learners, according to the norms of Chinese, tend to overuse expressions of regret when apologizing in English.

Theoretical accounts of L1 transfer have undergone considerable revision since the early days of SLA. Behaviorism believed that errors were the result of interference (negative transfer). The habits of the L1 were supposed to prevent the learner from learning the habits of the L2. Selinker in his IL theory, identified language transfer as one of the mental processes responsible for fossilization.

The learner's stage of development has also been found to influence L1 transfer. It is clear that transfer is governed by L2 learners' perceptions about what is transferable and by their stage of development. It follows that IL development cannot constitute a restructuring continuum. However, L2 learners may make use of their L1 knowledge along the way, but only when they believe it will help them in the learning task or when they have become sufficiently proficient in the L2 for transfer to be possible.

"Transfer" is yet another metaphor for explaining SLA. In some ways it is an inappropriate one. When money is transferred from one account into another, so one gains and the other loses. But, when language transfer takes place there is usually no loss of L1 knowledge. This fact has led to the choice of a better term for referring to the L1 transfers which might be "cross-linguistic influence".

### 9.4.2 The Role of Consciousness in SLA

Children seem to acquire their L1 without conscious effort. In contrast, L2 adult learners have to work hard and to study the language consciously. This comparison is not entirely accurate for L2 learners who are also capable of acquiring L2 in the same way as children's L1A. The role of consciousness becomes one of the most controversial issues in SLA.

Krashen has argued the need to distinguish "acquired" L2 knowledge and "learned" L2 knowledge. He claims that the former is developed subconsciously through comprehending input while communicating, while the latter is developed consciously through deliberate study of the L2.

However, Schmidt has pointed out that the term "consciousness" is often used very loosely in SLA and argues that there is a need to standardize the concepts that underlie its use. He distinguishes between consciousness as "intentionality" and consciousness as "attention".

"Intentionality" refers to whether a learner makes a conscious and deliberate decision to learn some L2 knowledge. It contrasts with "incidental learning", which takes place when learners pick up L2 knowledge through exposure. Schmidt argues that no matter whether learning is intentional or incidental, it involves conscious attention to features in the input. In other words, learning incidentally is not the same as learning without conscious attention.

Schmidt (1994: 18) also points to a third sense in which others can talk about consciousness in language learning. He reserves the terms understanding and awareness for explicit knowledge by saying: "awareness of a rule or generalization". He uses the term "awareness" to refer to whether learners are conscious of acquiring new L2 elements:

e.g. input → intake → L2 knowledge → output

Irrespective of whether learners learn implicitly or explicitly, it is widely accepted that they can acquire different kinds of knowledge. It is perhaps self-evident that all language users, including L2 learners, know rules that guide their performance without any awareness of what the rules consist of. Of course, they can always reflect on this implicit knowledge, thus making it explicit. It is also clear that L2 learners may have knowledge about the L2 (i.e. explicit knowledge) but be unable to use this

knowledge in performance without conscious attention.
### 9.4.3 Processing Operations
Another approach, which belongs to the mainstream of SLA in that it focuses close attention on learner language, has afforded a number of proposals. We shall examine two of them here: operating principles and processing constraints.
#### 9.4.3.1 Operating Principles in L1 Acquisition
Operating Principles (OPs) are based on the claim that "certain linguistic forms are more 'accessible' or more 'salient' to the child than others" (Slobin, 1979: 107). Slobin's book, *Psycholinguistics,* lists five OPs and five resulting universals. They are different from linguistic universals in that they are cognitive rather than linguistic in nature, and they characterize the way in which children perceive their environment and try to make sense of it and organize it.

The five OPs are described as: 1) OPs pay attention to the ends of words; 2) there are linguistic elements that encode relations between words; 3) OPs avoid exceptions; 4) underlying semantic relations should be marked overtly and clearly and 5) the use of grammatical markers should make semantic sense.

L1A **universals (Uni.)** are predicted from these OPs as follows:

**Uni. 1** (on 1 and 2): For any given semantic notion, grammatical realizations as postposed forms will be acquired earlier than realizations as preposed forms.

**Uni. 2** (on 3): The following stages of linguistic marking of a semantic notion are typically observed: (1) no marking; (2) appropriate marking in limited cases; (3) overgeneralization of marking; (4) full adult system.

**Uni. 3** (on 4): The closer a grammatical system adheres to one-to-one mapping between semantic elements and surface elements, the earlier it will be acquired.

**Uni. 4** (on 5): When selection of an appropriate inflection performing the semantic function is determined by arbitrary formal criteria, the child initially tends to use a single form in all environments.

**Uni. 5** Semantically consistent grammatical rules are acquired early and without significant error.

By 1985, the list of OPs had reached the number of 40, and had become much more sophisticated, using evidence from L1A in a range of languages. However, the OPs and universals above suffice to present a picture of the approach adopted.

### 9.4.3.2 Operating Principles in L2 Acquisition

Andersen and Shirai (1994) have investigated OPs in L2A. Andersen's principles are based on those of Slobin, but are then adapted to the learning of L2.

1) **The one-to-one principle:** an interlanguage system should be constructed in such a way that an intended underlying meaning is expressed with one clear invariant surface form or construction.

2) **The multifunctional principle:** the learners of English will often start with just one form for negation (e.g. *no the dog*; *he no go*), but once this form has been incorporated into their interlanguage, they are able to notice other forms and differentiate the environment in which they occur.

3) **The principle of formal determinism:** the clear, transparent encoding of the linguistic feature in the input forces the learner to discover the form-meaning relationship.

Considering the example of English negation above, the learner will be driven from the use of a single form to the use of multiple forms because the distribution of such forms in English is transparent (e.g. *don't* is used in preverbal environments, not with noun phrases, adverbs, etc.).

4) **The principle of distributional bias:** if a bias in the distribution of L1 and L2 makes it appear that L1 only occurs in environment A and L2 only occurs in environment B, when one acquires L1 and L2, L1 is restricted to environment A and L2 to environment B.

In Spanish, punctual verbs (e.g. *break*) occur mainly in the preterit form, and verbs of states (e.g. *know*) mainly in the imperfect form, making the preterit much more common in the input. L2 learners of Spanish reproduce this bias, and acquire the preterit form earlier.

5) **The relevance principle:** if two or more functors apply to a content word, try to place them so that the more relevant the meaning of a functor is to the meaning of the content word, the closer it is placed to the

content word.

Andersen's (1991) research on the L2A of Spanish verb morphology broadly supports the prediction that aspect should be encoded before tense, as it is most relevant to the lexical item it is attached to (the verb), and that tense would be next since it has wider scope than aspect, but is more relevant to the verb than subject-verb agreement, which would be last.

6) **The transfer to somewhere principle:** a grammatical form or structure will occur consistently in the IL as a result of transfer if and only if (1) natural acquisitional principles are consistent with the L1 structure; or (2) there already exists the potential for (*mis*-) generalization from the L2 input to produce the same form or structure.

Furthermore, in such transfer preference is given in the resulting IL to free, invariant, functionally simple morphemes that are congruent with the L1 and L2s, and to morphemes which occur frequently in the L1 and/or L2s.

7) **The reflexification principle:** when one cannot perceive the structural pattern used by the language one is trying to acquire, he uses his L1 structure with lexical items from the L2. Japanese learners of English sometimes use Japanese SOV word order in English in the early stages, with English lexical items.

In a detailed review of both L1A and L2A of tense and aspect, Andersen and Shirai made a conclusion of just three principles:

a) the Relevance Principle which guides learners to look for morphological marking relevant to the meaning of the verb;

b) the Congruence Principle which guides learners to associate verb morphology with verb types most congruent with the aspectual meaning of the verb inflection and;

c) the One-to-One Principle which causes learners to expect each newly discovered form to have one and only one meaning, function, and distribution.

## 9.4.4 Communication Strategies

A look should be necessarily taken at the mechanisms involved when learners use their acquired L2 knowledge in communication. As L2 learners who have tried to communicate know, they frequently experience problems in saying what they want to say because of their inadequate L2 knowledge.

In order to overcome these problems they resort to various kinds of communication strategies. If learners do not know a word in L2 they may "borrow" a word from their L1 or use another L2 word that is approximate in meaning (for example, "*worm*" for "*silkworm*"), or try to paraphrase the meaning of the word, or even construct an entirely new word (for example, "*picture place*" for "*art gallery*").

These strategies, with the obvious exception of those that are L1 based, are also found in the NSs' use. There have been a number of attempts to construct psycholinguistic models to account for the use of communication strategies.

The strategies are seen as part of the planning phase. They are called upon when L2 learners experience some kind of problem with an initial plan which prevents them from carrying it out. They can either abandon the initial plan and develop an entirely different one by means of a reduction strategy or try to maintain their original communicative goal by adopting some kind of achievement strategy.

As Selinker has pointed out, communication strategies constitute one of the processes responsible for learner errors. The choice of the strategies will reflect the learners' stage of development. L2 learners might be expected to switch from L1-based strategies to L2-based strategies as their L2 knowledge develops.

It would also be interesting to discover whether the use of communication strategies has any effect on SLA. For example, do learners notice the gap more readily as a result of having to use a communication strategy? Or does successful use of a communication strategy obviate the need for learners to learn the correct target-language forms? However, nothing is yet known about this.

### 9.4.5 Two Types of Computational Model

People have attempted to peer inside the "black box" of the learner's brain in order to identify some of the mental processes involved in constructing and using an IL. Of course, they cannot be viewed directly and can only be inferred from the various behaviors learners engage in. An attempt to distinguish a cognitive account from a behaviorist one is made to explain SLA in terms of mental processing.

The prevailing metaphor for explaining these processes has been that of the computer. The "black box" houses some kind of apparatus that extracts information from the "input", works on it, stores it, and subsequently uses it in "output". However, the actual type of apparatus involved and the nature of the computation performed remain a matter of some disagreement.

In particular, two radically different types of apparatus have been proposed. One type involves the idea of "serial processing". That is, information is processed in a series of sequential steps and results in the representation of what has been learned as some kind of "rule" or "strategy". This is the dominant version of the computational model in SLA and is evident in much of the preceding discussion.

The alternative type of apparatus involves that of "parallel distributed processing". This credits the learner with the ability to perform a number of mental tasks at the same time, and the ability to attend to both form and meaning while processing input. Models of parallel distributed processing reject the whole notion of "rule".

The second type sees mental structure as consisting of elaborate sets of weighted connections between separate items. Such a model helps to explain why some verbs are regularly used with -ed, some are sometimes used, and some never.

Not surprisingly, parallel distributed processing is controversial as it is against one of the central precepts of linguistics, namely that language is rule-governed.

## 9.5 Conclusion

What all the theories and approaches to Interlanguage have in common is that they apply models of input processing and L1 transfer to the SLA context. They do not generally have a great deal to say about the linguistic system that learners are constructing. They leave the task of analyzing the language rules underlying L2 productions to linguists interested in the formal properties of those systems.

What they are primarily interested in is the way in which the input is processed, given various constraints that operate on learners, and how these constraints change over time, that is, a transition theory. The "emergentist" linguists do not make this distinction between the formal linguistic system and processing mechanisms; they believe the two grow together and are inextricably linked.

 Points for Thinking

1. What are the characteristics and concepts of Interlanguage?
2. What are the social aspects of Interlanguage in language learning?
3. What are the discourse aspects of Interlanguage in language learning?
4. What are the psycholinguistic aspects of Interlanguage in language learning?
5. What are the significances of the IL study in SLA research?

 Further Reading

Andersen, R. and Shirai, Y. (1994). "Discourse motivations for some cognitive acquisition principles." *Studies in Second Language Acquisition* 16: 133 – 156.

Giles, H. and St. Clair, R. N. (Eds.) (1979). *Language and Social Psychology.* Oxford: Basil Blackwell.

Selinker, L. (1972). "Interlanguage." *Intenational Review of Applied Linguistics* 10: 209 – 231.

Selinker, L. (1992). *Rediscovering Interlanguage.* London: Longman.

Slobin, D. (1979). *Psycholinguisitics.* (2$^{nd}$ ed.) Gleview, IL: Scott, Foresman and Company.

Tarone, E.(1983). "On the variability of interlanguage systems." *Applied Linguistics* 4: 143—163.

# Chapter 10

# Researches on L2 Classroom Practice(I)

## 10.1 Introduction

It is noted that theorizing about SLA has its historic roots in reform movements connected to the practical business of language teaching. Howatt (1984) shows that this has been true since Renaissance times at least. Then, there is a question to answer: What kind of connections should this now relatively independent research field maintain, with its language teaching origins?

### 10.1.1 The Necessity of the Studies on Classroom Practice

The classroom is always one of the most important areas for SLA researchers. Much work has been concentrated on the following three perspectives:

1) comparative method studies, which seek to compare the effects of different teaching methods on L2 learning;

2) the effects of different types of interactional opportunities on L2 learning by going inside the "black box" of the classroom;

3) the effects of formal instruction, which attempts to intervene directly in the learning process by teaching specific properties of the L2 in order to address the question of whether instruction directed at specific grammatical items and rules has any effect on interlanguage development.

### 10.1.2 Research-derived Theory and Classroom Practice

It has been argued that the "scientific" findings of SLA should guide the practices of classroom teaching. Some recommendations are given from Input Hypothesis and the "Natural Approach" to language pedagogy.

Another one is the Teachability Hypothesis by Pienemann, who suggests that new L2 items might most effectively be taught in sequences that imitate empirically documented developmental sequences.

Ellis (1997) reviews a number of well-known difficulties with such a top-down, rationalist approach to linking research-derived theory and classroom practice. The findings of SLA research are not sufficiently secure, clear and uncontested, across different domains, to provide straightforward guidance for the teachers.

But, teaching is an art as well as a science, because of the constantly varying nature of the classroom as a learning community. There can be no "one best method", which applies at all times and in all situations, with various types of learners.

Instead, teachers "read" and interpret the changing dynamics of the learning context from moment to moment, and take what seem to be appropriate actions, in the light of largely implicit, procedural and pedagogic knowledge. This has been built up largely from their own previous experience, and usually derives only to a much more limited extent from L2 study or from organized L2 training.

### 10.1.3 The Co-work of the L2 Teachers and SLA Researchers

However, present SLA research offers a rich variety of concepts and descriptive accounts. Teachers are helped to interpret and make better sense of their own classroom experiences, and significantly broaden the range of pedagogic choices open to them.

SLA research has produced accounts of the interlanguage development, which show that L2 learners follow relatively invariant routes of learning, but that such routes are not linear, including phases of restructuring and apparent regression. Such accounts have helped teachers to understand patterns of learner error and its inevitability, and to accept the indirect nature of the relationship between what is taught and what is learnt.

The sub-field of research on SLA plays a special role in addressing concerns closer to the classroom teacher, and may offer opportunities for more direct involvement of teachers as research partners. But even SLA research is not identical with problem solving and development in language pedagogy, and does not ensure a shared agenda between teachers and researchers.

Researchers thus have a continuing responsibility to make their findings and their interpretations of them as intelligible as possible to a wider professional audience, with other preoccupations.

## 10.2 An Introduction to the History of L2 Teaching Methods

The relationship between L2A theory and L2 pedagogy is the focus of much discussion in the field of SLA research. Some researchers believe that the results of SLA studies can be helpful if applied cautiously to language pedagogy.

For example, research indicates that learners of English will acquire the third-person singular (-s) at a relatively late stage in the learning process. However, most textbooks present this form in early chapters as part of the simple present tense. This mismatch between what teachers teach and what learners are ready to learn can be easily corrected if the teacher are aware of SLA research findings and can adapt the textbook accordingly.

Some language teachers are eager to find out everything that research can tell them in order to optimize instructional practices, while others are cautious about applying the results of studies that do not appear to be relevant to their own classrooms and teaching contexts. Over the years, a number of attempts have been made to bring SLA research and language pedagogy together. The following section shows that language teaching methodologies reflect ideas about the processes and purposes of language learning.

### 10.2.1 L2 Teaching Methodology before the Mid of the 20$^{th}$ Century

One of the traditional teaching methods for FL teaching is the **Grammar Translation Method**, which was based on the purpose for language learning to master a tool for reading and literary translation. The premise is held that language learning is the same as an effortful intellectual exercise in logic and deduction.

Its goal was not oral communication; rather, learners were expected to develop explicit knowledge of language structure with constant reference to the L1. Accordingly, the approach used classical literary texts to teach the FL vocabulary and grammar. Success was measured by students' ability to translate sentences (in writing) from the FL into the L1 and vice versa, and these sentences served as exemplars of particular grammatical points rather than the carriers of real-world meanings.

With an increase in the demand for oral proficiency in FLs, this method gradually fell out of favor. It was replaced by a more "natural" approach called the **Direct Method**, which held that non-native languages, just like native languages, could be learned without translation and detailed grammar teaching. Teachers and researchers at the time had been noticing the ease with which children learned L1 and concluded that an approach emphasizing the importance of understanding and conveying meaning could be useful for adults as well.

Thus, as in L1A, spontaneous oral interaction in a modern conversational style of the target language was seen as crucial; the approach to grammar was inductive, and concrete, everyday vocabulary was emphasized. Proponents of the Direct Method argued that if teachers presented all information in the target language, using actions or pictures when necessary, the L2 learners could acquire the L2 naturally and directly.

### 10.2.2 L2 Teaching Methodology before 1980s

In the twentieth century, the period from the 1950s to the 1980s has been referred to as "the Age of Language Teaching Methodologies" because a number of quite detailed proposals for teaching approaches emerged during this time.

The **Audiolingualism** emphasized spoken language and maintained that grammar should be taught inductively. On the principles of behaviorism and drawing on contrastive analyses of the L1 and L2, the Audiolingual Method claimed that language learning was essentially habit formation, requiring mimicry, rote learning, feedback, extensive drills, or even over-learning to form habits. It was important to provide positive reinforcement for learners' correct responses while suppressing their errors.

After behaviorism fell out of favor in the 1960s, a new approach to L2 language teaching known as **Community Language Learning** began to receive more attention. L2 teachers and innovators made use of research insights in the fields of cognitive and educational psychology, which led them to develop more humanistic methods focusing on the social interaction and affective and interpersonal factors in learning.

Around this time, a method called the **Silent Way** also became more widespread. However, the rationale behind this approach was more concerned with cognition than with affect. Language is learned through problem-solving, and the teacher speaks only when necessary, thus encouraging students to discover the rules by themselves instead of relying on the teaching. It was seen as important for students to raise their awareness about the L2 and become autonomous learners.

### 10.2.3 L2 Teaching Methodology from 1980s to the Present

In the early 1980s, the **Natural Approach** became popular. Based on Krashen's Input and Natural Order Hypotheses, it was believed that if learners had a low enough affective filter, they would automatically acquire the target language when exposed to comprehensible input slightly above their current proficiency level.

But, with an increasing criticism of Krashen's theories, this approach began to give way to **Communicative Language Teaching** (CLT), which is one of the most commonly employed approaches in classrooms today.

CLT highlights communication as a means of facilitating language development. However, whereas the Natural Approach focused almost exclusively on speaking and paid much attention to meaning (with little attention to matters of form), CLT addresses all four basic skills. CLT also incorporates recent insights about the importance of active learner participation and the development of communicative competence, emphasizing that students need to be able to produce language in linguistically and culturally appropriate ways to carry out certain functions.

In CLT, the teacher's role is not so much as to provide comprehensible input, but rather to act as an advisor and facilitator, answering questions and creating learning situations in which students can engage in purposeful communication through learning tasks. These tasks typically focus on a particular communicative function with a meaningful purpose, such as making an invitation in an unrehearsed context.

It is important to remember that today most language teachers do not adhere strictly to just one method. Instead they use a combination of approaches, depending upon the goals of the lesson, the characteristics of their learners, and institutional factors. It may make more sense to view CLT as an overall approach reflecting theories about the nature of the processes and purposes for language learning.

## 10.3 Cross-language Competition between L1 and L2

According to the cognitive psychology and cognitive linguistics, the recent research on successful L2 learners suggests that lexical and semantic information in L1 is activated during both comprehension and production in L2. If this is the fact, then we might logically assume that less skilled L2 learners would be similarly affected by unintended L1 activation and might have a more difficult time controlling the cross-linguistic competition.

There is little psycholinguistic research investigating cross-linguistic competition in L2 learners. However, L2 teaching methods have long been aware of this competition and have been striving to minimize it.

### 10.3.1 Avoiding the Use of L1 in L2 Classroom

In examining L2 pedagogy, methods for teaching an L2 are predicated on notions of inhibiting L1 activation. In today's **communicative** L2 classroom, the use of L1 is typically avoided.

In teaching vocabulary, L2 teachers use various techniques that avoid L1, such as pictures, context, and miming, in an attempt to promote "form-meaning" connections for the L2 learners. The use of L1 is almost seen as detrimental to the L2 learning process. Maintaining L2 at all times and keeping learners in the L2 mode is a critical component of the communicative L2 classroom.

Historically, the **Direct Method** assumed that learners would acquire language much like children, through direct association of words and phrases with objects and actions and an enormous amount of input. The use of L1 and translation were strictly forbidden. New words were taught via the L2 paraphrases. In the same vein, the **Audiolingual Method** of the 1950s was to develop in learners the same abilities that NSs have, handling the language at an unconscious level. L1 was to be banned from the classroom and a "cultural island" was to be maintained.

In the 1970s **Total Physical Response** (TPR) was proposed by Asher in 1977. Its underlying philosophy is that language comprehension should develop before any oral participation, as it does with children. It is based on the belief that skills can be acquired more rapidly if you involve the sensory system. Accordingly, L2 teachers use oral commands and students show their understanding by performing an action. The L2 is the exclusive language of instruction.

In the 1970s, the **Natural Approach** emerged. This methodology was based on Krashen's theory of L2 acquisition. It claims that comprehensible input causes acquisition. The use of L2 was seen as the only tool for providing comprehensible input to the learners; L1 had no place in the Natural Approach of L2 learning.

**The Silent Way** was another method that avoided the L1, a method which used colored wooden sticks, language charts, and the L2 exclusively. This method seemed to be predicated on the notion of language control. Clearly, controlling any cross-linguistic interference was a critical aspect of this approach.

### 10.3.2　Rethinking of Cross-language Competition

The methods, in the past and today, whether intended to or not, are based on ideas about language activation and control. The evidence from the psycholinguistic literature overwhelmingly suggests that L1 words are active simultaneously in the proficient L2 learners. Therefore, as noted above, a regulatory mechanism must control cross-language competition in successful L2 learners.

The critical issues become how learners regulate the cross-linguistic activation and why some learners are more successful at it than others. There are many questions in L2 pedagogy that could be answered by psycholinguistic research. The studies on these issues hold important implications for teaching methods and psycholinguistic models alike.

Research on skilled bilingual lexical processing will help to inform an understanding of L2 acquisition. Similarly, many psycholinguistic models address skilled L2 learner processing but make no explicit claims about the nature of L1/L2 lexical competition during acquisition. Currently absent from the psycholinguistic literature is a comprehensive picture of how lexical activity changes and is controlled from early stages of learning through high levels of skilled performance.

In future it will be the focus on investigating the cognitive processes underlying the development of L2A and the proficient use of two languages by bilinguals.

## 10.4 Some Methods Used in L2 Classroom Research

### 10.4.1 The Psychometric Method

This Psychometric Method is evident through the comparative studies for proving relatedness as well as for reconstructing the system of the classroom learning and teaching. Researchers use this experimental method, in which pre-and post-tests are adopted, and experimental and control groups are arranged to investigate language gain from different teaching methods, materials and treatments.

The Psychometric Method is evident in correlational studies on the relationship between specific classroom behaviors and learning outcomes. It is possible, through comparing two groups, the equivalent of an experimental and a control group. It has the advantage that the participants are unaware that they are taking part in an investigation and it is certainly not as artificial as a laboratory setting.

But the studies suffer from a failure to validate the categories used to measure instructional features, as well as from a failure to establish theoretical links between processes being observed and learning outcomes. It is considered by some social scientists as not a true experiment because the researchers are unable to manipulate or control variables. For this reason it is sometimes referred to as a quasi-experiment.

## 10.4.2 The Interaction Analysis

The second method involves the use of a form or schedule consisting of a set of categories for coding specific classroom behaviors. Long (1986) distinguishes interaction analysis as: 1) each event in a category system is coded each time it occurs, and 2) each event in a sign system is recorded only once within a fixed time span, and then 3) in a rating scale, an estimate of the frequency of the occurrence of specific type of event is made after a period of observation.

When groups are working well, contributions build on each other. This is possible when participants contribute to the discussion in appropriate ways. The following eight categories of contribution(Rackham, 1971) can be used as an aid to analyzing patterns of group interaction:

| | Categories | Contributions |
|---|---|---|
| 1 | Seeking suggestions | This label is used when someone invites others to contribute their ideas, suggestions or proposals. |
| 2 | Suggesting | This can take some forms: e.g. *I suggest we do so, Let's do the following, Shall we do X, Y and Z?* or *Can I take your idea a stage further?* |
| 3 | Agreeing | This covers all types of supporting or backing up what has just been said. |
| 4 | Disagreeing | This covers all ways of opposing or withholding support for what has just been said: not only an outright disagreement: *No, I can't go along with that*, but also stating a difficulty, whether valid or not: *The snag is that ...* or *We are running short of time again*. |
| 5 | Seeking Clarification | Whenever someone asks for a recap or checks that he has understood what was intended, e.g. *Do you mean ...?* or, *What happens if A and B coincide*. |
| 6 | Clarifying | Responses to requests for explanations; also spontaneous summaries of a discussion. |
| 7 | Interrupting | Whenever someone breaks in to stop a member from finishing his or her contribution; or when everyone seems to be speaking at once. |
| 8 | Miscellaneous | In practice, it is difficult to assess all contributions quickly enough to categorize them, so any unspecified contribution can be put in this category rather than go unrecorded. |

An analyzing table was set out with the types of contribution down the side and the names of the participants on the top. The observer listens to each contribution during the discussion and puts a mark in the appropriate box. Afterwards the results can be shared either one-to-one with each individual or as a report back to the group.

|  | Group Interaction Analysis Sheet | | | |
| --- | --- | --- | --- | --- |
|  | Anne | Brian | Clair | David |
| Seeking suggestions |  |  |  |  |
| Suggesting |  |  |  |  |
| Agreeing |  |  |  |  |
| Disagreeing |  |  |  |  |
| Seeking Clarification |  |  |  |  |
| Clarifying |  |  |  |  |
| Interrupting |  |  |  |  |
| Miscellaneous |  |  |  |  |

Generally, the categories listed in a form reflected the researchers' assumptions and were not theoretically motivated. One problem is that researchers differ a lot in their research field, making comparison across studies difficult. Another problem is that it does not provide a complete picture of the language classroom because the behavior of the teacher and the learner is often treated separately.

Therefore, there is no basis for deciding which combination of features might be important. And the assumptions on which interaction is based can be questioned, thus casting doubt on the reliability and validity of the measurement.

### 10.4.3 The Discourse Analysis and Critical Discourse Analysis

The third method is **Discourse Analysis** (DA), or sometimes as **Critical Discouse Analysis** (CDA). It does not provide an answer to problems based on scientific research, but it enables access to the ontological assumptions behind a project, a statement, a method of research, or a set of classification. DA & CDA will enable to reveal the hidden motivations behind a text or behind the choice of a particular method of research to interpret that text.

In other words, DA & CDA will enable us to understand the conditions behind a specific problem and realize the essence of that problem. DA & CDA aims at viewing highly and gaining a comprehensive view of the problem. Expressed in the more trendy vocabulary, DA & CDA is nothing more than a deconstructive reading and interpretation of a problem or text.

DA & CDA is generally perceived as the product of the postmodernism. Postmodern theories conceive of every interpretation of reality and, therefore, of reality itself as a text. Every text is conditioned and inscribes itself within a given discourse, thus there comes into being the term Discourse Analysis.

DA & CDA serves as a device to study classroom transcripts and assign utterances to predetermined categories. It is an analysis of classroom discourse in linguistic terms, aiming to account for the joint contributions of teacher and student and to describe all the data. It is used to investigate different areas of the classroom, such as teachers' instructions, teachers' talks, teachers' questions, teachers' feedback, teachers' ways of error correction, the interaction between the teacher and learners, the interaction between learners, etc.

**10.4.4 The Ethnographic Method**

The fourth method is ethnographic in nature. It is not so much a method as a category of human-computer interaction research and has been adapted from sociology and anthropology. It is a method of observing human interactions in social settings and activities. It can also be described as the observation of people in their cultural context. There are a few terms that are related to ethnographic method with which the term **field study** is generally used interchangeably.

1) Contextual inquiry: a specific form of ethnographic method focusing on questioning or more exactly inquiry;
2) Observational study: a form of observing L2 users, without asking questions of why or how things are being done;
3) Observation: a form of focusing on the ethnographer joining in user activities to better understand the processes involved.

The above three activities frequently used together form the basis of a thorough ethnographic study. This method is naturalistic "uncontrolled" observation and description of classroom activities in order to obtain insight into the classroom as a cultural system. Some researchers take a regular part in the activities under study, while others only observe classroom activities as an outsider.

### 10.4.5 Comparative Method Studies (CMS)

The aim of Comparative Method Studies (CMS) is to analyze a situation, to examine its objectives and then to synthesize an improved, more efficient and effective method or system. The basic procedure of the study consists of six steps (known as SREDIM):

| | Procedure of Comparative Method Studies | |
|---|---|---|
| | Steps | Aims and Objectives |
| 1 | Selection | To *select* the work or area to be studied. |
| 2 | Recording | To *record* down appropriate and relevant data about the current situation. |
| 3 | Examination | To *examine* the recorded data critically. |
| 4 | Development | To *develop* alternative approaches to making improvements and choose the most appropriate. |
| 5 | Installment | To *install* the new method for making the required changes to the situation. |
| 6 | Maintenance | To *maintain* that new situation. |

In practice, the procedure consists of a cyclical process in which each step may be revisited according to the findings of subsequent steps. This process often begins with a rough pass of collecting and examining preliminary data, and progresses to a more detailed and thorough pass which results in the collection of more detailed and more complete data as the subject of a more rigorous examination.

The procedure is thus a convenient representation of what may be a complex process. CMS in SLA research is intended to find out which of two or more methods or approaches to language teaching is most effective in terms of learning.

However, studies failed to provide convincing evidence that one method was superior to another. Firstly, different teaching methods resemble each other in terms of what actually goes on in the classroom. Secondly, individual learners benefit from different types of instruction. Thirdly, language classes tend to offer very similar opportunities for learning irrespective of their methodological orientation.

## 10.5 Data Collection and Data Analysis

Gass and Selinker (2008: 52) pointed out that: "In recent years there has been increased attention paid to data collection and analysis." A central part of understanding the field of SLA is gained by hands-on experience in data collection, data analysis and data interpretation. In terms of data collection and data analysis, R. Ellis and Barkhuizen (2005) devoted most of an entire book to the various ways one can proceed, including a chapter on data collection. In addition, numerous books have dealt with specific data-collection procedures and approaches.

### 10.5.1 Data Collection and Its General Dimensions

Data collection is a term used to describe a process of preparing and collecting data as part of a process improvement or similar project. It usually takes place early on in an improvement project, and is often formalized through a data collection plan which often contains the following activity: 1) pre-collection activity, 2) collection and 3) post-collection activity.

The L1 data-collection methodologies have been characterized by Bennett-Kastor (1988) either as "naturally observed" or as elicited under "controlled observation". Of the data sources, she includes three types: 1) "indirect" or anecdotal evidence; 2) L1 "intuitions", especially as judgments of the acceptability of utterances; and 3) "raw" data, actually manifested in conversational and other naturally occurring forms.

Regardless of the practical approach or design adopted by different researchers, it has become clear that a variety of data-collection procedures is feasible. In the growth of the SLA research, the data-collection procedure enables its researchers to obtain the best sample of learners' performance potential.

The various approaches to the collection of data on learner performance in L2A will therefore be outlined, with a concern for the appropriate methodologies that ensure valid SLA analysis. The SLA researches will focus on the following primary questions (Chaudron, 2003):

- What procedures have been applied in SLA research, and what are the conditions and characteristics of each?
- How reliable and valid are the procedures and methods for collecting SLA data?
- As a specific outcome of the question of validity, what are the limits to interpretation from data collected by each procedure as reflections of underlying SLA performance/competence?
- As a matter of the generalizability of procedures, to what extent can procedures adopted for L1 research be applied in L2 research?
- What new or additional procedures or adaptations are possible or needed for L2 research?

A key concern of data-collection is 1) whether the particular methods employed have proven to be reliable and valid; 2) whether they have consistently led to successful elicitation of learners' language performance and, possibly, competence, and 3) whether the analysis of this performance matches other, independent measures of or expectations for the learners' production.

It is often impossible to tell from the collected data whether the forms produced are simply an artifact of the method. So many researchers today employ multiple measures, in order to differentiate the possible effects of the method employed from the stable or developing traits of the learners' underlying language capacity.

## 10.5.2 The Naturalistic Data Collection Procedures

The naturalistic/experimental dimension for classifying research methodologies by Nunan (1996) has been applied under various guises by many L2 theorists. To some extent, the naturalistic-experimental continuum may seem related, as well, to the "interlanguage continuum" distinction made by Tarone, with spontaneous free "vernacular" speech on one end and careful controlled speech on the other.

Some of the earliest approaches to and sources of productive data on

SLA involved observation of children's language use in play and normal interaction with parents and others. Procedures have gradually been elaborated for observing and recording children's (or adults') speech in such naturalistic settings. There are also recommendations for the use of video and audio-recording devices.

Naturalistic observation must be systematic, and details of the physical and verbal context must be recorded. The records help the researchers to retrieve sources of deictic reference, restrictive/non-restrictive relative clause contexts, and possible social-interactive events that would influence pragmatic meanings and interpretations. Assuming a context for observation in a naturally occurring social event, the advantage of data collected in this way is that:

1) The learner's production will be a true sample of his or her L2 speech, possibly in open communication with familiar colleagues or friends, and uninfluenced by artifactual aspects of an elicitation method, as well as potentially less influenced by the learner's careful monitoring or application of learned rules of production.

2) Also, extended research studies can collect very large amounts of learner production data in this manner, without substantially preparing new materials or altering any procedures for data collection.

As will be clear in later sections, the preparation of quality materials for eliciting more controlled speech forms is a highly complicated, intensive process. The disadvantages of naturalistic observation include a number of well-known limitations:

Firstly, the quality of recordings is obviously decisive. Secondly, the observer's written record may omit contextual features or distort speech production data if no independent recording is available. Thirdly, it is difficult to interpret the absence of structures in the learners' performance, and comprehension is typically not easily evaluated. Lastly, the naturalistic observation is usually highly labor-intensive, owing to the direct recording, and later transcription of the data.

This is why naturalistic observation is typically used in case studies of only a few children or a single classroom. In such research, the value of the data will depend more on the variability that arises through the natural interaction that might occur, or possible differences between the few subjects, or because the procedure is used in a longitudinal design to discover trends in acquisition.

## 10.5.3 The Method of Data Analysis Presented by Gass and Selinker

Gass and Selinker in their introductory SLA textbook (2008) have presented three data sets with a hypothesis for each, which are collected for the data analysis in a step-by-step fashion:

1) **Plurals (data set I)**: What are some possible interlanguage generalizations that might account for this particular pattern of IL plural marking?

The data of 19 utterances presented were collected from three adult native speakers of Cairene Arabic, intermediate to advanced speakers of English, shortly after they had arrived in the United States. The source was writings and conversations. Gass and Selinker try to get an answer to the question.

2) **Verb +-ing markers (data set II)**: The full force of the principle is that the acquisition of a grammatical form is variable, with the Verb + -*ing* form in intransitive sentences and the simple form in transitive sentences.

There are 10 utterances by an Arabic native speaker at the early stages of learning English. They had had no formal English instruction at the time of data collection. The sentences were gathered from spontaneous utterances with possible intention (context) of these utterances when the intention is not obvious from the forms produced.

3) **Prepositions (data set III)**: How can learners clearly realize that they do not know how to use prepositions appropriately in English and adopt the following strategy: using no preposition except in specifically constrained instances.

The data in this set concerns some English prepositions which are generally known to be among the most difficult items to learn in an L2 acquisition. Gass and Selinker describe the learners' behavior as involving a simplification strategy, although in this case that may be a dangerous generalization, for as Corder (1983; 1992) point out, learners cannot simplify what they do not know.

### 10.5.4 Some Difficulties in Data Analysis

In analyzing L2 data there can be considerable difficulties in determining what the targeted structure is. The results from the analyzed data can be different depending on the methodology used for data analysis, and there can also be differences in the results when using a similar methodology by different researchers or analysts. There is an additional problem particularly existing in attempting to deal with the role of the learner's L1 in his/her L2 learning process.

One final related point has to do with the entire notion of "target" from the learner's perspective. Gass and Selinker have discussed the difficulty in assessing what the native language forms are that the learner brings to the L2 learning situation. They argued that: "we cannot pretend to know precisely what knowledge base a learner brings to the learning situation, nor can we pretend to understand what target language model the learner has adopted" (2008: 70).

## 10.6 Conclusion

This chapter has discussed the relationship between SLA researchers and the L2 classroom practice. There is a brief introduction to L2 teaching methodology with cross-linguistic attitudes to the avoidance of L1 in the teaching. It also presents some researching methodologies and a means for data collection and data analysis with a review on different methodologies. We next move to a discussion on classroom interactions together with the role of the teacher and performances of the learners within L2 classroom contexts.

 Points for Thinking

1. Why is there the necessity of the SLA studies on classroom teaching and learning?
2. What are the L2 teaching methods and approaches from 1980s to the present?
3. What is the competition between L1 and L2 in the development of

language teaching methodology?
4. What are the major methods adopted in L2 research in classroom contexts?
5. How do SLA researchers carry out data collection and data analysis?

 Further Reading

Asher, J. (1977). *Learning Another Language through Actions: The Complete Teacher's Guidebook.* Los Gatos, CA: Sky Oaks Productions.

Ellis, R. (1994). *The Study of Second Language Acquisition.* Oxford: Oxford University Press.

Ellis, R. and Barkhuizen, G. (2005). *Analysing Learner Language.* Oxford: Oxford University Press.

Gass, S. and Selinker, L. (2008). *Second Language Acquisition: An Introductory Course.* 3$^{rd}$ Edition. Hillsdale, NJ: Lawrence Erlbaum.

Howatt, A.P.R. (1984). *A History of English Language Teaching.* Oxford: Oxford Uni. Press

Long, M. H. (1980). *Input, Interaction and Second Language Acquisition.* University of California, Los Angeles, PhD dissertation.

Selinker, L. (1992). *Rediscovering Interlanguage.* London: Longman.

# Chapter 11

# Researches on L2 Classroom Practice(II)

## 11.1 Direct Involvement of Classroom Interaction Research

The present SLA research offers a rich variety of concepts and descriptive accounts. They can help teachers to interpret and make better sense of their own classroom experiences, and significantly broaden the range of pedagogic choices open to them. It has produced descriptive accounts of the interlanguage development, which show that learners follow relatively invariant routes of learning.

The SLA research accounts have also helped teachers to understand patterns of learner error and its inevitability, and more generally, to accept the indirect nature of the relationship between what is taught and what is learnt. Similarly, in some recent literature, discussions have great potential to stimulate teacher reflections on the classroom interaction when enacting their own roles as L2 guides and interlocutors.

## 11.2 An Introduction to Classroom Interaction

### 11.2.1 The Aspects of Classroom Interaction

There is a continuing necessity for dialogue between the "practical theories" of classroom educators, and the more decontextualized and abstract ideas deriving from programmes of research. But SLA research is not often identical with problem solving and development in language pedagogy, and does not ensure a shared agenda between teachers and researchers.

The failure of finding the global method studies led to the development of another approach called **classroom process research**, which was based on the following three basic premises:

1) a rejection of the notion that classrooms differ on a single variable such as "method" or "approach";

2) an emphasis on describing fully the instructional activities as a way of generating rather than just testing hypothesis;

3) the priority of direct observation of the classroom lessons and processes.

The goal of such research was to discover and describe how teachers carry out and accomplish classroom lessons. SLA researchers viewed language lessons as socially constructed events and sought to understand how they took place. Initially, such research was not guided by SLA theories, but attention was increasingly shifted to the examination of instructional events in relation to the kinds of interactional theories discussed in previous chapter.

### 11.2.2 The Nature of L2 Classroom Interaction

The term Classroom Interaction refers to the events that teachers and students talk, communicate or negotiate with each other in the classroom. Dialogue, or conversation, is the medium through which most classroom interaction takes place, so the study of classroom discourse is the study of the process of face-to-face classroom teaching.

Classroom discourse mediates between pedagogic decision-making and the outcomes of language instruction. Teachers usually plan their lessons by making selections with regard to what to teach (form the syllabus), how to teach (choosing the proper methods or approaches) and also perhaps the nature of the social relationships they should encourage to establish (considering the teaching atmosphere).

The interaction provides learners with opportunities to encounter input or to practise the L2. And it also creates in the learners a "state of receptivity", defined as "an active openness, a willingness to encounter the language and the culture". The following is the diagram of Classroom Interaction:

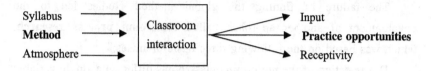

The interactions are not usually designed in advance of a lesson, but they display different and predictable characteristics. The following issues will be addressed: 1) the structure and general characteristics of classroom discourse; 2) types of language use; 3) turn taking; and 4) differences between classroom and naturalistic discourse.

### 11.2.3 The Structure of Classroom Interaction

A discourse of classroom interactions consists generally of three phases:

1) **an opening phase**: the participants are going to conduct a lesson as opposed to some other activities;

2) **an instructional phase**: information is exchanged between the teacher and the students;

3) **a closing phase**: participants are reminded of what went on in the core of the lesson.

Sinclair and Coulthard (1975) provide a hierarchical model of classroom discourse. They identify the following ranks in the structure of a lesson:

(1) lesson, (2) transaction, (3) exchange, (4) move, and (5) act.

**A lesson** has only a vaguely defined structure, consisting of an unordered series of transactions. **A transaction** is ill defined and is made up of preliminary, one or more medial and terminal exchanges. **A teaching exchange** has the most clearly defined structure. It consists of **an initiating move, a responding move, and a follow-up move.** This pattern of exchange is called "**IRF**". Each move is realized by means of various **acts**—the smallest unit of discourse. For example,

T: Ask Allan what his name is. (**I**: initiating )
S: What's your name? (**R**: responding)
T: Good. (**F**: follow-up)

This model is not designed to account for language lessons, but it fits well with small modifications.The structure is likely to arise in teacher-controlled classroom discourse. Other types of structures are also likely to be found. Even in strictly teacher-controlled discourse, students in the L2 classroom often produce an additional response after the follow-up move:

T: What do you do every morning? (**I**: initiating)

S: I brush my teeth. (**R**: responding)

T: You brush your teeth every morning. (**F**: follow-up)

S: I brush my teeth every morning. (**A**: additional responding)

### 11.2.4 The Characteristics of Classroom Interaction

With regard to the characteristics of classroom discourse, the system developed by Allen et al. (1984) is called the **Communicative Orientation in Language Teaching (COLT)**. It is different from other systems. It not only reflects current theories of communicative competence and communicative language teaching but researches into L1 and L2 to provide a means of comparing some aspects of classroom discourse with natural language outside the classroom.

The **COLT** system divides into two parts. The first part is **a description of classroom activities** designed for real time coding. It consists of a set of general categories to be broken down into subcategories. The main unit of analysis is **activity type** (drill, translation, discussion, game and dialogue). Each activity is then described in terms of **participant organization** (whole class, group work, or individual work), **content** (the subject matter of the activities), **student modality** (skills involved in the activity), and **materials** (type, length, and source/purpose).

The second part is **communicative features**. Seven communicative features are identified relating to the use of the L2: whether and to what extent there is **an information gap**, sustained speech, whether the focus is on code or message, the way in which incorporation of preceding utterances takes place, discourse initiation, and the degree to which linguistic form is restricted.

Such a system provides a basis for investigating which interactional features are important for language acquisition. The following table illustrates the interaction in analytical and experiential lessons:

A. Analytical instruction

| Utterance | Communicative features |
|---|---|
| T: What's the date today? | L2/pseudo-request/minimal speech |
| S1: April 15th. | L2/predictable information/ultra minimal speech/ limited form |
| T: Good. | L2/comment/minimal speech |
| T: What's the date today? | L2/pseudo-request/minimal speech |
| S2: April 15th. | L2/predictable information/ultra minimal speech/ limited form |
| T: Good. | L2/comment/minimal speech |

B. Experiential instruction

| Utterance | Communicative features |
|---|---|
| T: What did you do on the weekend? | L2/genuin request/minimal speech |
| S: I went to see a movie. | L2/giving unpredictable information/minimal speech/unrestricted form |
| T: That's interesting. What did you see? | L2/comment/elaboration (genuine request for information)/sustained speech |
| S: E.T. I really liked it. He is so cute. | L2/giving unpredictable information/sustained speech/unrestricted form |
| T: Yes. I saw it too and really liked it. Did anyone else see it? | L2/comment/expansion/elaboration (genuine request for information)/sustained speech |

## 11.3 Types of Language Use in Classroom Interaction

Classroom interaction can also be described by identifying the different types of language use or interaction in L2 classrooms. Researchers provide several different accounts of it.

1. Macro-analysis of language teaching and learning (Allwright, 1980) identifies three basic elements:

1) Samples: instances of the target language, in isolation or in use;

2) Guidance: instances of communication concerning the nature of L2;

3) Management activities: ensuring the profitable occurrence of the

above two.

These elements are not mutually exclusive, as instances of guidance and management activities automatically provide samples. They vary according to their relative proportion; their distribution between teacher and learner, their sequencing, and the language used (L1/L2).

2. McTear (1975) makes a distinction between interactions focusing on code itself and those focusing on genuine meaning exchange:

1) Mechanical: no exchange of meaning is involved;

2) Meaningful: meaning is contextualized but there is still no information conveyed;

3) Pseudo-communicative: new information is conveyed but in a manner that is unlikely in naturalistic discourse;

4) Real communication: spontaneous speech resulting from the exchange of opinions, jokes, classroom management.

Mechanical and meaningful language use focuses on the code, while pseudo-communicative and real communication on genuine information exchange.

3. Van Lier (1988) proposes a much more complicated framework, and he distinguishes **goal** and **address**. The former is the overall purpose of an interaction, and the latter refers to who is talking to whom. There are three goals in communication:

1) **Core goals**, where focus is on the language itself (medium), on some other content (message), or embedded in some ongoing activities such as model-building;

2) **Framework goals** associated with the organization and management of classroom events;

3) **Social goals.**

Researches show that learning in English lessons occurred most commonly in interactional events with core goals where there was an element of spontaneous language use. In Van Lier's framework classroom discourse divides into four types:

1) Type 1 occurs when the teacher controls neither topic nor activity, as in the small talk sometimes found at the beginning of a lesson;

2) In type 2 the teacher controls the topic but not the activity. It

occurs when the teacher makes an announcement, gives instructions or delivers a lecture;

3) Type 3 involves teacher control of both topic and activity, as teacher elicits responses in a language drill;

4) In type 4 the teacher controls the activity but not the topic, as in small-group work where the procedural rules are specified. The students are free to choose the topic.

The above frameworks are not designed to serve as schemes for coding classroom behaviors. It is often not clear what unit of classroom discourse they are intended to relate to. Their advantage is that they provided a tool for understanding classroom interaction and how it might affect learning. Their disadvantage is that they do not permit precise quantification, and thus cannot easily be used in experimental or correlational research.

## 11.4 Turn Taking in Classroom Discourse

In the naturalistic discourse, turning-taking in classroom interaction is likely to be characterized by: 1) only one speaker speaks at a time; 2) a speaker can select the next speaker by nominating or by performing the first part of an adjacent pair; 3) a speaker can alternatively allow the next speaker to self-select; and 4) speakers compete to take the next turn.

Turn-taking in classroom discourse is different from that in natural discourse. However, it does not differ from that in general subject classrooms. Studies show that turns were always allocated by the teacher in L2 classrooms, and the right to speak returned to the teacher when a student turn was finished, and the teacher had the right to interrupt and stop a student turn.

Van Lier identified the following turn-taking behaviors in L2 classrooms:

1) **Topic**: the turn is off-stream (discontinuing), introduces something new, or denies/disputes a proposition in a previous turn.

2) **Self-selection**: selection originates from the speaker.

3) **Allocation**: the turn selects next speaker.

4) **Sequence**: the turn is independent of sequence.

According to his study, many of the teacher's utterances were undirected and the learners frequently did self-select. But so far there have been no studies investigating different types of turn taking on acquisition, probably because of its difficulty.

## 11.5 Differences between Classroom and Naturalistic Discourse

Because classroom affords opportunities to communicate as well as to learn, two types of discourses can co-exist. Kramsch (1985) suggests that the nature of classroom discourse be determined by the roles the participants adopt, the nature of the learning task, and the kind of knowledge that is targeted.

**Instructional discourse** arises when the teacher and the students act out institutional roles. The tasks are concerned with transmission and reception of information and are controlled by the teacher, and there is a focus on knowledge as a product and on accuracy.

**Natural discourse** is characterized by more fluid roles established through interaction, with tasks that encourage equal participation in the negotiation of meaning, and a focus on the interactional process itself and on fluency.

Studies show that natural discourse seldom occurs in L2 classroom although the potential exists. There is very little negotiation of meaning in L2 classrooms and learners have limited opportunities to participate.

The teacher's control over the discourse is the main reason for the prevalence of pedagogic discourse. In the classroom setting discourse rights are invested in the teacher, who has the right to participate in all exchanges, such as to initiate exchanges, to decide on the length of exchanges, to close exchanges, to include or exclude participants. Learners are placed in a dependent position.

Researchers disagree with each other on the role played by pedagogic discourse in SLA. Some believe that it has negative effect on SLA; others think that it is inevitable and desirable because formal instruction does appear to result in faster learning and higher levels of ultimate achievement.

## 11.6 The Teacher's Role in Classroom Interaction

### 11.6.1 The Teacher Talk

Teacher talk is defined as a type of modified language used by teachers when addressing language learners. It has attracted the attention of researchers because of its potential effect on learners' comprehension. Research results show that teachers modify their speech when addressing L2 learners in the classroom in a number of ways and also that they are sensitive to their learners' general proficiency level.

These modifications are mostly the same as those found in foreigner talk. Some appear to have special characteristics, and can be described in terms of the following:

(1) **Amount of talk**. The teacher takes up around two-thirds of the talking time.

(2) **Functional distribution**. Teachers dominate all classroom activities.

(3) **Rate of speech**. Teachers speak at a slower rate.

(4) **Pauses**. Teachers are likely to make use of longer pauses to L2 learners.

(5) **Phonology, intonation, articulation, and stress**. Teachers appear to speak more loudly and to make their speech more distinct when addressing L2 learners.

(6) **Modifications in vocabulary**. Lexical simplifications are frequently used.

(7) **Modifications in syntax**. Utterances addressing the learner tend to be shorter, simpler, and ungrammatical teacher talk is rare.

(8) **Modifications in discourse**. Teachers use more self-repetitions with L2 learners.

However, it is not clear what constitute optimal teacher talk and on what basis teachers make modifications. It is supposed that teachers may aim at hypothetical average learner. In this case, input is not likely to be tuned accurately to the level of many of the learners. Another hypothesis is that teacher talk may provide an optimal environment for successful language learning in the elementary school.

### 11.6.2 The Issues of Error Treatment in Classroom

Error Treatment (ET) concerns the way in which teachers and other learners respond to learners' errors. It is discussed in terms of whether errors should be corrected, when, how, and by whom. Very few studies have investigated the effect of error treatment on acquisition. There are three main issues that have been identified concerning error treatment.

The first issue is terminological in nature. "Feedback", "repair" and "correction" are used to refer to the general area of error treatment: 1) feedback is a cover term for the information provided by listeners on the reception and comprehension of messages in two types (cognitive feedback and emotive feedback); 2) repair is an attempt to identify and remedy communication problems; 3) correction refers to attempts to deal with linguistic errors and to supply "negative evidence" that draw the learners' attention to the errors they have made.

The second issue concerns learners' attitudes towards error treatment. Research results show that learners like to be corrected by their teachers and want more correction than they are usually provided with. In contrast, Krashen warns that correction is both useless for acquisition and dangerous in that it may lead to a negative affective response.

The third issue concerns who performs the treatment. In natural conversations, repairs are made by the speaker himself. In classroom context, other-initiated and other-completed repair can be expected because discourse rights are unevenly invested in the teacher. In the language-centered phase, errors were identified by the teacher but the learners should do correction. But, in the content phase, the learners themselves more often corrected errors.

### 11.6.3 The Teacher's Inconsistency in Error Treatment

A point that should be noted is that teachers are inconsistent in their error treatment. They often give more than one type of feedback simultaneously, and many of their feedback moves go unnoticed by students. Teachers respond positively even when the learners continue to make the same error. They correct an error in one part of the lesson but ignore it in another.

Some researchers think that this inconsistency is inevitable and even desirable. It reflects the teacher's attempt to cater to individual differences among learners, but others argue that it is harmful.

There are few studies investigating the effect of error treatment on acquisition. It indicates that error treatment may not be successful in the short term, but may be so in the long run because it helps to raise the learner's consciousness.

### 11.6.4 Teachers' Questioning in Classroom Interaction

Teachers ask a lot of questions in their teaching. This can be accounted for by the teacher's control over the discourse. A question is likely to occupy the first part of the three-phase IRF exchange. A lot of efforts have been made to clarify teachers' questions, and here are several main clarifications as the following:.

1. Barnes' four types of classification (1989)
   (1) **Factual questions** ("what?") that request the facts;
   (2) **Reasoning questions** ("how?" and "why?") that fall into two sub-types: closed (with only one answer) and open (permitting a number of answers);
   (3) **Open questions** that do not require any reasoning;
   (4) **Social questions** that influence students' behaviors by control or appeal.

2. Long and Sato's classification (1983)
   (1) **Echoic questions** which ask for the repetition of an utterance or confirmation: ("all right?" "Ok?" "What do you mean?" "Did you say 'he'?")
   (2) **Epistemic questions** which serve the purpose of acquiring information, fall into four types: referential, display, expressive and rhetorical.
   (3) **Referential questions** are genuinely information seeking, while display questions "test" the learner by eliciting known information.
   (4) **Expressive questions** are used for expressing the speaker's feelings or emotion and questions for the rhetorical effects.

3. Other Researchers' classification

Other researchers put emphasis on various aspects of teachers' questions and classify them differently accordingly. For example, Hakansson and Lindberg (1988) classify teachers' questions into three formal categories:

(1) **nexus questions** which can be answered with "yes" or "no";

(2) **alternative questions** which provide the responder with an alternative to select from;

(3) **X-questions** in which there is an unknown element, as in *wh-*questions.

The above results are not conclusive. There have been no clear idea of the nature of teachers' questions as they have so far received only superficial treatment.

Firstly, students' patterns of questioning need to be investigated in order to have complete picture of questions in classroom settings.

Secondly, more attention should be paid to the sociocultural context of questioning strategies. Teachers from different social backgrounds might display questioning patterns accordingly.

## 11.7 Learner Participation

Learners are usually restricted to a passive role in classroom situations. They have limited opportunities to participate productively in the activities. If opportunities for using L2 resources were important, then learning would be inhibited in the classroom.

### 11.7.1 Quantity of Participation

There have been no clear evidence that the amount of learners' participation in the activities affect their rate of development. SLA studies concerning the relationship between amount of learner participation and proficiency/achievement have produced mixed results. Even if they are significantly correlated, it is not clear yet about the directionality because all of them are correlational in nature. It might be the case that proficiency causes participation, or they have interactive effects.

### 11.7.2 Quality of Participation

Therefore, the amount of participation may not be a key factor. However, high-quality participation may be so. According to the comprehensible output hypothesis, acquisition is promoted when there are opportunities for pushed output.

Factors that seem to determine the quality of learner participation in classroom settings include: 1) the degree of control the learners exercise over the discourse; 2) the kind of activity they are involved in; 3) the learners' volunteered or nominated responses; 4) the teacher's policy regarding the distribution of practice opportunities; and 5) individual differences that affect the degree of anxiety experienced.

The SLA research showed that the situations where the learner had control of the talk, were characterized by a wide variety of communicative acts and syntactic structures, whereas the situations where the teacher had control, seemed to produce one-word utterances, short phrases, and formulaic chunks. Activity types also determine the quality of participation. Learners had more freedom in a role-play situation than in a teacher-led discussion. They behaved in a much more natural way in the former than in the latter.

However, according to Ellis (2000), interactions derived from controlled language practice such as pattern drills, though characterized by strict teacher control, should be considered as "social event" involving personal investment on the part of the learner. Therefore, it is important not to over-emphasize the restrictive nature of learner participation in teacher-controlled interaction.

## 11.8 Classroom Interaction in the L2 Learning

### 11.8.1 Tasks and Classroom Interaction

Motivated partly by proposals for "a task-based syllabus", the study of tasks has drawn much of researchers' attention. A task in the language classroom is defined as an activity designed to engage the learner in using the language communicatively or reflectively in order to arrive at an outcome other than that of learning a specified feature of the L2. It can be real-world activity or a contrived, pedagogic activity.

The variables affecting the interaction can be classified into those that relate to the task itself and those that relate to the participants performing the task. Tasks can be classified on the basis of two general dimensions:

Firstly, there are procedures for conveying the information as: 1) **who** holds it; 2) **who** conveys it; 3) **who** requests it; 4) **who** gives feedback on comprehension; 5) **the direction** of the information flow; 6) **whether** the information-exchange is required or optional and 7) **the degree** of the preciseness required.

Secondly, there is the task resolution—**whether** it is divergent or convergent.

Other important variables include the linguistic and cognitive requirements of the task and the social-linguistic context in which the task is carried out. Another important question concerning the study of tasks is that what and how to measure an interaction. Results from the research by Long show that:

(1) **Two-way tasks** produce more negotiation of meaning than **one-way tasks**;

(2) **Planned tasks** stretch IL further and promote destabilization more than **unplanned tasks**. When learners have time to plan their output, they tend to produce more complex and more target-like language;

(3) **Closed tasks** produce more negotiation work and more useful negotiation work than **open tasks**.

## 11.8.2 Group Work in Classroom Interaction

Group work (including pair work) is considered an essential feature of communicative language teaching (Long and Porter, 1985) because: 1) it **increases** practice opportunities; 2) it **improves** the quality of student talk; 3) it **helps** to individualize instruction; 4) it **promotes** a positive affective climate; and 5) it **motivates** learners to learn.

And from the perspective of psycholinguistics, it provides the kind of input and opportunities for output that promotes rapid SLA. Research results indicate that:

Students working in small groups produced a greater quantity of language and also high quality language than students in a teacher-fronted, lockstep classroom setting did. They have more opportunities for language production and produce greater variety of language use in initiating discussion, asking for clarification, interrupting, competing for the floor, and joking.

Interaction between learners can provide the interactional conditions that facilitate acquisition more readily than can interaction that involves teachers. However, what we should bear in mind is that interlanguage talk is less grammatical than teacher talk, and exposure to incorrect peer input may lead to fossilization.

The factors affecting the quality of the talk include sex and the proficiency level of the learners. SLA researches show that speech produced by female learners is on the whole of better quality. The results show that learners with lower proficiency level generally get better quality input from those with higher proficiency level, but, in contrast, learners with higher proficiency level get more opportunities to practise.

To sum up, learners benefit from interacting in group work. They will have more opportunity 1) to speak, 2) to negotiate meaning and content, and 3) to construct discourse collaboratively. This may help acquisition. They are also exposed to more ungrammatical input. It is possible that group work may not aid the development of sociolinguistic competence. Less is known about the ideal composition, but studies show that mixed gender and mixed proficiency pairs may be optimal.

## 11.9 The Relationship between Classroom Interaction and SLA

### 11.9.1 L2 Learning in the Communicative Classroom

Some researchers propose that the most effective way of developing successful L2 competence in a classroom is to give the learners more opportunities to participate in discourse directed at the exchange of information. According to this view, lack of comprehensible input and/or output may lead to the failure of many classrooms.

Studies show that learners can learn naturally in a communicative classroom setting. This shows that the communicative classroom is effective in promoting SLA. However, the problem with these studies is that they are mainly concerned with elementary level learners.

Other studies suggest that communicative classroom may not be so successful in promoting high levels of linguistic competence. And students who were taught by means of communicative methods produced little evidence of syntactic development.

Therefore, communicative classroom setting may not be sufficient to ensure the development of higher linguistic and sociolinguistic competence, although they may be successful in developing fluency and effective discourse skills. Communication in that language does not guarantee full target language competence.

### 11.9.2 Effect of Classroom Interaction on L2 Learning

Some correlational studies investigated the relationship between various aspects of classroom interaction and either proficiency or learners' output. Results showed that some measures of interaction (e.g. teachers' use of metalanguage, overt correction, and vocabulary explanation) were correlated with performance on language tests. And different types of behaviors were related to different kinds of language proficiency.

A structured teaching style involves teacher-directed practice activities or question-answer sequences. Wong-Fillmore (1982) distinguished two basic types of classroom organization in a longitudinal study of L2 learners:

1) teacher-directed classrooms: interactions involve the teacher and the L2 learners;
2) learner-centered organization: interactions take place between teacher and individual students and also among the learners themselves.

Results showed that successful L2 learning occurred in classes that had a high proportion of L2 learners and also in classes that were mixed in composition (more native-English speaking children). Conversely, much less learning took place in mixed teacher-directed classes and open classes with a large number of L2 learners.

From these studies we can conclude that what is more important is access to plentiful, well-formed input tailored to the level of the learner.

Wong-Fillmore's study shows that factors which contribute to L2 learning are grouped into two sets: 1) class organization, and 2) characteristics of teacher talk.

The important characteristics of teacher talk include: 1) a clear separation of L1/L2 languages; 2) an emphasis on communication and comprehension by ensuring message redundancy; 3) the avoidance of ungrammatical teacher-talk; 4) the frequent use of patterns and routines and repetitiveness; 5) tailoring questions to suit the learners' level of proficiency; and 6) general richness of language.

## 11.10 Conclusion

It is premature to draw any conclusion for the relationship between interaction and L2 acquisition. But, there is evidence to support the following statements:

1) Opportunities to negotiate meaning may help the acquisition of L2 vocabulary.
2) Pushing L2 learners to reformulate their utterances to make them more target-like may lead to greater grammatical accuracy in the long term.
3) Teacher-controlled "pedagogic discourse" may contribute to the acquisition of formal language skills, while learner-controlled "natural discourse" may aid the development of oral language skills.
4) Learners need access to well-formed input that is tailored to their own level of understanding. This can be achieved in teacher-directed lessons with a clearly defined structure and well-adjusted teacher talk.
5) Listening to others in teacher-led classes may be more important for learning than direct learner participation.

Points for Thinking

1. What are the aspects and the nature of classroom interaction in the SLA studies?
2. What are the types of language use in classroom interaction?
3. What are the differences between classroom and naturalistic discourse?
4. What is the role of language teachers in classroom interaction?
5. What is the significance in carrying out the study on learner participation?

Further Reading

Allwright, R. (1988). *Observation in the Language Classroom*. Harlow: Longman.

Kramsch, C. (1993). *Context and Culture in Language Teaching*. New York: Oxford University Press.

Sinclair, J. M. and Coulthard. M. (1975). *Towards an Analysis of Discourse*. London: Oxford Uni. Press.

Van Lier, L.(1988). *The Classroom and the Language Learner*. London: Longman.

Wong-Fillmore, L. (1982). "Instructional language as linguistic input: second language learning in classroom." In Wilkinson, L. (Ed.). *Communicating in the Classroom*. New York: Academic Press.

# Chapter 12

# Conclusion

## 12.1 A Brief Review of the Book

Having come to the end of our introduction to current studies in SLA research, we are left with a reinforced impression of great diversity. It is impossible for a single book to cover the entire range of SLA research, let alone the whole of the topics in its field. Nevertheless, we have tried the best to present as much as possible.

In Chapter 1, there are the major SLA terms together with plausible definitions, defined characteristics and its theoretical applications. In Chapter 2, the presentation has been done to a variety of views on the nature of language, on the language learning process and the L2 learners. In Chapter 3, a review is given on the studies on the developmental patterns in L1 acquisition and their importance in L2 learning. In Chapter 4 and 5, another review is done on the recent history of SLA research and then Chomskian theory of Universal Grammar which brought a revolutionary change of views on language and language learning. It is noted that the SLA research accounts for only a portion of the complex phenomenon of second language acquisition. In Chapter 6 and 7, there is a further presentation of the association with Cognitive Theorists, such as Processing Approaches, Connectivism and L2 Processing theories. There are also the discussion of Functional Perspectives, Functionalist Contributions, Sociocultural Perspectives and Sociolinguistic Perspectives on SLA. In Chapter 8, the role of language universals is discussed for the acquisition of a second language as well as for the acquisition of phonology and the tense/aspect system. In Chapter 8, the concepts of Gass's Input—Interaction—Output model are presented to an explanation of how these ideas are relevant to acquisition itself. In Chapter 9, there is a review on the role of Selinker's Interlanguage in SLA with a discussion on social, discoursal, psycholinguistic aspects of Interlanguage. Chapter 10 and Chapter 11 have examined how L2 teachers' instruction can (or cannot) affect L2 learning; and how L2 learners' participations in classroom activities can help L2 acquisition. This chapter is simply a general conclusion.

## 12.2 An Integrated View of SLA Research

As has become clear throughout this introductory book, the L2 learning or acquisition is a multifaceted endeavor. In order to fully understand the SLA theory and L2 learning process, one must consider what is possibly learned and what is seemingly not learned, as well as the language contexts in which that L2 learning/acquisition takes place. The latter includes the various influences on the L2 learning process that is the focus of the main SLA research and investigation.

Different research groups are pursuing theoretical agendas that centre on very different parts of the total language learning process. As many researchers have placed the modeling of learner grammars at the heart of their study, others focus on language processing, or on second language interaction. Each research tradition has developed its cluster of specialized research procedures, ranging from the grammaticality judgment tests associated with Universal Grammar-inspired research, to the naturalistic observation and recording practiced by ethnographers and language socialization theorists.

On the whole, grand synthesizing theories, which try to encompass all aspects of SLA in a single model, have not received general support. Rather than a process of theory reduction and consolidation, it is found that new theoretical perspectives (such as connectionism or sociocultural theory) have entered the field.

## 12.3 Main Achievements of Recent SLA Research

The wealth of SLA studies can be taken into account as they have been carried out in the last 40 years or so. Plenty of significant results and achievements can be noted in SLA theorizing from a variety of origins:

1. Linguistically, an application of Chomskian UG approach to the modeling of L2 competence has led to an increasingly sophisticated and interconnected extension of proposals around the "LAD". Krashen originally brought about the possible contents of that mysterious LAD into SLA research.

One complication is that some UG specialists hold a growing view that different aspects of language knowledge are relatively autonomously learnt and stored. The UG approach has also been as an instrument in providing sheer linguistic descriptions of learner language, and has been useful in documenting the linguistic development of L2 learners and in explaining some cross-linguistic influences.

2. Cognitively, the main and great evolutionary progress has been the formation of information processing models. They have been applied to some domains complementary to grammar learning. There is also an application of Anderson's ACT model to the acquisition of learning strategies.

As far as grammar learning itself is concerned, connectionist models have offered a more radical challenge to traditional linguistic views. They have proposed that they may do it without the conventional help of abstract grammar rules and symbolic representations. They have also suggested that a much more primitive network with some associated links can lay foundations for language learning and performance. However, the empirical data and evidence supporting such claims still remains limited, and controversial in its interpretation, let alone application.

3. In the functionalist tradition, recent researches have grown substantially to an understanding of the process of L2 development, and especially the major role played by the theory of pragmatics and lexis in

L2 learners' interlanguage communication, particularly in their beginners' stages. Different kinds of studies also suggest the L2 variability can be accounted for by building-up and developing the links between language form and its function.

4. In terms of descriptive perspective, SLA researchers have also got to learn much from recent studies on the contexts within which L2 communication takes place and the types of interactions in which L2 learners become so much engaged. They have also begun seriously to look into the connections between interactional engagement and SLA studies.

5. In the different approaches, the interactionist, sociocultural and sociolinguistic perspectives all have interest in the issues of SLA research. Interactionist and sociocultural research, both in their different ways, display how the ongoing feature of L2 interaction can systematically affect the language learning opportunities which it makes available. They have started to show how learners actually use these opportunities for L2 interaction.

The sociolinguistic perspective has demonstrated how learners' engagement in L2 interaction is influenced by power relations and other cultural factors. These cultural factors are not unchangeably fixed, but can be renegotiated as L2 learners have built up their new identities.

However, there remains a major limitation shared by all the above particular disciplines. The interactionist tradition in particular is not so successful as expected. There is a continuing scarcity of researches which may help track and document learners' language development in detail over time, and link their progressive control of linguistic structure to an account of their interactional experiences.

Those researchers in the sociocultural tradition have obviously recognized, even in extensive studies, that the links have up to now been established on a limited scale, only in an aspect of small "patches" of language knowledge. It has not yet been seen the systematic connections over the accounts of interlanguage development as the evidence provided by the functionalist theory, with developmental accounts of L2 negotiation, scaffolding, interaction, etc.

## 12.4 SLA Research and Language Education

In Chapter 10 and 11, it has been noted that theorizing about SLA has its historic roots in reform movements linked to the practice of language teaching and learning in the classroom. Howatt (1984) argues that this has been the case since the age of Renaissance times at least. In the second half of the 20$^{th}$ century, however, SLA has become a much more autonomous field of enquiry, based on its own independent and scientific rationale.

But what kind of connections should SLA now relatively independent investigating field maintain, with its language teaching origins? From time to time, this issue has been argued that the scientific findings of SLA should guide the practices of teachers in their classroom teaching. The obvious example is a group of recommendations that flowed from Krashcn's Input Hypothesis, in the form of the "Natural Approach" to language pedagogy.

Another example introduced briefly in Chapter 6 is the Teachability Hypothesis. The hypothesis was advanced by Pienemann, and he suggests that new L2 items might be most effectively taught in some sequences that imitate empirically documented developmental sequences.

Ellis (1997), with such a top-down, rationalist approach, reviews a number of well-known difficulties to linking research-derived theory and language classroom practice. SLA research is carried out across broad enough domains. Its findings are not sufficiently secure, clear and uncontested to provide straightforward rationales and guidance for the teacher.

The findings from the SLA research are not generally put foreword in ways accessible and meaningful to language teachers. The agenda of SLA research does not always necessarily focus on the issues which L2 teachers are most conscious of as problematic.

But most importantly, any teaching is an art as well as a science, and irreducibly so, because of the constantly changing nature of the classroom situation as a learning community. There can be no "one best method or approach", however much research evidence supports it. No method or approach is possibly to suit all times and all situations, with every type of learner.

On the contrary, teachers would "read" and interpret the dynamic change of the learning context from time to time. They just take what seems to them to be appropriate actions, in the light of largely implicit knowledge of proceduralized pedagogy. This has been deeply rooted over time from their own previous teaching experience. The knowledge usually derives, to a much more limited extent, from study or from organized training.

However, present SLA research offers a rich variety of different and descriptive concepts. It can help L2 teachers to possibly interpret and make better sense of their own classroom teaching experiences. It can significantly broaden their eye-views and also broaden the range of pedagogic choices open to them.

For example, SLA research has already proposed descriptive accounts of the course of interlanguage development. These accounts show that L2 learners follow relatively some invariant routes of interlanguage development, but that such routes are not simply linear, including phases of restructuring and apparent regression.

Such accounts have helped L2 teachers to understand some patterns of learners' errors and its inevitability in learning. Teachers would more generally accept the indirect nature of the relationship between what is taught and what is learnt.

Similarly, in the recent research literature, discussions about the role of recasts and negative evidence in learning about scaffolding, or about language socialization have great potential to stimulate L2 teachers' reflections on the pedagogic choices available to them, when enacting their own roles as L2 guiders and interlocutors in the classroom activities.

## 12.5 Future Directions for SLA Research

For the predicatable future, it seems that SLA will be considered and treated as a modular phenomenon, with different researching programmes focusing on different issues. The influence is unlikely to diminish from the linguistic knowledge and L1 competence on the modeling of L2 development, so that it can be expected to see continuing efforts in SLA research. There exists a need for the application of successive theories of UG approach, Functional Perspectives and Sociolinguistic theory to the SLA research.

On the other hand, the general learning theories derived from cognitive psychology, and neural science has been applied to the SLA research. It can also be expected to continue the attempts to bear on SLA such diverse theories of general learning, as connectionism and Vygotskyan sociocultural theory. But more theories and approaches are sure to follow what the SLA has achieved so far.

Although it can be sure that these different strands within SLA will maintain their self-direction and individual interest. However, they attempt to set up interconnection between them and examine the links between different learning "modules" in a systematic way. Such a process will continue to prove a fruitful way of enhancing a better and fuller understanding of the particular modular domains. Much of the recent researches have examined a variety of interfaces in detail, for example between syntax and morphology, between the lexicon and syntax, or between semantics and syntax, or between semantics and pragmatics.

From a viewpoint of methodology, one progressive development within certain disciplines of SLA research is the frequent use of Computer-aided Instruction (CAI) in the classroom and computer-aided techniques for analyzing L2 data. The research on child language has shown the potential of computer-aided analysis for dealing with corpus data, for example, by using software such as the CHILDES package in the project by MacWhinney (2000a; 2000b).

In the research to devise proper and effective tools for data analysis, the development of electronic L2 corpora is making possible the more systematic linkage of L2 grammar development together with L2 interaction. The instruments also facilitate researchers much closer attention to L2 lexis and lexico-grammar, and to the role of lexical chunking and routines in L2 use and SLA. Recent achievements in computer technology have also enabled the quick development of computer modeling of the SLA researches, for example, the application of connectionism to SLA research in the recent years.

But by any large, such kind of technical devices do not challenge the fundamental issues and assumptions of SLA research. However, there are a number of critiques which have developed of autonomous applied linguistics and the SLA research, from more socially engaged perspectives. They can be found in those contemporary theoretical discussions, and also proposals for more socially engaged approaches of the SLA research, on the one hand (Block, 1996), and for the interpretations of L2 use and learning by the post-modern theory on the other.

Post-modernism offers a relativist critique of the attempts to regard human activity as part of a grand scheme, driven by the notions of progressive development of any kind (Brumfit, 1997). As far as language is concerned, it highlights the existing problems of textuality, and the complex relationship between language and any kind of external reality: "we are positioned by the requirements of the discourse we think we adopt, and our metaphors of adoption hide the fact that *it* adopts *us*". (Brumfit, 1997: 25)

The post-modernist concept of intertextuality—the idea that all language use is a patchwork of borrowings from previous users—has been claimed to be of central importance for SLA study (Hall, 1995). The critical and post-modern commentary on SLA, however, has not given up its central modernist assumptions. It will be a task of the future to tell how much impact it eventually exerts on programmes of L2 empirical enquiry. This evolution will evidently be related to more extensive ongoing debates in the field of social sciences.

Considering the relationship between SLA research and classroom language teaching, the sub-field of SLA research plays a special role in addressing the issues somewhat closer to those of the classroom teacher. It may offer opportunities for more direct involvement of teachers as research partners or an SLA researcher.

But it should be clear that SLA research is not identical with problem solving and development in language pedagogy. It does not ensure a shared agenda between L2 teachers and SLA researchers. There is a constant need for a dialogue between the practical theories of classroom teaching, and the more decontextualized and abstract ideas deriving from SLA research programmes.

SLA researchers thus have a continuing responsibility to make their findings and their interpretations of SLA theories as intelligible as possible to a wider professional audience of language teachers. It is expected that more SLA researches and findings continue to contribute usefully to the dialogue of theory and practice in language acquisition.

## Points for Thinking

1. What is a general and integrated view of the SLA research?
2. What are the main findings and achievements in the SLA research?
3. What is the relationship between the SLA research and classroom language teaching?
4. What are the language teachers' response to the findings and theories on language teaching and learning?
5. What is your understanding and future expectation of the SLA research?

## Further Reading

Block, D. (1996). "Not so fast: some thoughts on theory dulling, relativism, accepted findings and the heart and soul of SLA." *Applied Linguistics* 17: 63 – 83.

Brumfit, C.J. (1997). "Theoretical practice: applied linguistics as pure and practical science." *AILA Review* 12: 18 – 30.

Hall, J.K. (1995). "(Re)creating our worlds with words: a sociohistorical perspective of face-to-face interaction." *Applied Linguistics* 16: 206 – 232.

MacWhinney, B. (2000a). *The CHILDES Project: Tools for Analyzing Talk. Volumn 1: Transcription Format and Programs* (3$^{rd}$ ed.). Mahwah, NJ: Lawrance Erlbaum.

MacWhinney, B. (2000b). *The CHILDES Project: Tools for Analyzing Talk.*

*Volumn 2: The database* (3$^{rd}$ ed.). Mahwah, NJ: Lawrence Erlbaum.

Towell, R. and Hawkins, R. (1994). *Approaches to Second Language Acquisition*. Clevedon: Multilingual Matters.

# REFERENCES

Abunuwara, E. (1992). "The structure of the trilingual lexicon." *European Journal of Cognitive Psychology* 4:311 – 313.

Adamson, H. D. (1988). *Variation Theory and Second Language Acquisition*.Washington, DC: Georgetown University Press.

Adjemian, C. (1976). "On the nature of interlanguage systems." *Language Learning* 26: 297 – 320.

Adjemian, C. (1983). "The transferability of lexical properties." In S. Gass and L. Selinker (Eds.). *Language Transfer in Language Learning*. Rowley, MA: Newbury House, pp.250 – 268.

Aitchison, J. (1989) *The Articulate Mammal*. London: Routledge, as referenced in Willis, Shortall & Johns (2001:68).

Akmajian, A., Demers, R., Farmer, A. and Harnish, R. (1995). *Linguistics: An Introduction to Language and Communication*. Cambridge, MA: MIT Press.

Aljaafreh, A. and Lantolf, J.P. (1994). "Negative feedback as regulation and second language learning in the Zone of Proximal Development." *Modern Language Journal* 78:465 – 483.

Allwright, D. (2005). "From teaching points to learning opportunities and beyond." *TESOL QUARTERLY* 39(1): 9 – 31.

Allwright, R. L. (Ed.) (1975). *Working Papers: Language Teaching Classroom Research*. University of Essex, Department of Language and Linguistics.

Allwright, R. L. (1977). "Language learning through communication practice." *ELT Documents* 76/3 (reprinted in Brumfit and Johnson 1979).

Allwright, R.L. (1979). "Abdiction and responsibility in language teaching." *Studies in Second Language Acquisition*, Vol. 2 No. 1.

Allwright, R. L. (1980). "Turns, topics and tasks: patterns of participation in language Learning and teaching." In D. Larsen -Freeman (Ed.). *Discourse Analysis in Second Language Research*. Rowley: Newbury House.

Allwright, R. (1988). *Observation in the Language Classroom*. Harlow: Longman.

Allen, P. et al. (1984). "The communicative orientation of language teaching: an observation scheme." In J.Handscombe, R. Orem & B. Taylor (Eds.). *On TESOL '83. The Question of Control*. Washington, DC: TESOL.

Ammar, A. and Spada, N. (2006). "One size fits all? Recasts, prompts and L2 learning." *Studies in Second Language Acquisition* 28:543 – 574.

Andersen, R. (1983). "Transfer to somewhere." In S. Gass and L. Selinker (Eds.).

*Language Transfer in Language Learning.* Rowley, MA: Newbury House, pp. 177 – 201.

Andersen, R. (1984). "The one-to-one principle of interlanguage construction." *Language Learning* 34:77 – 95.

Andersen, R. (1990). "Models, processes, principles and strategies: second language acquisition inside and outside the classroom." In B. VanPatten and J. F. Lee (Eds.). *Second Language Acquisition* (R) (*Foreign Language Learning*, pp. 45 – 78). Clevedon, UK: Multilingual Matters.

Andersen, R. (1991). "Developmental sequences: the emergence of aspect marking in second language acquisition." In T. Huebner and C. Ferguson (Eds.). *Crosscurrents in Second Language Acquisition and Linguistic Theories.* Amsterdam: John Benjamins, pp.305 – 324.

Andersen, R. and Shirai, Y. (1994). "Discourse motivations for some cognitive acquisition principles." *Studies in Second Language Acquisition* 16:133 – 156.

Anglin, J. M. (1993). "Vocabulary development: a morphological analysis." *Monographs for the Society for Research in Child Development* 58 (10, No.238).

Ard, J. (1989). "A constructivist perspective on non-native phonology." In S. Gass and J. Schachter (Eds.). *Linguistic Perspectives on Second Language Acquisition.* Cambridge: Cambridge University Press, pp.243 – 259.

Ard, J. and Gass, S. (1987). "Lexical constraints on syntactic acquisition." *Studies in Second Language Acquisition* 9:235 – 255.

Ardilla, A. (2003). "Language representation and working memory with bilinguals." *Journal of Communication Disorders* 36:233 – 240.

Asher, J.(1977). *Learning another Language through Actions: The Complete Teacher's Guidebook.* Los Gatos, CA: Sky Oaks Productions.

Ayoun, D. (2001). "The role of negative and positive feedback in the second language acquisition of the passé composé and imparfait." *Modern language Journal* 85:226 – 243.

Baddeley, A. D. (2000). "The episodic buffer: a new component of working memory?" *Trends in Cognitive Sciences* 4:417 – 423.

Baddeley, A. D. (2003a). "Working memory and language: an overview." *Journal of Communication Disorders* 36:189 – 208.

Baddeley, A. D. (2003b). "Working memory: looking back and looking forward." *Neuroscience* 4:29 – 839. Rowley, MA: Newbury House.

Baker, C. and Jones, S. P. (Eds.) (1998). *Encyclopedia of Bilingualism and Bilingual Education.* Clevedon, UK: Multilingual Matters.

Bard, E., Robertson, D. andSorace, A. (1996). "Magnitude estimation of linguistic acceptability." *Language* 72:32 – 68.

Bardovi-Harlig, K. (1987). "Markedness and salience in second-language acquisition." *Language Learning* 37:385 – 407.

Bardovi-Harlig, K. (2000). "Tense and aspect in second language acquisition: form, meaning, and use." *Language Learning Supplement*. Malden, MA: Blackwell.

Bardovi-Harlig, K. (2006). "Interlanguage development: main routes and individual paths." In K. Bardovi-Harlig and Z. Darnyei (Eds.). *Themes in SLA Research. AILA Review* 19:69 – 82. Amsterdam: John Benjamins.

Bardovi-Harlig, K. (2007). "One functional approach to second language acquisition: the concept-oriented approach." In B. VanPatten and J. Williams (Eds.). *Theories in Second Language Acquisition: An Introduction*. Mahwah NJ: Lawrence Erlbaum Associates, pp.57 – 75.

Bardovi-Harlig, K. and Darnyei, Z. (1998). "Do language learners recognize pragmatic violations? Pragmatic versus grammatical awareness in instructed L2 learning." *TESOL Quarterly* 32:233 – 262.

Bardovi-Harlig, K. and Hartford, B. (1996). "Input in an institutional setting." *Studies in Second Language* 18:171 – 188.

Barnes, D.(1969). *Language, the Learner and the School*. Harmondsworth, Middlesex: Penguin Books.

Barnes, D. (1989). "Language in the secondary classroom." In Barnes, D., Britton, J. and Torbe. M. (Eds.). *Language, the Learner and the School*. London: Heinemann.

Bates, E. and MacWhinney, B. (1982). "Functionalist approach to grammar." In E. Wanner and L. Gleitman (Eds.). *Language Acquisition: The State of the Art*. New York: Cambridge University Press, pp.173 – 218.

Bates, E., Bretherton, I. & Snyder, L. (1988). *From First Words to Grammar: Individual Differences and Dissociable Mechanisms*. New York: Cambridge University Press.

Bayley, R. and Preston, D. (Eds.) (1996). *Second Language Acquisition and Linguistic Variation*. Amsterdam: John Benjamins.

Beck, M. L. and Eubank, L. (1991). "Acquisition theory and experimental design: a critique of Tomasello and Herron." *Studies in Second Language Acquisition* 13:73 – 76.

Benati, A. (2004). "The effects of structured input activities and explicit information on the acquisition of the Italian future tense." In B. VanPatten (Ed.). *Processing Instruction: Theory, Research, and Commentary*. Mahwah, NJ: Lawrence Erlbaum Associates, pp.207 – 225.

Bennett-Kastor, T. (1988). *Analyzing Children's Language: Methods and Theories*. Oxford: Blackwell.

Bhatia, T. (2006). "Introduction to part I." In T. Bhatia and W. Ritchie (Eds.). *The Handbook of Bilingualism*. Malden, MA: Blackwell, pp.5 – 6.

Bhatia, T. and Ritchie, W. (Eds.) (2006). *The Handbook of Bilingualism*. Malden, MA: Blackwell.

Bialystok, E. (1997). "The structure of age: in search of barriers to second language acquisition." *Second Language Research* 13:116 – 137.

Bialystok, E. (2001a). *Bilingualism in Development: Language, Literacy and Cognition*. Cambridge, UK: Cambridge University Press.

Bialystok, E. (2001b). "Metalinguistic aspects of bilingual processing." *Annual Review of Applied Linguistics* 21:169 – 181.

Bialystok, E. and Hakuta, K. (1994). *In Other Words: The Science and Psychology of Second-Language Acquisition*. New York: Basic Books.

Birdsong, D. (1992)."Ultimate attainment in second language acquisition." *Language* 68: 706 – 755.

Block, D. (1996)."Not so fast: some thoughts on theory dulling, relativism, accepted findings and the heart and soul of SLA." *Applied Linguistics* 17: 63 – 83.

Bloomfield, L. (1933). *Language*. New York: Holt.

Bogaards, P. (2001). "Lexical units and the learning of foreign language vocabulary." *Studies in Second Language Acquisition* 23:321 – 343.

Bogaards, P. and Laufer, B. (Eds.) (2004). *Vocabulary in a Second Language: Selection, Acquisition and Testing*. Amsterdam: John Benjamins.

Bohannon, J.N. et al.(1990). "No negative evidence revisited: beyond learnability or who has to prove what to whom." *Developmental Psychology* 26:221 – 226.

Bohannon, J.N. et al. (1996)."Useful evidence on negative evidence." *Developmental Psychology* 32:551 – 555.

Bourdieu, P. (1977). "The economics of linguistic exchanges." *Social Science Information* 16:645 – 668.

Braine, M. (1971). "The Acquisition of Language in Infant and Child." In Reed, C.E. (Ed.) *The Learning of Language*. New York: Appleton-Center-Crofts. Quoted in Jean Aitchison. *The Articulate Mammual*. London: Huchison, 1973, p.74.

Braidi, S.M. (1995). "Reconsidering the role of interaction and input in second language acquisition." *Language Learning* 45:141 – 175.

Bresnan J. (Ed.) (1982). *The Mental Representation of Grammatical Relations*. Cambridge, Massachusetts: MIT Press.

Brown, H. et al. (Eds.) (1977). *On TESOL 77*. Washington D.C.: TESOL.

Brown, R.O.(1973). *Early Syntactic Development*. Cambridge, MA: MIT Press.

Brumfit, C.J. (1997). "Theoretical practice: applied linguistics as pure and practical science." *AILA Review* 12:18-30.

Carlisle, R. (1998). "The acquisition of onsets in a markedness relationship: a longitudinal study." *Studies in Second Language Acquisition* 20:245-260.

Carroll, S. (2000). *Input and Evidence: The Raw Material of Second Language Acquisition.* Amsterdam: John Benjamins.

Carroll, S. (2007). "Autonomous induction theory." In B. VanPatten and J. Williams (Eds.). *Theories in Second Language Acquisition: An Introduction.* Mahwah, NJ: Lawrence Erlbaum Associates.

Cenoz, J. (2005). Review of T. Bhatia and W. Ritchie (Eds.). "Handbook of Bilingualism." *Studies in Second Language Acquisition* 27:638-639.

Chamot, A., Barnhardt, S., El-Dinary, P. B. and Robbins, J. (1999). *The Learning Strategies Handbook.* New York: Longman.

Chapelle, C. (2001). *Computer Applications in Second Language Acquisition: Foundations for Teaching, Testing and Research.* Cambridge: Cambridge University Press.

Chapelle, C. and Green, P. (1992). "Field independence/dependence in second language acquisition research." *Language Learning* 42:47-83.

Chaudron, C. (1985b). "Intake: on models and methods for discovering learners' processing of input." *Studies in Second Language Acquisition* 7:1-14.

Chaudron, C. (1988). *Second Language Classrooms: Research on Teaching and Learning.* Cambridge: Cambridge Uni. Press.

Chaudron, C. (2001). "Progress in language classroom research: evidence from *The Modern Language Journal*, 1916-2000." *The Modern Language Journal* 85:57-76.

Chaudron, C. (2003). "Data collected in SLA research." In Doughty, C and Long, M. (Eds.). *The Handbook of Second Language Acquisition.* MA: Blackwell, pp.762-828.

Chomsky, N. (1959). "Review of B. F. Skinner's Verbal Behavior." *Language* 35:26-58.

Chomsky, N. (1968). *Language and Mind.* New York: Harcourt Brace Jovanovich.

Chomsky, N. (1981).*Lectures on Government and Binding.* Dordrecht, the Nether-lands: Foris.

Chomsky, N. (2000).*New Horizons in the Study of Language and Mind.* Cambridge: Cambridge University Press.

Chomsky, N. (2002). *On Nature and Language.* Cambridge: Cambridge University Press.

Clahsen, H. (1984). "The acquisition of German word order: a test case for cognitive approaches to L2 development." In Anderson, R. (Eds.). *Second Language: A Crosslinguistic Perspective.* Rowley, MA: Newbury House, pp. 219-242.

Clahsen, H. and Felser, C. (2006). "Grammatical processing in language learners." *Applied Psycholinguistics* 27:3 – 42.

Clark, H. and Clark, E. (1977). *Psychology and Language: An Introduction to Psycholinguistics*. New York: Harcourt Brace.

Clark, E.V. (1993.). *The Lexicon in Acquisition*. New York: Cambridge University Press.

Coady, J. and Huckin, T. (Eds.) (1997). *Second Language Vocabulary Acquisition*. Cambridge: Cambridge University Press.

Cohen, A. (1998). *Strategies in Learning and Using a Second Language*. London: Longman.

Cohen, A. (2005). "Strategies for learning and performing L2 speech acts." *Inter-cultural Pragmatics* 2:275 – 301.

Cohen, A. and Macaro, E. (2007). *Language Learner Strategies: Thirty Years of Research and Practice*. Oxford: Oxford University Press.

Comrie, B. (1981). *Language Universals and Language Typology*. Chicago: University of Chicago Press.

Cook, V. (1986). "The basis for an experimental approach to second language learning." In V. Cook (Ed.). *Experimental Approaches to Second Language Learning*. Oxford: Pergamon Press, pp.3 – 21.

Cook, V. (1988). *Chomsky's Universal Grammar*. Oxford: Basil Blackwell.

Cook, V. (1996). *Second Language Learning and Language Teaching*, 2nd ed. London: Edward Arnold.

Cook, V. (1997). *Inside Language*. London: Edward Arnold.

Cook, V. (Ed.) (2003). *Effects of the Second Language on the First*. Clevedon, UK: Multilingual Matters.

Corder, S. P. (1967). "The significance of learner's errors." *International Review of Applied Linguistics* 5:161 – 169.

Corder, S.P. (1971). "Idiosyncratic Dialects and Error Analysis." In Richards, J.C. (Ed.) (1984). *Error Analysis: Perspectives on Second Language Acquisition*. London: Longman, pp.158 – 171.

Corder, S.P. (1977). "Simple codes' and the source of the learner's heuristic hypothesis." *Studies in Second Language Acquisition* 1:1 – 10.

Corder, S. P. (1981). *Error Analysis in Interlanguage*. Oxford: Oxford University Press.

Corder, S. P. (1983). "A role for the mother tongue in language learning." In S. Gass and L. Selinker (Eds.). *Language Transfer in Language Learning*. Rowley, MA: Newbury House, pp.85 – 97.

Corder, S. P. (1992). "A role for the mother tongue." In S. Gass and L. Selinker (Eds.). *Language Transfer in Language Learning*, 2nd ed. Amsterdam: John Benjamins, pp.

18 - 31.

Coulthard, M. (1977). *An Introduction to Discourse Analysis.* London: Longman.

Coulthard, M. (1985). *An Introduction to Discourse Analysis.* (2nd edition). London: Longman.

Day, B (Ed.) (1986). *Talking to Learn: Conversation in Second language Acquisition.* Rowley, Mass: Newbury House.

deJong, N. (2005). "Can second language grammar be learned through listening? An experimental study." *Studies in Second Language Acquisition* 27:205 - 234.

DeKeyser, R. (1993). "The effect of error correction on L2 grammar knowledge and oral proficiency." *Modern Language Journal* 77:501 - 514.

DeKeyser, R. (2003). "Implicit and explicit learning." In C. Doughty and M. H. Long (Eds.). *The Handbook of Second Language Acquisition.* Oxford: Blackwell, pp. 313 - 347.

De la Fuente, M.J. (2002). "Negotiation and oral acquisition of L2 vocabulary." *Studies in Second language Acquisition* 24:81 - 112.

Demuth, K.(1996). "Collecting spontaneous production data." In D. McDaniel, C. McKee and H. SmithCairns (Eds.). *Methods for Assessing Children's Syntax.* Cambridge, MA: MIT Press, pp.3 - 22.

Deuchar, M. and Quay, S. (2000). *Bilingual Acquisition: Theoretical Implications of a Case Study.* Oxford: Oxford University Press.

Dietrich, R., Klein, W. and Noyau, C. (1995). *The Acquisition of Temporality in a Second Language.* Philadelphia: John Benjamins.

Donato, R. (1994). "Collective scaffolding in second language learning." In Lantolf, J.P. and Appel, G. (Eds.). *Vygotskian Approaches to Second Language Research.* Norwood, NJ: Ablex Publishing Corporation, pp.33 - 56.

Donato, R. and MacCormick, D. (1994). "A sociocultural perspective on language learning strategies: the role of mediation." *Modern Language Journal* 78:453 - 464.

Dornyei, Z. and Otto, I. (1998). "Motivation in action: a process model of L2 motivation." *Working Papers in Applied Linguistics* 4: 43 - 69. London: Thames Valley University.

Dornyei, Z. (2003). *Questionnaires in Second Language Research: Construction, Administration, and Processing.* Mahwah, NJ: Lawrence Erlbaum Associates.

Doughty. C. (1991)."Second language instruction does make a difference: evidence from an empirical study of SL relativization." *Studies in Second Language Acquisition* 13:431 - 469.

Doughty, C. (2001)."Cognitive underpinnings of focus on form." In P. Robinson (Ed.). *Cognition and Second Language Instruction.* Cambridge: Cambridge University

Press, pp.206 – 257.

Doughty, C. (2003)."Instructed SLA: constraints, compensation, and enhancement." In C. Doughty and M. H. Long (Eds.). *The Handbook of Second Language Acquisition*. Oxford: Blackwell, pp.256 – 310.

Doughty, C. and Long, M. H.(2000). "Eliciting second language speech data." In L. Menn and N. Bernstein Ratner (Eds.). *Methods for Studying Language Production*. Mahwah, NJ: Lawrence Erlbaum Associates, pp.149 – 177.

Doughty, C and Long, M.H. (2003).*Handbook of Second Language Acquisition*. Oxford: Blackwell, pp.55 – 77.

Duff, P. (2008).*Case Study Research in Applied Linguistics*. New York: Taylor & Francis.

Eckman, F. (2007). "Hypotheses and methods in second language acquisition: testing the noun phrase accessibility hierarchy on relative clauses." *Studies in Second Language Acquisition* 29:321 – 327.

Edwards, J. (2006)."Foundations of bilingualism." In T. Bhatia and W. Ritchie (Eds.). *The Handbook of Bilingualism*. Oxford: Blackwell, pp.5 – 29.

Ehrman, M. and Leaver, B. L. (2003). "Cognitive styles in the service of language learning." *System* 31:391 – 415.

Eimas, P.D. and Nygaard, L.C. (1992). "Contextual coherence and attention in phoneme monitoring." *Journal of Memory and Language* 31:375 – 395.

Eimas, P.D.et al. (1990). "Attention and the role of dual codes in phoneme monitoring." *Journal of Memory and Language* 29:160 – 180.

Ellis, N. (2001)."Memory for language." In P. Robinson (Ed.). *Cognition and Second Language Instruction*. Cambridge, UK: Cambridge University Press.

Ellis, N. (2002)."Frequency effects in language processing: a review with implications for theories of implicit and explicit language acquisition." *Studies in Second Language Acquisition* 24:143 – 188.

Ellis, N. C. (2005). "At the interface: dynamic interactions of explicit and implicit language knowledge." *Studies in Second Language Acquisition* 27:305 – 352.

Ellis, N. (2007)."The associate -cognitive Creed." In B. VanPatten and J. Williams (Eds.). *Theories in Second Language Acquisition: An Introduction*. Mahwah, NJ: Lawrence Erlbaum Associates.

Ellis, R. (1984). *Classroom Second Language Development: A Study of Classroom Interaction and Language Acquisition*. Oxford, UK: Pergamom.

Ellis, R. (1985).*Understanding Second Language Acquisition*. Oxford: Oxford University Press.

Ellis, R. (1994).*The Study of Second Language Acquisition*. Oxford: Oxford University Press.

Ellis, R. (1997).*Second Language Acquisition*. Oxford: Oxford University Press.

Ellis, R. (Ed.) (2000). *Learning a Second Language through Interaction*. Amsterdam: John Benjamins.

Ellis, R. (2005)."Measuring implicit and explicit knowledge of a second language: a psychometric study." *Studies in Second Language Acquisition* 27:141 – 172.

Ellis, R. (2007)."The differential effect of corrective feedback on two grammatical structures." In A. Mackey (Ed.). *Conversational Interaction and Second Language Acquisition: A Series of Empirical Studies*. Oxford: Oxford University Press, pp. 339 – 360.

Ellis, R. and Barkhuizen, G. (2005). *Analysing Learner Language*. Oxford: Oxford University Press.

Ellis, R. and He, X. (1999). "The roles of modified input and output in the incidental acquisition of word meanings." *Studies in Second Language Acquisition* 21:285 – 301.

Faerch, C. et al. (1984). *Learner Language and Language Learning*. Clevedon, UK: Multilingual Matters.

Faerch, C. and Kasper, G. (1980). "Processes in foreign language learning and communication." *Interlanguage Studies Bulletin* 5:47 – 118.

Faerch, C. and Kasper, G. (1986). "The role of comprehension in second language learning." *Applied Linguistics* 7:257 – 274.

Faerch, C. and Kasper, G. (1987). "From product to process – introspective methods in second language research." In C. Faerch and G. Kasper (Eds.). *Introspection in Second Language Research*. Clevedon, UK: Multilingual Matters, pp.5 – 23.

Farrar, M. J. (1992). "Negative evidence and grammatical morpheme acquisition." *Developmental Psychology* 28: 90 – 98.

Ferguson, C. (1971). "Absence of copula and the notion of simplicity: a study of normal speech, baby talk, foreigner talk and pidgins." In Dell Hymes (Ed.). *Pidginization and Creolization of Languages*. Cambridge: Cambridge University Press, pp.141 – 150.

Ferguson, C. (1975). "Towards a characterization of English foreigner talk." *Anthropological Linguistics* 17:1 – 14.

Ferguson, C. (1977). "Baby talk as a simplified register." In C. E. Snow & C. A. Ferguson (Eds.). *Talking to children: Language input and acquisition*. Cambridge, UK: Cambridge University Press, pp.247 – 258.

Ferguson, C. (1984). "Repertoire universals, markedness, and second language acquisition." In W. Rutherford (Ed.). *Language Universals and Second Language Acquisition*. Amsterdam: John Benjamins, pp.247 – 258.

Ferguson, C. & DeBose, C. (1976). "Simplified registers, broken languages and pidginization." In A. Valdman (Ed.). *Pidgin and Creole Linguistics*. Bloomington: Indiana University Press, pp.99–125.

Flege, J. E. (2007). "Language contact in bilingualism: phonetic system interactions." In J. Cole and J. I. Hualde (Eds.). *Laboratory Phonology* 9. Berlin: Mouton de Gruyter, pp.353–382.

Foster-Cohen, S. (1999). *An Introduction to Child Language Development*. London: Longman.

Fries, C. (1945). *Teaching and Learning English as a Foreign Language*. Ann Arbor: University of Michigan Press.

Fromkin, V., Rodman, R. and Hyams, N. (2007). *An Introduction to Language*, 8th ed. Boston, MA: Heinle.

Gallaway, C. and Richards, B.R. (1994). *Input and Interaction in Language Acquisition*. Cambridge: Cambridge Uni. Press.

Gardner, R. C. and Lambert, W. (1972). *Attitudes and Motivation in Second Language Learning*. Rowley, MA: Newbury House.

Gardner, R. C. & MacIntyre, P. D. (1992). "A student's contribution to Second Language Learning: Part I, Cognitive Factors." *Language Teaching* 25:211–220.

Gardner, R. C. & MacIntyre, P. D. (1993). "A student's contribution to Second Language Learning: Part I, Affective Factors." *Language Teaching* 26:1–11.

Gardner, R. C., Masgoret, A. M., Tennant, J. and Mihic, L. (2004). "Integrative motivation: changes during a year-long intermediate-level language course." *Language Learning* 54:1–34.

Gass, S. (1979a). *An Investigation of Syntactic Transfer in Adult Second Language Acquisition*. Unpublished doctoral dissertation, Indiana University, Bloomington.

Gass, S. (1979b). "Language transfer and universal grammatical relations." *Language Learning* 29: 327–344.

Gass, S. (1986). "An interactionist approach to L2 sentence interpretation." *Studies in Second Language Acquisition* 8:19–37.

Gass, S. (1997). *Input, Interaction, and the Second Language Learner*. Mahwah, NJ: Lawrence Erlbaum Associates.

Gass, S. (2003). "Input and interaction." In C. Doughty and M. H. Long (Eds.). *The Handbook of Second Language Acquisition*. Oxford: Basil Blackwell, pp.224–255.

Gass, S. and Mackey, A. (2000). *Stimulated Recall Methodology in Second Language Research*. Mahwah, NJ: Lawrence Erlbaum Associates.

Gass, S. and Mackey, A. (2007). *Data Elicitation for Second and Foreign Language Research*. Mahwah, NJ: Lawrence Erlbaum Associates.

Gass, S. and Madden, D. (1985). *Input in Second Language Acquisition*. Rowley, Mass.: Newbury House.

Gass, S. and Schachter, J. (Eds.) (1989). *Linguistic Perspectives on Second Language Acquisition*. Cambridge: Cambridge University Press.

Gass, S. and Selinker, L. (Eds.) (1992). *Language Transfer in Language Learning*. Amsterdam: John Benjamins.

Gass, S. and Selinker, L. (2008). *Second Language Acquisition: An Introductory Course* (3$^{rd}$ Edition). Hillsdale, NJ: Lawrence Erlbaum Associates.

Gass, S. and Varonis, E.M. (1994). "Input, interaction and second language production." *Studies in Second Language Acquisition* 16:283–302.

Gass, S. and Selinker, L. (1994). *Second Language Acquisition: An Introductory Course*. Hillsdale, NJ: Lawrence Erlbaum Associates.

Gass, S. M. & Varonis, E. M. (1989). "Incorporated repairs in nonnative discourse." In M. Eisenstein (Ed.) *The Dynamic Interlanguage: Empirical Studies in Second Language Variation*. New York: Plenum Press, pp.71–86.

Gattegno, C. (1976). *The Common Sense of Teaching Foreign Languages*. New York: Educational Solutions. Amsterdam: John Benjamins.

Giles, H. (1973)."Accent mobility: a model and some data." *Anthropological Linguistics* 15:87–109.

Giles, H. (1978)."Linguistic differentiation between ethnic groups." In H. Tajfel (Ed.). *Differentiation between Social Groups*. London: Academic Press, pp.361–393.

Giles, H. and St. Clair, R. N. (Eds.). (1979).*Language and Social Psychology*. Oxford: Basil Blackwell.

Giles, H. and Smith, P. M. (1979). "Accommodation theory: optional levels of convergence." In H. Giles and R. N. St. Clair (Eds.). *Language and Social Psychology*. Oxford: Basil Blackwell, pp.45–65.

Giles, H. (Ed.) (1984). "The dynamics of speech accommodation." *International Journal of the Sociology of Language* 46.

Giles, H. (Ed.) (2002). *Law Enforcement, Communication and Community*. Amsterdam: John Benjamins.

Giles, H. and Wiemann, J. M. (1987). "Language, social comparison and power." In C. R. Berger and S. H. Chaffee (Eds.). *The Handbook of Communication Science*. Newbury Park, CA: Sage, pp.350–384.

Giles, H. et al. (2005). "Communication accommodation: law enforcement and the public." *Center on Police Practices and Community (COPPAC)*. Retrieved on October 27, 2006 from http://repositories.cdlib.org/isber/coppac/articles_chapters/

Golinkoff, R.M. et al. (2002). "Young children can extend motion verb labels to point-light displays." *Developmental Psychology* 38: 604 - 614.

Golinkoff, R.M. & Hirsh-Pasek, K. (2008). "How toddlers begin to learn verbs." *Trends in Cognitive Science* 12:397 - 403.

Gopnik, A and Meltzoff, A. N. (1986). "Relations between semantic and cognitive development in the one-word stage: the specificity hypothesis." *Child Development* 57:1040 - 1053.

Gregg, K. (1990)."The variable competence model of second language acquisition and why it isn't." *Applied Linguistics* 11:364 - 383.

Hakansson, G. and Lindberg, I. (1988). "What's the question? Investigating second language classroom." In Kasper (Ed.). *Classroom Research. AILA Review* 5:73 - 88.

Hakuta, K. (1974). "A preliminary report on the development of grammatical morphemes in a Japanese girl learning English as a second language." *Working Papers on Bilingualism* 3:18 - 43.

Hakuta, K. (1976). "A case study of a Japanese child learning English as a second language." *Language Learning* 26: 321 - 351.

Hall, J.K. (1995). "(Re)creating our worlds with words: a sociohistorical perspective of face-to face interaction." *Applied Linguistics* 16:206 - 232.

Han, Z. (2002)."A study of the impact of recasts on tense consistency in L2 output." *TESOL Quarterly* 36:543 - 572.

Harris, V. (2003)."Adapting classroom-based strategy instruction to a distance learning context." *TESL-EJ* 7:1 - 19.

Hatch, E. (1978). "Introduction." In E. Hatch (Ed.). *Second Language Acquisition: A Book of Readings*. Rowley, MA: Newbury House, pp.1 - 18.

Hearth, S.B. (1983).*Ways with Words*. Cambridge: Cambridge Uni. Press.

Hearth, S.B. (1986)."What no bedtime story means: narrative skills at home and school." In Schieffelin, B.B. and Ochs, E. (Eds.). *Language Socialization across Culture*. Cambridge: Cambridge Uni. Press.

Horwitz, E. K. (2001). "Language anxiety and achievement." *Annual Review of Applied Linguistics* 21:112 - 126.

Howatt, A.P.R. (1984). *A history of English Language Teaching*. Oxford: Oxford Uni. Press.

Howatt, A.P.R. (1988). "From structure to communicative." *Annual Review of Applied Linguistics* 8:14 - 29.

Huang, J. and Hatch, E.(1978). "A Chinese child's acquisition of English." In E. Hatch (Ed.). *Second Language Acquisition: A Book of Readings*. Rowley, MA: Newbury House, pp.118 - 131.

Izumi, S. et al. (1999)."Testing the output hypothesis: effects of output on noticing andsecond language acquisition." *Studies in Second Language Acquisition* 21:421–452.

Izumi, S. and Bigelow, M. (2000)."Does output promote noticing and second language acquisition?" *TESOL Quarterly* 34:329–378.

Jakobson, R. (1941/1968) (Trans.A.R. Keiler). *Child Language, Aphasia and Phonological Universals*. The Hague: Mouton.

Jiang, N. (2004)."Semantic transfer and its implications for vocabulary teaching in a second language." *Modern Language Journal* 88:416–432.

Johnson, J., Prior, S. and Artuso, M. (2000). "Field dependence as a factor in second language communicative production." *Language Learning* 50:529–567.

Jordan, G. (2005). *Theory Construction in Second Language Acquisition*. Amsterdam: John Benjamins.

Kaplan R. and Bresnan J. (1982). "Lexical-functional grammar: a formal system for grammatical prepresentation." In Bresnan (Ed.). *The Mental Representation of Grammatical Relations*. Cambridge, MA: MIT Press, pp.173–281.

Kasper, G. (2004). "Participant orientations in German conversation-for-learning." *Modern Language Journal* 88:551–567.

Kasper, G. and Dahl, M.(1991). "Research methods in interlanguage pragmatics." *Studies in Second Language Acquisition* 13:215–247.

Katona, G. (1940). *Organizing and Memorizing: Studies in the Psychology of Learning and Teaching*. New York: Columbia University Press.

Kellerman, E. (1979). "Transfer and non-transfer: where we are now." *Studies in Second Language Acquisition* 2:37–57.

Kellerman, E. (1985). "Dative alternation and the analysis of data: a reply to Marzurkewich." *Language Learning* 35:91–101.

Kellerman, E. (1987). *Aspects of Transferability in Second Language Acquisition*. Doctoral dissertation, Katholieke University le Nijmegen.

Kellerman, E. and Sharwood Smith, M. (1986). *Cross-linguistic Influence in Second Language Acquisition*. Elmsford, NJ: Pergamon.

Klein, W. and Perdue, C.(1992). *Utterance Structure: Developing Grammars Again*. Philadelphia: John Benjamins.

Kramsch, C. J. (1985). "Classroom interaction and discourse options." *Studies in Second Language Acquisition* 7(2):169–183.

Kramsch, C. (1985). "Literary texts in the classroom: a discourse." *The Modern Language Journal* 69(4):356–366.

Kramsch, C. (1993). *Context and Culture in Language Teaching*. New York: Oxford University Press.

Kramsch, C. & Kramsch, O. (2000). "The avatars of literature in language study." *The Modern Language Journal* 84(4):553 – 573.

Krashen, S. (1981). *Second Language Acquisition and Second Langauge Learning*. Oxford: Pergamom.

Krashen, S. (1982). *Principles and Practice in Second Language Acquisition*. Oxford: Pergamon.

Krashen, S. (1983). "NewMark's ignorance hypothesis and current second language acquisition theory." In Gass, S. and Selinker, L. (Eds.). *Language Transfer in Language Learning*. Rowley, MA: Newbury House, pp.135 – 153.

Krashen, S. (1985). *The Input Hypothesis: Issues and Implications*. New York: Longman.

Krashen, S. (1998). "Comprehensible output?" *System* 26:175 – 182.

Krashen, S. and Scarcella, R. (1978). "On routines and patterns in second language acquisition and performance." *Language Learning* 28:283 – 300.

Krashen, S. and Terrell, T. (1983). *The Natural Approach: Language Acquisition in the Classroom*. Hayward, CA: Alemany Press.

Lantolf, J.P. and Thorne, S. (2006). *Sociocultural Theory and the Genesis of Second Language Development*. Oxford: Oxford University Press.

Lantolf, J. P. and Thorne, S. (2007). "Sociocultural theory and second language learning." In B. VanPatten and J. Williams (Eds.). *Theories in Second Language Acquisition: An Introduction*. Mahwah, NJ: Lawrence Erlbaum Associates, pp.201 – 224.

Larsen-Freeman, D. (1975a)."The acquisition of grammatical morphemes by adult ESL students." *TESOL Quarterly* 9:409 – 430.

Larsen-Freeman, D. (2006)."The emergence of complexity, fluency, and accuracy in the oral and written production ofthe Chinese learners of English." *Applied Linguistics* 27:590 – 619.

Larsen-Freeman, D. and Long, M. (1991). *An Introduction to Second Language Acquisition Research*. London: Longman.

Leaver, B. L., Ehrman, M. and Shekhtman, B. (2005). *Achieving Success in Second Language Acquisition*. Cambridge: Cambridge University Press.

Lee, J. (2007). *The Inside of the L2 Lexicon and Semantic Overgeneralization*. Ms. Michigan State University.

Leopold, W.(1939). *Speech Development of a Bilingual Child. Vol. I: Vocabulary Growth in the First Two Years*. Evanston, IL: Northwestern University Press.

Leopold, W.(1948). "The study of child language and infant bilingualism." *Word* 4:1 – 17.

Lieven, E.V.M. (1994). "Crosslinguistics and crosscultural aspects of language addressed to children." Chapter 3 in Gallaway, C. and Richards, B. R. (Eds.). *Input and Interaction in Language Acquisition*. Cambridge: Cambridge Uni. Press, pp.56 – 73.

Lightbown, P. (1983). "Exploring relationships between developmental and instructional sequences in L2 acquisition." In H. Seliger and M. H. Long (Eds.). *Classroom Oriented Research in Second Language Acquisition*. pp.217-243.

Lightbown, P. and Spada, N. (2006). *How Languages are Learned*. Oxford: Oxford University Press.

Long, M. H. (1980). "Input, Interaction and Second Language Acquisition." Unpulished doctoral dissertation, University of Pennsylvania, Philadelphia.

Long, M. H. (1983a). "Native speaker/non-native speaker conversation and the negotiation of comprehensible input." *Applied Linguistics* 4:126-141.

Long, M. H. (1983b). "Linguistic and conversational adjustments to non-native speakers." *Studies in Second Language Acquisition* 5:177-193.

Long, M. H. (1985). "Input and second language acquisition theory." In Gass, S. and Madded, C.G. (Eds.). *Input in Second Language Acquisition*. Rowley, MA: Newbury House, pp.377-393.

Long, M. H. (1990). "Maturational constraints on language development." *Studies in Second Language Acquisition* 12:251-285.

Long, M. H. (1996). "The role of the linguistic environment in second language acquisition." In Ritchie, W. C. and Bhatia, T. K. (Eds.). *Handbook of Second Language Acquisition*. San Diego, CA: Academic Press, pp.413-468.

Long, M. H. (2003). "Stabilization and fossilization in interlanguage development." In C. Doughty and M. H. Long (Eds.). *The Handbook of Second Language Acquisition*. Malden, MA: Blackwell, pp.487-535.

Long, M. H. and Porter, P. (1985). "Group work, interlanguage talk, and second language acquisition." *TESOL Quarterly* 19: 207-228.

Long, M. H. and Sato, C. J. (1983). "Classroom foreigner talk discourse: forms and functions of teacher's questions." In Seliger, H. W. and Long, M. H. (Eds.). *Classroom Oriented Research in Second Language Acquisition*. Rowley MA: Newbury House, pp.268-285.

Long, M. H. et al. (1998). "The role of implicit negative feedback in SLA: models and recasts in Japanese and Spanish." *Modern Language Journal* 82:357-371.

Loschky, L. (1994). "Comprehensible input and second language acquisition: what is the relationship?" *Studies in Second Language Acquisition* 16:303-323.

Lyster, R. (1998). "Negotiation of form, recast, and explicit correction in relation to error types and learner repair in immersion classrooms." *Language Learning* 48: 183-218.

Lyster, R. and Ranta, E. (1997). "Corrective feedback and learner uptake: negotiation of form in communicative classrooms." *Studies in Second Language Acquisition*

19:37 – 61.

Macaro, E. (2001). *Learning Strategies in Foreign and Second Language Classrooms*. London: Continuum Press.

Mackey, A. (1999). "Input, interaction and second language development." *Studies in Second Language Acquisition* 21:557 – 587.

Mackey, A. (2002). "Beyond production: learners' perceptions about interactional processes." *International Journal of Educational Research* 37:379 – 394.

Mackey, A. (2006). "Feedback, noticing and instructed second language learning." *Applied Linguistics* 27:405 – 430.

Mackey, A. and Gass, S. (2005). *Second Language Research: Methodology and Design*. Mahwah, NJ: Lawrence Erlbaum Associates.

Mackey, A. and Philip, R. (1998). "Conversational interaction and second language development: recasts, responses and red herrings?" *Modern Language Journal* 82: 338 – 356.

Mackey, A. et al. (2000). "How do learners perceive implicit negative feedback?" *Studies in Second Language Acquisition* 19:37 – 66.

MacIntyre, P. D. and Noels, K. A. (1994). "The Good Language Learner: a retrospective review." *System* 22:269 – 280.

MacIntyre, P. D. & Gardner, R. C. (1994). "The effects of induced anxiety on cognitive processing in computerized vocabulary learning." *Studies in Second Language Acquisition* 16:1 – 17.

MacWhinney, B. (Ed.) (1999). *The Emergence of Language*. Mahwah, NJ: Lawrence Erlbaum Associates.

MacWhinney, B. (2000a). *The CHILDES Project: Tools for Analyzing Talk. Vol. 1: Transcription Format and Programs*. (3$^{rd}$ Ed.). Mahwah, NJ: Lawrence Erlbaum Associates.

MacWhinney, B. (2000b). *The CHILDES Project: Tools for Analyzing Talk. Vol. 2: The Database*. (3$^{rd}$ Ed.). Mahwah, NJ: Lawrence Erlbaum Associates.

MacWhinney, B. (2001). "The competition model: the input, the context, and the brain." In Robinson, P. (Ed.). *Cognition and Second Language Instruction*. Cambridge: Cambridge Uni. Press, pp.60 – 90.

Markee, N. (2000). *Conversation Analysis*. Mahwah, NJ: Lawrence Erlbaum Associates.

McDonough, K. (2005). "Identifying the impact of negative feedback and learners' responses on ESL question development." *Studies in Second Language Acquisition* 27:79 – 103.

McDonough, K. (2007). "Interactional feedback and the emergence of simple past activity verbs in L2 English." In A. Mackey (Ed.). *Conversational Interaction and Second*

Language Acquisition: A series of Empirical Studies. Oxford: Oxford University Press, pp.323 – 338.
McDonough, K. and Mackey, A. (2006). "Responses to recasts: repetitions, primed production, and linguistic development." Language Learning 56:693 – 720.
McLaughlin, B. (1987).Theories of Second Language Learning. London: Edward Arnold.
McLaughlin, B. (1990a). "Restructuring." Applied Linguistics 11:113 – 128.
McLaughlin, B. (1990b)."The relationship between first and second languages: language proficiency and language aptitude." In B. Harley, P. Allen, J. Cummins and M. Swain (Eds.). The Development of Second Language Proficiency. Cambridge: Cambridge University Press, pp.158 – 178.
McLaughlin, B. and Heredia, R. (1996)."Information-processing approaches to research on second language acquisition and use." In W. Ritchie and T. Bhatia (Eds.). Handbook of Second Language Acquisition. San Diego: Academic Press, pp.213 – 228.
McLaughlin, B., Rossman, T. and McLeod, B. (1983). "Second language learning: an information processing perspective." Language Learning 33:135 – 158.
McTear, M. F. (1975). "Structures and categories of foreign language teaching sequences." In Allrigh. R. (Ed.). Working Papers: Language Teaching Classroom Research. University of Essex, Department of Language and Linguistics.
McTear, M. F. (1985). Children's conversation. New York: Basil Blackwell Inc.
McTear, M. (2002). "Spoken dialog technology: enabling the conversational interface." ACM Computing Surveys 34(1): 90 – 169.
Mercer, N. (1995).The Guided Construction of Knowledge: Talk amongst Teachers and Learners. Clevedon: Multilingual Matters.
Mercer, N. (1996)."Language and the guided construction of knowledge." In Blue, G. and Mitchell, R. (Eds.). Language in Education. Clevedon: BAAL/Multilingual matters, pp.28 – 40.
Milroy, L.(1987). Observing and Analyzing Natural Language. Oxford: Blackwell.
Morgan, J.L. et al.(1995). "Negative evidence on negative evidence." Developmental Psychology 31:180 – 197.
Nassaji, H. and Swain, M. (2000). "A Vygotskian perspective on corrective feedback in L2: the effect of random versus negotiated help in the learning of English articles." Language Awareness 9(1):34 – 51.
Nesmer, W. (1971) "Approximative systems of foreign language learners." In Richards, J. C.(Ed.) (1984). Error Analysis: Perspectives on Second Language Acquisition. London: Longman, pp.55 – 63.
Nicholas, H. et al.(2001). "Recasts as feedback to language learners." Language Learning

51:719 – 758.

Ninio, A. and Snow, C. (1999). "The development of pragmatics: learning to use language appropriately." Invited chapter, in T. K. Bhatia & W. C. Ritchie (Eds.). *Handbook of Language Acquisition*. (Prefinal Version). New York: Academic Press, pp.347 – 383.

Nobuyoshi, J. and Ellis, R. (1993). "Focused communication tasks and second language acquisition." *ELT Journal* 47:203 – 210.

Norton, B. (2000). *Identity and Language Learning*. Harlow: Pearson Education.

Nunan, D. (1996). "Issues in second language acquisition research: examining substance and procedure." In W. C. Ritchie and T. K. Bhatia (Eds.). *Handbook of Second Language Acquisition*. New York: Ritchie and Bhatia, pp.349 – 374.

Ochs, E. (1988). *Culture and Language Development: Language Acquisition and Language Socialization in a Samoan Village*. Cambridge: Cambridge Uni. Press.

Ochs, E. and Schieffelin, B.B. (1984). "Language acquisition and socialization: three developmental stories and their implications." In Shweder, R. and le Vine, R. (Eds.). *Culture Theory: Essay on Mind, Self and Emotion*. Cambridge: Cambridge Uni. Press, pp.276 – 320.

Ochs, E. and Schieffelin, B. B. (1995). "The impact of language socialization on grammatical development." In Fletcher, P. and MacWinney, B. (Eds.). *The Handbook of Child Language*. Oxford: Oxford Uni. Press.

Ohta, A. S. (2000). "Rethinking interaction in SLA: developmentally appropriate assistance in the zone of proximal development and the acquisition of L2 grammar." In Lantolf, J. P. (Eds.). *Sociocultural Theory and Second Language Learning*. Oxford: Oxford Uni. Press.

Ohta, A.S. (2001). *Second Language Acquisition Processes in the Classroom: Learning Japanese*. Mahwah, NJ: Lawrence Erlbaum Associates.

Oliver, R. and Mackey, A. (2003). "Interactional context and feedback in child ESL classrooms." *Modern Language Journal* 87:519 – 533.

Oller, J. and Ziahosseiny, S. (1970). "The Contrastive Analysis Hypothesis and spelling errors." *Language Learning* 20:183 – 189.

Oxford, R. (1993). *Style Analysis Survey (SAS)*. University of Alabama.

Oxford, R. (1999). "Learning strategies." In B. Spolsky (Ed.). *Concise Encyclopedia of Educational Linguistics*. Oxford: Elsevier, pp.518 – 522.

Panova, I. And Lyster, R. (2002). "Patterns of corrective feedback and uptake in an adult ESL classroom." *TESOL Quarterly* 36:573 – 595.

Pei, M. (1966). *How to Learn Languages and What Languages to Learn*. New York: Harper and Row.

Peirce, B. N. (1995). "Social identity, investment, and language learning." *TESOL Quarterly* 29: 9-31.

Perdue, C. (Ed.) (1982). *Second Language Acquisition by Adult Immigrants: A Field Manual*. Strasbourg: European Science Foundation.

Pica, T. (1994)."Research on negotiation: what does it reveal about second-language learning conditions, processes and outcomes?" *Language Learning* 44:493-527.

Pica, T. et al. (1987)."The impact of interaction on comprehension." *TESOL Quarterly* 21:737-758.

Pica, T. et al. (1993). "Choosing and using communication tasks for second language instruction." In G. Crookes and S. Gass (Eds.). *Tasks and Language Learning: Integrating Theory and Practice*. Clevedon: Multilingual Matters, pp.9-34.

Pienemann, M. (1998). *Language Processing and Second Language Development: Processability Theory*. Philadelphia: John Benjamins.

Pienemann, M. (1999). *Language Processing and Second Language Development: Processability Theory*. Amsterdam: John Benjamins.

Pienemann, M. (2007). "Processability theory." In B. VanPatten and J. Williams (Eds.). *Theories in Second Language Acquisition: An Introduction*. Mahwah, NJ: Lawrence Erlbaum Associates, pp.137-154.

Pienemann, M. and Johnson, M. (1987). "Factors influencing the development of language proficiency." In Nunan, D. (Ed.). *Applying Second Language Acquisition Research*. Adelaide, Australia: National Curriculum Resource Center, pp.45-141.

Pine, J. M. (1994)."The language of primary caregivers." In Gallaway, C. and Richards,B. R. (Eds.). *Input and Interaction in Language Acquisition*. Cambridge: Cambridge University Press, pp.15-37.

Pinker, S. (1989). *Learnability and cognition*. Cambridge, MA: MIT Press.

Pinker, S. (1995). *The language Instinct*. London: Harper.

Plann, S. (1977). "Acquiring a second language in an immersion situation." In Brown, H. et al. (Eds.). *On TESOL 77*. Washington D.C: TESOL, pp.204-212.

Poole, D. (1992). "Language socialization in the second language classroom." *Language learning* 42:593-616.

Porter, J. (1977)."A cross-sectional study of morphemes acquisition in first language learners." *Language Learning* 27:47-62.

Porter, J. (1986)."How learners talk to each other: input and interaction in task-centered discussions." In Day (Ed.). *Talking to Learn: Conversation in Second Language Acquisition*. Rowley, Mass: Newbury House.

Preston, D. (1989). *Sociolinguistics and Second Language Acquisition*. Oxford: Basil Blackwell.

Rackham et al. (1971). *Developing Interactive Skills*. Northampton: Wellens Publishing.

Ravem, R. (1968). "Language acquisition in a second language environment." *International Review of Applied Linguistics* 6:165 – 185. (Reprinted in 1974) In J. Richards (Ed.). *Error Analysis*. London: Longman, pp.124 – 133.

Ravem, R. (1970). "The development of Wh-questions in first and second language learners." Occasional Papers, Language Centre, University of Essex. (Reprinted in 1974) In J. Richards (Ed.). *Error Analysis*. London: Longman, pp.134 – 155.

Richards, J.(1974). "A Non-Contrastive Approach to Error Analysis." In Richards, J. (Ed.). *Error Analysis: Perspectives on Second Language Acquisition*. Essex: Longman, pp.172 – 188.

Richards, B.J. and Gallaway, C. (1994). "Conclusions and directions." Chapter 11 in Gallaway, C. and Richards, B. J. (Eds.). *Input and Interaction in Language Acquisition*. Cambridge: Cambridge Uni. Press, pp.253 – 269.

Rocca, S. (2007). *Child Second Language Acquisition: A Bi-Directional Study of English and Italian Tense – Aspect Morphology*. Amsterdam: John Benjamins.

Rosa, E. and Leow, R. (2004). "Awareness, different learning conditions, and L2 development." *Applied Psycholinguistics* 25:269 – 292.

Schachter, J. (1988). "Second language acquisition and its relationship to Universal Grammar." *Applied Linguistics* 9:219 – 235.

Schieffelin, B.B. (1985). "The acquisition of Kaluli." In Slobbin, D.I. (Ed.). *The Cross-linguistic Study of Language Acquisition*, Volume 1. Hillsdale, NJ: Lawrence Erlbaum Associates, pp.525 – 595.

Schieffelin, B.B. (1990). *The Give and Take of Everyday Life: Language Socialization of Kaluli Children*. Cambridge: Cambridge Uni. Press.

Schmidt, R. (1990)."The role of consciousness in second language learning." *Applied Linguistics* 11:129 – 158.

Schmidt, R. (1994). "Deconstructing consciousness in search of useful definitions for applied linguistics." *AILA Review* 11:11 – 26.

Schmidt, R. (2001)."Attention." In P. Robinson (Ed.). *Cognition and Second Language Instruction*. Cambridge: Cambridge University Press, pp.3 – 32.

Schumann, J. (1978a). *The Pidginization Process: A Model for Second Language Acquisition*. Rowley, MA: Newbury House.

Schumann, J. (1978b)."The acculturation model for second language acquisition." In R. Gingras (Ed.). *Second Language Acquisition and Foreign Language Teaching*. Arlington, VA: Center for Applied Linguistics, pp.27 – 50.

Scovel, T. (2001). *Learning New Languages: A Guide to Second Language Acquisition*. Boston: Heinle and Heinle.

Seliger, H. W. and Shohamy, E. (1989). *Second Language Research Methods*. London: Oxford University Press.

Selinker, L. (1972). "Interlanguage." *Intenational Review of Applied Linguistics* 10:209 – 231.

Selinker, L. (1992). *Rediscovering Interlanguage*. London: Longman.

Service, E., Simola, M., Metsaenheimo, O. and Maury, S. (2002). "Bilingual working memory span is affected by language skill." *European Journal of Cognitive Psychology* 13:383 – 407.

Sharwood Smith, M. (1993). "Input enhancement in instructed SLA: theoretical bases." *Studies in Second Language Acquisition* 15:165 – 179.

Sharwood Smith, M. and Truscott, J. (2005). "Stages or continua in second language acquisition: a MOGUL solution." *Applied Linguistics* 26:219 – 240.

Shehadeh, A. (2002). "Comprehensible output, from occurrence to acquisition: an agenda for acquisitional research." *Language Learning* 52:597 – 647.

Sinclair, J. M. and Coulthard. M. (1975). *Towards an Analysis of Discourse*. London: Oxford Uni. Press.

Singleton, D. (1999). *Vocabulary Learning in Another Language*. Cambridge: Cambridge University Press.

Slobin, D. (1973). "Cognitive prerequisites for the development of grammar." In Ferguson, C. and Slobin, D. (Eds.). *Studies of Child Language Development*. New York, NJ: Holt, Rinhart & Winston.

Slobin, D. (1979). *Psycholinguisitics*. (2$^{nd}$ ed.). Gleaview, IL: Scott Foresman & Company.

Slobin, D. (1985). "Crosslinguistic evidence for the language-making capacity." In Slobin, D. (Ed.). *The Crosslinguistic Study of Language Acquisition*. Vol. 2. Hillsdale, NJ:Lawrence Erlbaum Associates, pp.1159 – 1249.

Slobin, D. (1985—1997). *The Crosslinguistic Study of Language Acquisition*. Vol. 1 – 5. Hillsdale, NJ: Lawrence Erlbaum Associates.

Snow, C.E. (1994). "Beginning from baby talk: twenty years of research on input and interaction." In Gallaway, C. and Richards, B.R. (Eds.). *Input and Interaction in Language Acquisition*. Cambridge: Cambridge Uni. Press, pp.3 – 12.

Sokolov, J.L. and Snow, C.E. (1994). "The changing role of negative evidence in theories of language development." In Gallaway, C. and Richards, B.J. (Eds.). *Input and Interaction in Language Acquisition*. Cambridge: Cambridge Uni. Press, pp.38 – 55.

Spada, N. (1997). "Form-focused instruction and second language acquisition: a review of classroom and laboratory research." *Language Teaching* 30:73 – 87.

Spada, N. and Fröhlich, M. (1995). *COLT Observation Scheme. Communicative Orientation of Language Teaching Observation Scheme: Coding Conventions and*

*Applications*. Sydney: National Centre for English language Teaching and Research (NCETR), Macquarie University.

Sternberg, R. J. (1997). *Thinking Styles*. New York: Cambridge University Press.

Storch, N. (2003). "Patterns of interaction in ESL pair work." *Language Learning* 52: 119 – 158.

Swain, M. (1985)."Communicative competence: some roles of comprehensible input and comprehensible output in its development." In Gass, S. and Nadden, C.G. (Eds.). *Input in Second Language Acquisition*. Rowley, MA: Newbury House, pp.235 – 253.

Swain, M. (1995)."Three functions of output in second language learning." In Cook, G. andSeidlhofer, B. (Eds.). *Principle and Practices in Applied Linguistics: Studies in Honour of H.G. Widdowson*. Oxford: Oxford Uni. Press, pp.125 – 144.

Swain, M. (2000). "The output hypothesis and beyond: mediating acquisition through collaborative dialogue." In Lantolf, J. (Ed.). *Sociocultural Theory and Second Language Learning*. Oxford: Oxford Uni. Press, pp.97 – 114.

Swain, M. and Cumming, A.(1989). "Beyond methodology: behind research." In J.H. Esling (Ed.). *Multicultural Education and Policy: ESL in the 1990s*. Toronto: OISE Press, pp.88 – 106.

Swain, M. and Lapkin, S. (1998) "Interaction and second language learning: two adolescent French immersion students working together." *Modern Language Journal* 82 (3):320 – 337.

Tarone, E. (1979). "Interlanguage as chameleon." *Language Learning* 29(1):181 – 191.

Tarone, E. (1983). "On the variability of interlanguage systems." *Applied Linguistics* 4: 143 – 163.

Terrell, T. D.(1986). "Acquisition in the natural approach: the binding/access framework." *Modern Language Journal* 75:52 – 63.

Tomasello, M. (1988). "The role of joint attentional process in early language development." *Language Sciences* 10:69 – 88.

Tomasello, M. (2001). "Perceiving intentions and learning words in the second year of life." In M. Bowerman & S. Levinson (Eds.). *Language Acquisition and Conceptual Development*. Cambridge, UK: Cambridge University Press, pp.132 – 158.

Tomasello, M. (2003). *Constructing a Language: A Usage-based Theory of Language Acquisition*. Cambridge, MA: Harvard University Press.

Tomasello, M. (2006). "Why don't apes point?" In N. J. Enfield & S. C. Levinson (Eds.). *Roots of Human Sociality: Culture, Cognition, and Interaction*. Oxford, UK: Berg, pp.506 – 524.

Tomasello, M. & Camaioni, L. (1997). "A comparison of the gestural communication of apes and human infants." *Human Development* 40:7 – 24.

Tomasello, M., Carpenter, M., Call, J., Behne, T. & Moll, H. (2005). "Understanding and sharing intentions:the origins of cultural cognition." *Behavioral and Brain Sciences* 28:675-735.

Tomasello, M. & Farrar, J. (1986). "Joint attention and early language." *Child Development* 57:1454-1463.

Toohey, K. (2000). *Learning English at School: Identity, Social Relations and Classroom Practice*. Clevedon: Multilingual Matters.

Toohey, K. (2001). "Disputes in child L2 learning." *TESOL Quarterly* 35:257-278.

Toohey, K. and Norton, B. (2001). "Changing perspectives on good language learners." *TESOL Quarterly* 35:307-322.

Towell, R. and Hawkins, R. (1994). *Approaches to Second Language Acquisition*. Clevedon: Multilingual Matters.

Trahey, M. (1996). "Positive evidence in second language acquisition: some long-term effects." *Second Language Research* 12:111-139.

Valian, V. (1990). "Null subject: a problem for parameter-setting models of language Acquisition." *Cognition* 35:105-122.

Van Lier, L. (1988). *The Classroom and the Language Learner*. London: Longman.

VanPatten, B. (1996). *Input Processing and Grammar Instruction: Theory and Research*. Norwood, NJ: Ablex.

VanPatten, B. (2002). "Processing instruction: an update." *Language Learning* 52:755-803.

VanPatten, B. and Cadierno, T. (1993). "Explicit instructions and input processing." *Studies in Second Language Acquisition* 18:495-510.

Vygotsky, L. S. (1978). *Mind in Society: The Development of Higher Psychological Processes*. Cambridge, MA: Harvard University Press.

Watson-Gegeo, K. A. and Nielsen, S. (2003). "Language sociolization in SLA." In Doughty, C and Long, M.H. (Eds.). *Handbook of Second Language Acquisition*. Oxford: Blackwell, pp.55-77.

Wexler, K. and Culicover, P. W. (1980). *Formal Principles of Language Acquisition*. Cambridge, MA: MIT Press.

Wilkinson, L. (Ed.) (1982). *Communicating in the Classroom*. New York: Academic Press.

Williams, J. (1999). "Memory, attention, and inductive learning." *Studies in Second Language Acquisition* 21:1-48.

Williams, J. and Lovatt, P. (2003). "Phonological memory and rule learning." *Language Learning* 53:67-121.

Wong-Fillmore, L. (1982). "Instructional language as linguistic input: second language learning in classroom." In Wilkinson, L. (Ed.). *Communicating in the Classroom.* New York: Academic Press.

Wong-Fillmore, L. (1985). "When does teacher talk work as input?" In Gass, S. and Madden, D. (Ed.). *Input in Second Language Acquisition.* Rowley, Mass.: Newbury House.

Zobl, H. (1980). "The formal and developmental selectivity of L1 influence on L2 acquisition." *Language Learning* 30:43 – 57.

Zobl, H. (1982). "A direction for contrastive analysis: the comparative study of developmental sequences." *TESOL Quarterly* 16:169 – 183.

Zuengler, J. (1989). "Performance variation in NS-NNS interactions: ethnolinguistic difference, or discourse domain?" In S. Gass, C. Madden, D. Preston, and L. Selinker (Eds.). *Variation in Second Language Acquisition: Discourse and Pragmatics.* Clevedon, UK: Multilingual Matters, pp.228 – 244.